THE
ANTINUCLEAR
MOVEMENT

Revised Edition

SOCIAL MOVEMENTS PAST AND PRESENT

Irwin T. Sanders, Editor

THE
ANTINUCLEAR
MOVEMENT

Revised Edition

Jerome Price

TWAYNE PUBLISHERS
A DIVISION OF G. K. HALL & CO. • BOSTON

The Antinuclear Movement, Revised Edition

Copyright 1990 by G. K. Hall & Co.
First Edition copyright 1982 by G. K. Hall & Co.
All rights reserved.

Published by Twayne Publishers
A division of G. K. Hall & Co.
70 Lincoln Street, Boston, Massachusetts 02111

Copyediting supervised by Barbara Sutton
Book production by Janet Z. Reynolds
Typeset in Century Oldstyle by Compset, Inc.

Printed on permanent/durable acid-free paper
and bound in the United States of America.

Library of Congress Cataloging in Publication Data

Price, Jerome.
     The antinuclear movement / Jerome Price.—Rev. ed.
       p.   cm.—(Social movements past and present)
     Bibliography: p.
     Includes index.
     ISBN 0-8057-9735-1 (alk. paper).—ISBN 0-8057-9736-X (pbk. :
alk. paper)
      1. Antinuclear movement—United States. I. Title. II. Series.
HD9698.U52P74 1989
333.79'24'0973—dc20   89-15537
                                      CIP

Contents

About the Author

Jerome Price was born in Tampa, Florida. His family moved first to England near London and then to Mississippi, where he graduated from Millsaps College in Jackson. He received his M.A. from Western Kentucky University and thereafter worked in Germany. He attended Rutgers University, where he earned his Ph.D. in sociology in 1979. He has taught at Virginia Polytechnic Institute and State University and at the University of Maine, Presque Isle. He is currently a lecturer in sociology at the University of Maine, Portland, and a financial consultant in Kennebunkport.

Preface to the Revised Edition

The 1990s will not see the demise of the antinuclear movement. During the course of revising this study, I became certain that as long as the democratic process survives, on the one hand, and as long as nuclear power is used to produce electricity and make nuclear weapons on the other, there will still be advocates and opponents of nuclear power. The revisions I have made mostly address political developments in the Reagan-Bush era and the renewed vigor of the movement since Chernobyl. The 1980s have forced me to reevaluate the role of environmentalists in the antinuclear movement and to consider new issues—primarily military nuclear wastes and the trend toward linking the nuclear fuel cycle with the production of nuclear weapons. In the 1980s, at the local community level, opposition to nuclear-waste dump sites proposed by the Department of Energy and to emergency evacuation plans mobilized many citizens over the nuclear issue for the first time.

The continuing efforts of scientists and environmentalists to fight the Nuclear Regulatory Commission over safety issues and radioactive wastes has kept the core of the movement intact. Meanwhile, direct action waned after the large demonstrations of the late 1970s. The movement became even more entrenched internationally—the greatest expansion of nuclear power in the 1980s was outside the United States, especially in Europe. As antinuclear goals diffused in the face of a strong counterattack, grassroots opposition moved ideologically more in the direction of the Green movement.

I have incorporated new sociological studies of the antinuclear movement that have appeared since this book's first edition in 1982. There is also further analysis of the potential for nuclear terrorism.

Coincidentally, I am writing this preface on the day after George Bush defeated Michael Dukakis for president of the United States—with a campaign that made the most explicit attack on liberalism this country has seen since the 1950s. The impact that the Bush presidency will have on the antinuclear movement in the next four years is not entirely predictable, but I anticipate that existing Republican nuclear policies will be continued. The Hart-Simpson Amendment prohibited the recycling of commercial nuclear wastes for the manufacture of nuclear weapons, but activists should be prepared for Bush administration efforts to allow it.

During the last eight years of American political life, I have seen made what seem to me to be tragic errors. I have become personally more committed to the goals of the antinuclear movement than I was when I wrote the first edition in the late 1970s. I am also less restrained now by conventional academic approaches to the study of political issues than I was then. I salute groups that fight the NRC over safety issues, and I salute the thousands of individuals who attend public meetings and rallies in support of antinuclear goals.

But I am also compelled to make a suggestion to the movement's leaders—that they now focus more of their attention on the Department of Energy. In fact, one of the critical issues that has emerged in the 1980s involves the DOE. Put simply, the Department of Energy has been given a military mission—to research and develop nuclear weapons. Only if the Pentagon had been given this mission could the situation have turned out more disastrously. In the present DOE, solar energy, conservation, coal conversion, energy efficiency, and other alternative technologies are not likely to receive much attention unless they have military implications. Civilian energy research and development must be separated from the national defense, and the Department of Energy must not be subordinated to the military.

An issue of particular importance in the 1990s may be over a DOE decision to build a modular, high-temperature gas-cooled (helium) reactor to produce tritium in a new Idaho plant for use in nuclear weapons. This concept is being offered as an alternative to conventional light-water reactors as well as to coal- and gas-fired power plants linked to acid rain and the greenhouse effect. If this is to be a prototype of a new generation of planned nuclear reactors, does this mean DOE will finally admit that the current generation of nuclear reactors are technological dinosaurs? A second issue might be over how well founded the safety of this system is as it uses ceramic-covered grains of uranium as fuel, which are thought to render impossible a meltdown of fuel elements and release of radioactive materials. Although at this writing a commitment has not yet been made to the modular HTGCR concept by the Department of Energy, this would be of major significance to the nuclear controversy.

The antinuclear movement should continue to pressure the Nuclear Regulatory Commission on safety issues and the Department of Energy on radioactive-waste disposal. But renewed efforts to produce nonnuclear energy could be greatly enhanced if the Democratic party itself were to make these issues an important part of their platform in the 1990s. The best solution to the worldwide proliferation of nuclear technology would be a competitive array of new energy technologies that would make nuclear energy less desirable.

In the first edition I concluded that the greatest threat of nuclear disaster was in the Third World. But with the enormous expansion of nuclear power in Europe, a major accident is as likely to occur in France, the nation most committed to nuclear power. Human error played a greater role at Chernobyl and Three Mile Island than did technological weakness; human error could occur anywhere in the world. Terrorist acts could still occur. At the grassroots level, the Green movement is important in perpetuating environmental consciousness, but that movement should also advocate positive solutions to force political leaders to take up the challenge of creating a nonnuclear twenty-first century. In the United States, this may best be achieved through presidential politics aimed at changing the mission of the Department of Energy.

Republican ascendancy in the White House and in the federal bureaucracy means that initiative for policy change must come from the House or the Senate. Here the antinuclear movement could realize its positive goals. To sustain its protracted struggles with the NRC and the DOE, it requires access to resources that only organized groups such as the Union of Concerned Scientists have. Grassroots pressure on political leaders to take positive steps for the future should have equal footing with grassroots antinuclear efforts.

The survival of social movements has never seemed more tenuous than in the last decade. But the antinuclear movement still won much of that battle. Even with administration support, it is unlikely that more nuclear power plants will be constructed. Within twenty or thirty years, scores of concrete-entombed decommissioned nuclear power plants may have become permanent parts of America's landscape. On the other hand, dams, solar plants, conversion plants, and similar technology could also be built if the Department of Energy were genuinely committed to efficient, clean, and advanced nonnuclear options.

I appreciate the opportunity given to me by Irwin Sanders and Athenaide Dallett to revise this book. I wish also to thank my friends who climbed up the hundred highest peaks of New England with me, which is how we have kept our sanity in the mid-1980s. These excursions lifted us out of the stresses of our jobs in corporate and bureaucratic America, where conservatives are well entrenched. As a matter of fact, in a few days I will be hiking in the mountainous area of western Maine, near the Quebec border. Yesterday I signed a local referendum petition to ban cruise-missile testing in the very same area. Every day we are faced with a nuclear issue.

Jerome Price
Portland, Maine

Preface (1982)

In the 1970s, when the search for alternative sources of energy to replace fossil fuels began, nuclear power seemed to be the solution to our energy problems. Its proponents claimed that nuclear power was a clean and safe source of energy with a "flawless record," one of the twentieth century's greatest scientific and technological achievements. By controlling the fission of atoms, enormous quantities of energy could be released to provide heat that would run electric turbines indefinitely. We seemed to have found a source of energy that would free us from dependence on imported oil and provide nations with a plentiful supply of energy for aeons with no threat to human life.

This confidence has been seriously eroded. Opponents of nuclear power assert that it is already a "failed technology" and that it exists only because of massive government subsidies. The possibility of more nuclear accidents like the one at Three Mile Island and uncertainty about what to do with radioactive wastes continue to be major sources of contention between antinuclear activists and the nuclear establishment.

I first became interested in the antinuclear movement in a dissertation proposal to analyze the role of scientists in policy formation in Project Independence. It soon became apparent to me that government energy policy was focused on nuclear power. I decided to narrow my study to examine why nuclear energy was considered preferable to alternatives such as solar and hydroelectric power. It was disconcerting for me to discover that nuclear technology is not as safe as people generally assumed, and is moreover clearly linked to nuclear-weapons proliferation.

As I became more deeply immersed in studying nuclear power and the controversy it was generating, I realized that a social movement was in the making. I initially followed the development of the antinuclear movement as an interested observer, but this interest soon developed into active participation. Most movement participants do not realize they are involved in a social movement, believing that movement involvement is defined solely by attendance at rallies and demonstrations. But involvement in a social movement also involves less tangible activities such as the awakening of one's political and social conscience. The larger "movement" during the 1960s included civil rights activism, revolutionism, anti–Vietnam War activities, and at least sympathy for myriad groups articulating a new political consciousness. What puts the antinuclear movement in the same stream is the common spirit of social change.

For a new generation the antinuclear movement provides a view of the world and political activity that keeps the liberal tradition alive in an era when religious fundamentalism and New Right philosophy appear to be ascendant. The 1960s generation inherited such issues as the vestiges of a plantation society, militarism in Southeast Asia, and oppressive cultural traditionalism. The 1970s and 1980s generations have inherited radioactive wastes, potential core meltdowns, two nuclear superpowers, and innumerable smaller muclear-armed nations. The catalysts that press people into social action change from generation to generation, but the fight for liberalism continues to enjoy a steady infusion of energy.

Although Seabrook and Diablo Canyon garner much attention as media events, the real locus of the antinuclear movement is in a plethora of environmentalist, labor, church, women's, and local citizens' activist groups. While younger activists may choose to demonstrate outside nuclear power plants, others are more restrained and devote themselves to petitioning and other less visible movement activities. Organized groups like the Union of Concerned Scientists and the Natural Resources Defense Council rely on professionals—scientists, lawyers, and others—who are able to sustain themselves while fighting powerful interests. This is a tribute to the viability of the democratic process in the United States during a period that is seemingly dominated by archconservatives.

Some observers believe that the antinuclear movement is now irrelevant because few nuclear power stations are being ordered. Nothing could be farther from the truth. By the end of the 1980s the number of nuclear power plants in operation worldwide almost doubled, while aging plants have increased risks of accidents, and radioactive wastes will continue to accumulate. A moratorium on the development of nuclear power has not been achieved.

The book first gives an overview of the history and origins of the antinuclear campaign and shows how it grew into a movement of great significance. I explore the values of diverse antinuclear groups, their organizational histories, and their ideologies. The episodic antinuclear movements of the 1950s and 1960s preceded its environmentalist phase and its eventual emergence as a distinctive movement. The antinuclear movement now spans three decades, and it is as strong in Western Europe as in the United States.

After reading the overview of the movement, the reader may want to turn to the first appendix, which is an excursion into the general social-science theory of social movements—specifically resource-mobilization and social-action theory. (Second and third appendixes give information on the nuclear fuel cycle and the structure of the nuclear industry for those who are not certain how nuclear energy is used to produce electricity.)

Subsequent chapters are concerned with subgroups within the movement: environmentalists, scientists, and direct-action groups. Each subgroup has contributed in unique ways to the movement. These chapters describe the people and the organizations they created to bring about social change.

After analyzing and describing environmentalists', scientists', and direct-action groups, I examine the consequences of the antinuclear movement, particularly on the energy policy of the Carter administration, on public opinion, and on international nuclear policy. The movement's greatest impact was on the Democratic party in the late 1970s, but a reversal of priorities in the Reagan administration turned around many gains the antinuclear movement had made.

The final chapter attempts to place the movement in the context of more general problems facing modern societies.

Social movements constantly undergo change, and the antinuclear movement is no exception. New groups and coalitions come into existence, and tactics are changed when efforts meet with failure. The challenge of studying social movements lies in the fact that they are not frozen in time but rather are made up of living, acting people who are always redefining their roles and creating innovative strategies for change.

Chapter One

The Emergence of the Antinuclear Movement

Along the beautiful coastal area near Wiscasset, not far from Bar Harbor and Acadia National Park, the large dome of Maine Yankee, a nuclear power plant, rises above the surrounding forest. Although this seemingly innocuous power station produces one-third of Maine's electricity, in the 1980s the people of that state were given the choice of shutting down the plant in three successive referendums. These referendums were aimed at forcing the utilities to actively pursue alternative sources of energy. If one of these nuclear referendums had succeeded, an existing nuclear power plant would have been closed down and a national precedent would have been set. It would have represented a substantial victory for the antinuclear movement.[1] The referendums failed, as nearly 60 percent voted against a shutdown—primarily because of unwillingness to pay higher electricity bills. But over 40 percent of the voters did express their opposition to nuclear energy.

Maine is a small state with just over a million inhabitants, many of whom struggle as potato farmers or depend on the seasonal tourist trade or public relief. Why would such a large proportion of its voters have been willing to risk having to import more foreign oil should Maine Yankee close? The results of the referendums were widely perceived as votes of no confidence in nuclear power and in support of alternatives such as solar, wind, and hydroelectric power.

Voting is a simple act, but understanding the complex issues involved in the controversy and the conflicting interests of competing groups is

1

much more complicated. The groups and organizations that formed the opposition to Maine Yankee under the banner of the Maine Nuclear Referendum Committee are similar to hundreds of antinuclear groups that have emerged in every state and in many Western European nations. Pronuclear groups formed a countermovement under the auspices of Save Maine Yankee. Hundreds of thousands of dollars were spent to woo the electorate to one position or another. Nuclear power is no longer the special province of government and industry; it is a public issue in which citizens now play a decisive role.

How did the antinuclear movement emerge, and what are the goals and ideology of groups active in the movement? What is the history of the controversy over nuclear power? How did the movement grow and become a force in the politics of Western Europe? Has the movement been successful? These questions do not lend themselves to easy answers, but we must try to answer them if we are to comprehend the implications of the movement.

Historical Precursors (1945–60)

In August 1939, physicists Eugene Wigner, Leo Szilard, and Albert Einstein wrote a letter to President Franklin D. Roosevelt warning him that Nazi scientists were investigating the feasibility of building an atomic weapon using a nuclear chain reaction. In response, the Manhattan Project was formed, under the direction of General Leslie R. Groves. The project culminated in the explosions of two atomic bombs over Hiroshima and Nagasaki in 1945, killing over 100,000 people. The age of atomic energy had begun.[2]

At the conclusion of World War II, the Truman administration was committed to international control of the atom. The Baruch Plan was proposed by the United Nations in 1946 to establish an international corporation for the peaceful application of nuclear energy. The plan, like the proposals of Secretary of War Henry Stimson, provided for the United States and the Soviet Union to share atomic secrets.

Many scientists, too, were liberal and internationalist. A movement developed among scientists to prevent the military from controlling nuclear energy. The scientists of the Federation of American Scientists, led by J. Robert Oppenheimer, had worked in the Manhattan Project. The federation's efforts helped to bring about the McMahon Act in December 1945, in which the military was subordinated to playing an operating or technical-level role. The McMahon Act mandated *civilian control of the atom.*[3]

But the success of Oppenheimer and the federation in preventing full military control of the atom backfired on them. The military had opposed the Baruch Plan, but as the cold war erupted domestically, a nationalist obsession with military power erupted. Franz Schurmann has argued that this conflict between nationalists and internationalists was resolved only in a bipartisan ideology of national security.[4] In this ideology, liberals looked to the United Nations as the solution to the problems of war and revolution symbolized by Germany and Russia; the United Nations would facilitate demilitarization and transfer surplus wealth to the poor. On the other hand, nationalists embraced Britain as the symbol of international capitalism and feared Russia as the symbol of the revolutionary poor. To prevent the spread of communism, they rallied to the cause of General Douglas MacArthur and Chiang Kai-shek. The compromise doctrine of national security established that all policy decisions regarding nuclear energy would be made by the federal government and the military.

Atomic weapons had given the United States the status of an international superpower. Suspicions fell on the critics of nuclear power rather than on the guardians of nuclear secrets. In the McCarthy era, national-security issues brought before the public cast suspicions of communist sympathy on those who were critical of an area as sensitive as nuclear policy. Indeed, virulent anticommunism created an atmosphere in which dissenting to nuclear policy was tantamount to treason. Only ten months after the Americans exploded a fusion device, the Soviet Union did so too.[5] In what many today believe was an extreme act of scapegoating, Julius and Ethel Rosenberg were tried and executed for espionage in passing vital atomic energy secrets to the Soviet Union.

In a military campaign to suppress the dissent of the internationalist scientists, the scientists were increasingly maligned personally or denied security clearances. They lost their administrative power over nuclear energy to other government appointees. They were then discredited in a congressional investigation by Senator Hickenlooper, with the result that Oppenheimer lost his security clearance. Government secrecy in matters of nuclear energy was firmly established.[6]

The next major development was the Atoms for Peace proposal, made by President Eisenhower before the United Nations in December 1953. It called for international cooperation and the sharing of nuclear materials. (This has been a feature of U.S. government policy to the present day and is the basis for its stated refusal to export nuclear technology to nations that it believes will use nuclear materials for nuclear weaponry.) However, the slogan "atoms for peace" was used for American propaganda purposes in its relations with nonnuclear nations, and it also allowed limited control over nuclear research that led to nuclear-weapons development in other parts of the world. Atoms for Peace proved infamous twenty years later, when India detonated an atomic bomb with materials that had been supplied to it by Canada under the Atoms for Peace program.

In the early 1950s, a debate ensued over who should build and control nuclear power plants: the government or private industry. In a conflict between a private utility and a public corporation, the Dixon-Yates controversy of the mid 1950s, government control of commercial public power was at stake.[7] Legislation to establish government financing of the Tennessee Valley Authority was viewed by Republicans as "creeping socialism." However, private-enterprise advocates of commercial nuclear power were given support when President Eisenhower appointed Lewis Strauss, a New York financier, to head the Atomic Energy Commission. Later, the first civilian nuclear power plant was built under *private* control in 1957 in Shippingport, Pennsylvania (utilizing a design taken directly from the early submarine reactors developed by the navy). Government subsidies of nuclear-research centers aided this development. Between 1939 and 1971, it is estimated the government invested over $52 billion in atomic energy, and, over half that amount was spent for military programs.[8] Critics of nuclear power argue that without government subsidies of nuclear research and facilities—in particular, the uranium-enrichment plants in Tennessee—nuclear energy would be prohibitively expensive as a source of commercial power.

Radioactive fallout from nuclear-weapons testing gave a new direction in the activities of scientists opposing government policies. In 1962, Linus Pauling was awarded the Nobel Peace Prize for his efforts to ban the testing of nuclear weapons in the atmosphere. Herman Müller, who had been awarded a Nobel prize for his work with fruit flies, publicly warned that radiation could cause genetic mutations. A paper written by Müller was suppressed by the Atomic Energy Commission (AEC).[9] During the late 1950s, the public began to express opposition to government military nuclear policy. This was indirectly expressed in an alienated youth movement—the beatniks—in the United States and Britain. The beatniks, predecessors of hippies whose social accoutrements included sandals, jazz, bongo drums, and beards, had a "let's live for today" philosophy that stemmed from a belief that they would die soon in a nuclear war. The Cold War era was beginning to break apart, and when a young, liberal President was elected, dramatic changes were set into motion. The culmination of these changes was the Test Ban Treaty, signed in 1962 by President John F. Kennedy, that barred the detonation of nuclear weapons in the atmosphere.

Antinuclear Episodes (1960–68)

Several episodes occurred during the 1960s that indicated public resistance to both commercial and military uses of nuclear power. One was the Ban the Bomb movement in Britain. Under the spiritual leadership of Bertrand Russell, large numbers of people marched from the village of Aldermaston to London to protest the American Polaris missile base in Scotland and the use of Britain as an American military arsenal. [10] In Wyoming County, Pennsylvania, citizens became embroiled in a controversy over the proposed Meshoppen nuclear power plant.

The Meshoppen plant was supported both by President Kennedy and by Glenn Seaborg, then chairman of the Atomic Energy Commission. But a group of Quakers and a citizens' committee composed of dentists, county officials, businessmen, and housewives appeared before a Senate Select Committee to try to block the proposed reactor due to the threat of radiation danger. [11] They feared that low-level radiation from the plant would have damaging effects on public health, including infant mortality and cancer.

Ernest Sternglass, a scientist at the University of Pittsburgh, opened the controversy by warning of an increase in cancer deaths due to radiation from nuclear power plants. Strontium-90 from radioactive fallout was linked in the minds of local residents to the contamination of milk. By associating nuclear reactors with infant deaths, Sternglass quickly gained a reputation as a prophet of doom. He was joined in his scientific views by John Gofman, who was then a nuclear chemist and a physician at Livermore National Laboratory in California. An AEC scientist who was assigned the task of refuting Sternglass initially concluded that Sternglass had underestimated the socioeconomic reasons for infant deaths in Wyoming County, *but* he also said that there was a significant relationship between radioactivity and infant mortality. The AEC responded by requiring the scientist, Dr. Arthur Tamplin, to submit his speeches to the commission for prior approval. A paper Tamplin was to have presented before the American Association for the Advancement of Science was censored, and his staff was transferred to other departments.[12]

In the early 1970s, Sternglass, Gofman, and Tamplin became important leaders of the antinuclear movement. Gofman was a member of the Committee on Nuclear Responsibility, while Tamplin became a professional staff member of the Natural Resources Defense Council. The elder critic, Linus Pauling, also became active in the movement two decades after he initially warned of the dangers of radiation. Government repression only resulted in more active public dissent by scientists.

These early episodes of antinuclear activity in the 1960s dissipated somewhat when the Nuclear Nonproliferation Treaty was signed in 1968 by President Lyndon B. Johnson. The treaty placed nuclear materials used for commercial power in the United States under the regulatory power of the International Atomic Energy Agency. Social activists became much more involved in the antiwar movement, which reached its peak in the late 1960s, as well as in other movements for change, including those of youth, women, blacks, prisoners, and numerous other aggrieved groups in American society.

The issue of low-level ionizing radiation, raised by scientists in the Meshoppen controversy, resurfaced in the mid-1980s. Higher-than-normal incidences of children dying of leukemia were reported in a study conducted by the Massachusetts Department of Health in the population living near the Pilgrim reactor in Plymouth, Massachusetts. In Maine similar findings for residents living near Maine Yankee were refuted, but in Britain a study found higher rates of leukemia for residents who lived near any nuclear facility, not just nuclear power plants.[13]

But scientific evidence of the effect of radiation on health is still surprisingly inconclusive, given the seriousness of the issue. In the early 1980s, the Kemeny Commission report on Three Mile Island concluded that one of the greatest lacks of knowledge is of the effect of low-level radioactive wastes on human organisms.[14] In 1988, the National Institutes of Health began a study of excess cancer deaths, or "leukemia clusters," in areas surrounding all U.S. nuclear power plants. The low-level ionizing radiation controversy persists even after more than twenty-five years. Aside from a lack of research, the controversy also involves the question of whether the effects of low-level radiation are cumulative and genetically transmitted, or are harmful only if they exceed an unknown threshold level.[15]

The Environmentalist Phase (1968–72)

In the 1970s, the ecology and environmentalist movements emerged and drew attention to a broad range of environmental problems, such as air pollution, strip mining, water pollution, and the quality of life. Some of the mystery of nuclear power was stripped away when citizens' groups began to regard nuclear plants as ecological concerns. The antinuclear movement entered its environmentalist phase when the issue of thermal pollution of the environment by nuclear power plants became an issue.

Nuclear power plants discharge immense quantities of hot water from their cooling systems. Several large fish kills occurred near a nuclear plant at Oyster Creek, New Jersey, and at a nuclear-fuels-reprocessing plant in West Valley, New York. The issue of thermal pollution was not as emotion-laden as the issue of radiation hazards and did not involve questions of national security. But perhaps its most important effect was to lessen the power of the Atomic Energy Commission.

Since its inception, the AEC had been one of the most arrogantly directed agencies in the federal government. But environmentalist organizations in the early 1970s found that they could use the 1969 National Environmental Policy Act to challenge the nuclear establishment on the effects of nuclear power on the ecology of local areas. The most important result of the environmentalist phase was to pave the way for legal intervention in AEC licensing hearings for new plants. The landmark 1971 *Calvert Cliffs* federal court ruling required environmental impact statements to be made before the AEC could issue a construction permit for a nuclear power plant. This opened the door to chip away at the authoritarian power of the commission. (The new confidence of citizens' groups may have been reflected in the use of the term *nuclear energy* for commercial nuclear power, for the term *atomic energy* seems more associated with military power and unassailable governmental bodies such as the AEC.)

Thermal pollution was a short-lived issue, for the problem was not that severe and could be corrected through the construction of cooling towers (although this added substantially to the cost of nuclear power plants). Some of the fish kills had been the results of accidental discharges, and other evidence indicated that warmer waters around nuclear plants had actually been breeding grounds for several types of fish.

A typical nuclear power controversy during the environmentalist phase was that over a proposed nuclear power plant at Cayuga Lake, in upstate

New York. Scientists and citizens feared that ecological damage to the lake would result from a proposed plant.

The university professors who opposed the Cayuga Lake plant were joined by physicians, local politicians, the local Chamber of Commerce, the League of Women Voters, and the Sierra Club. Dorothy Nelkin, in a 1971 study of the Cayuga Lake controversy, found that Republicans generally viewed the conflict from the perspective of the national interest in new energy supplies and progress, while Democrats were more likely to oppose construction of the plant. Those involved in scientific research funded by the utility company were criticized by their peers in the scientific community; these opposing scientists were more concerned with policy analysis and wrote public speeches, participated in citizens' committees, and wrote position papers. Nelkin observed that the contribution of these scientists was diminished both by company management and by critics in their eagerness to support their own point of view.[16]

Scientific agreement on the possible environmental damage of the plant was never definitively established. Nelkin found that scientists from nearby Cornell University were divided as to whether the credibility of science would be threatened if they took a position on the issue at a time when the evidence for possible ecological damage was inconclusive.[17] However, the subtle disagreement among scientists never became a rigid cleavage.

In the legal hearings, scientists could not provide objective knowledge about the effects of nuclear power. The adversary process of the legal system had little relation to normal scientific processes. Two political scientists who observed licensing proceedings for nuclear power plants proposed in Midland, Michigan, and Vernon, Vermont, reported in 1974 that the proceedings were geared to promoting nuclear power and to confirming previously made decisions to build the plants.[18] Citizen intervenors in the hearings had limited financial resources and lacked experts to provide technical criticisms, and they frequently could not comprehend the complex technical testimony given by company scientists and engineers. When scientists testified against the plant, attorneys would seize upon existing gaps in scientific knowledge to portray them as deliberately attempting to hide information that would damage their case. This created a situation in which scientists came to avoid testifying in the hearings in order not to have their competence challenged by lawyers all too willing to embarrass them. Small groups of citizens were thus consigned to helplessness before the "steam-roller of agency arrogance, expert elitism, and stacked-deck proceedings." This led citizens to become prone to "know-nothingism, blind antitechnology and antigovernment sentiment, pessimism, and doom forecasting."[19]

Despite these problems, the tactic of citizen intervention quickly became a major part of the strategy of the coalescing antinuclear movement. If the environmentalist phase of antinuclear activities was modestly successful, it was because the government had been favorably disposed to regulate the environmental consequences of modern technology.

A Large-scale Movement Arises

Nuclear energy was controversial from the very beginning, and a number of opposition movements existed, first among scientists, then among disenchanted beatniks, and finally among the professional upper middle class. So the largescale antinuclear movement that has garnered mass media publicity since the early 1970s must be viewed as a continuation of earlier struggles. Nonetheless, it became a large-scale social movement with a distinct identity *only* after the devastating 1973–74 energy crisis. The Yom Kippur war between Egypt and Israel and the OPEC embargo on oil to supporters of Israel was a turning point in recent history. The ensuing energy crisis itself was the result of an accumulation of factors, but never before had world political instability, mercantilist economic policies, and world recession been factors in energy shortages. High inflation and unemployment turned the public away from the oil corporations, thought to be culprits in the crisis, and a movement developed within the liberal wing of the Democratic party for divestiture of their holdings.

After "brownouts" in the Northeast in 1970 due to electricity shortages, President Richard M. Nixon attempted to deal with the problem through "Clean Energy" proposals. Nixon proposed a successful demonstration of the fast breeder reactor by 1980 and federal support for alternative-energy resources. The fast breeder has the technological advantage of producing more fuel than it consumes, but in the 1980s it is still nowhere near a successful demonstration in the United States; in 1966, the experimental Fermi breeder reactor in Detroit experienced a partial meltdown.[20] The other Clean Energy proposals were for increased federal monies for sulfur oxide control, conversion of coal into a gaseous fuel, underground transmission of electricity, offshore oil and gas leases, government reorganization of energy agencies, and assessment of solar energy by the National Aeronautics and Space Administration and the National Science Foundation.

Many of these proposals became the basis of energy policy in later administrations. President Jimmy Carter attempted to cut support for the fast breeder reactor and greatly increased research expenditures for solar energy, conservation, and coal conversion. President Ronald Reagan reversed the Carter policies by restoring funding for the fast breeder reactor and all but eliminating federal support for solar-energy technology and conservation. Offshore oil and gas leases, often opposed by environmentalists, also accelerated in the Reagan era, while government reorganization of energy agencies accomplished little in the way of basic change of energy policy.[21]

In a struggle both within Congress and between Congress and the Nixon White House, President Nixon asked Congress to create the Federal Energy Administration and the Energy Research and Development Administration. These interim agencies were later incorporated into a large-scale Department of Energy. The interim plan was opposed by Senator Henry Jackson from the State of Washington, who wanted direct enactment of a Department of Energy. Dixie Lee Ray, chairman of the AEC (later governor of Washington state), supported the Nixon plan for a new agency to take over the research and management of nuclear installations and a second agency, the Nuclear Regulatory Commission, to be responsible for licensing and regulating nuclear power plants.[22]

The conflict of interest between the promotion and regulatory functions of the AEC was the first political issue of the coalescing antinuclear forces. They could not see how the Atomic Energy Commission could both promote and regulate nuclear power, and they believed this to be an obstacle to creating a new energy agency to research alternative-energy technologies and energy conservation. Congressional infighting among Senators Jackson, Ribicoff, and Kennedy and among Representatives Udall, Holifield, and McCormack made passage of a reorganization bill difficult.

The real opening for antinuclear forces came when Senator Abraham Ribicoff of Connecticut held hearings on amendments designed to strengthen the safety requirements of nuclear power plants. Cooperating with Friends of the Earth and National Intervenors, Senator Edward Kennedy introduced an amendment requiring that antinuclear intervenors in regulatory and licensing hearings be subsidized. In the House of Representatives, the amendments were vigorously opposed by the influential Representative Holifield of California. Senator Kennedy and Representative Udall of Arizona then pressed for assurances that the new energy agency would develop nonnuclear technologies as well as protect the environment.

Ralph Nader entered the battle by calling the commitment to nuclear power "technological suicide." When the Sierra Club and Friends of the Earth joined Nader and called for a moratorium on nuclear power development, the antinuclear movement was born. Senator Ribicoff held more hearings in March 1974 and warned of safety hazards from dependence on nuclear energy. Theodore B. Taylor, a nuclear physicist who had designed many of the most advanced weapons for the Defense Department, appeared before the committee to warn of the dangers of nuclear theft and sabotage. His contentions were refuted by Dixie Lee Ray and Ralph Lapp, a nuclear consultant. The interchange was broadcast on national television.

Representative Holifield succeeded in blocking the Kennedy amendments to subsidize intervenors, clearing the way for the Energy Reorganization Act of 1974. The AEC was abolished, and the Energy Research and Development Administration (ERDA) and an independent Nuclear Regulatory Commission (NRC) were established. President Gerald Ford appointed Robert Seamans, former secretary of the air force, as director of ERDA, and William Anders, a former AEC member, as chairman of the NRC. Despite new commitments and significant government reorganization, ERDA budget expenditures did not shift from nuclear energy to conservation and alternative-energy technologies. When Carter succeeded Ford, Congress went back to the original plan for a large energy superagency and created the Department of Energy to replace ERDA. The structure of the Nuclear Regulatory Commission remained secure until the accident at Three Mile Island.

Significant Events in the Nuclear Controversy (1973–80)

Almost as suddenly as the national political elite split over government reorganization to manage the energy crisis, resolution came swift and certain: the nuclear option was validated, and commitment to it was strengthened. The antinuclear movement was born, and momentum intensified from that point on.[23]

The safety of nuclear power plants now became an important issue. The public was awakened to the controversy through a CBS broadcast about dangers in the commercial nuclear-power industry. Writing about Theodore Taylor, the physicist who had done nuclear-weapons research,

John McPhee sounded the alarm in *The Curve of Binding Energy* 1974, which became essential reading for antinuclear groups forming throughout the nation.

Weakness had also been shown within the nuclear establishment. Shortly before its demise, the AEC had released the Rosenbaum report regarding the inadequacy of nuclear safeguards, then had dramatically overreacted to its own report by ordering armed guards around nuclear installations. The Montsanto Mound Laboratory in Miamisburg, Ohio, discovered that plutonium was leaking into the Erie Canal. A flood of internal memoranda were covertly released from within the AEC, confirming popular suspicion that nuclear power was not as safe or clean as proponents believed.

The government countered in 1974 by releasing a massive report on reactor safety by a research team under Norman Rasmussen at MIT. Intended to be a definitive study demonstrating the statistical improbability of a nuclear accident, the Rasmussen report was immediately challenged by both the Sierra Club and the Union of Concerned Scientists— groups whose criticisms of the safety of emergency core-cooling systems in reactors had helped prepare the ground for a movement.

When it was apparent that the Capitol Hill battle had been lost, Ralph Nader organized the first antinuclear conference, Critical Mass '74, in Washington, D.C. Workshops were held, and groups throughout the United States learned some of the basics of forming antinuclear organizations. At about the same time, Karen Silkwood, a worker at the Kerr-McGee plutonium-reprocessing facility in Oklahoma, was killed in an automobile accident. Her death brought the National Organization for Women and the labor movement into the antinuclear movement and cast doubt on the safety of workers in nuclear facilities. With speculation that the "accident" may have been intended, Silkwood's death also gave the movement a symbolic martyr, the first activist to die as a result of participation in the movement. This was analogous to the Kent State incident during the movement to end the Vietnam war.

Natural events also created a sense of urgency. A geologic fault that could result in an earthquake was discovered at Diablo Canyon in California, the site of a nuclear power plant under construction. In March 1975, a fire broke out at the Browns Ferry reactor in Alabama, burning through the cables controlling the emergency cooling system. If the reactor had not been shut down in time, a major nuclear accident could have occurred.

The antinuclear movement gained more attention in mid-1975, when the American Physical Society released a study critical of reactor safety. Representative Lee Aspin requested the NRC to withdraw a license for the shipment of nuclear materials to South Korea, and Senator Henry Jackson publicly opposed nuclear exports to South Africa. This criticism of nuclear power from within the political and scientific establishment gave the movement credibility.

The Brown's Ferry incident prompted Hugh Carey, then governor of New York, to announce his support of a nuclear moratorium in that state, and a moratorium bill was also introduced into the state legislature of Nebraska. Businessmen and Professional People in the Public Interest and the Izaak Walton League scored one of the first movement victories when they obtained a permanent stay against the Bailly, Indiana, plant construction because the site was too near major population centers. However, the stay was reversed by the U.S. Supreme Court four months later.

The need for international cooperation on the nuclear-safeguards issue was demonstrated when West Germany announced the sale of a complete nuclear fuel cycle to Brazil, which had not signed the Nuclear Nonproliferation Treaty. President Ford responded only by asking Congress for private industry control of future uranium-enrichment plants. Local groups, however, were becoming more active on issues related to the safety of plants in the United States. In Pennsylvania, LeHigh Common Cause voted to oppose nuclear power, while the Vermont state legislature was persuaded by the Vermont Public Interest Research Group to pass a bill requiring legislative approval of new nuclear power plants. Colorado Public Interest Research Groups filed suit to force the Environmental Protection Agency to regulate radioactive-water discharges from nuclear facilities. (Later, the U.S. Court of Appeals made the Environmental Protection Agency set water-pollution standards for all nuclear facilities.) In New York, the Safe Energy Coalition attempted to introduce a bill to prohibit the construction of any new nuclear power plants in the state but did not get legislative support, and an Iowa citizens' group blocked the licensing of a nuclear power plant until a commercial system could handle its wastes.

There was a lull in the movement during the summer of 1975 after this flurry of activity. Nuclear advocates were given a boost when Saudi Arabia announced a $15 billion electrification and desalinization plan that would include twenty-five agro-industrial complexes and a national power grid generated by nuclear power—despite the fact that uranium prices had tripled, casting doubt on the future of nuclear-fuel supply. Gulf Oil later pleaded nolo contendere to charges of price-fixing in the uranium market with the Canadian government. In other areas of controversy, the NRC officially opposed the idea of a federal security force to protect nuclear materials, challenging the argument that nuclear power would require a national security state. In New York, the Council on Economic Priorities charged Con Edison with a misleading public-relations campaign about savings from the operation of the Indian Point nuclear reactors, while Ralph Nader publicly requested the NRC and the EPA to alert two hundred New Mexico uranium miners and their families that their drinking water contained high levels of radioactive substances. Billy Jack Productions announced its intention to film a documentary on the strange circumstances surrounding Silkwood's death.

Everywhere the nuclear establishment was on the defensive. A group called Citizen Alert opposed an ERDA decision choosing Nevada as the site for storage of high-level radioactive wastes. Safe Power for Maine began a petition drive for a referendum calling for a seven-year moratorium on nuclear power, while Concerned Citizens of Tennessee opposed a proposed nuclear complex in Hartsville. National Public Radio Corporation filed a Freedom of Information suit against the Justice Department to gain access to the files of its investigation into the death of Karen Silkwood, and on 13 November 1975, nuclear opponents scheduled a rally in New York City to coincide with the first anniversary of the death of Silkwood. Ralph Nader groups requested that evacuation plans in the event of a nuclear accident be released, and he coordinated efforts to block the automatic passing of uranium price increases to consumers. Two important suits were filed against the NRC with long-range implications. The Natural Resources Defense Council, the Sierra Club, and Businessmen and Professional People in the Public Interest succeeded in getting the NRC to prepare an environmental impact statement on the handling of wastes from light-water nuclear reactors. The Sierra Club and the Natural Resources Defense Council filed a petition to intervene in hearings on the Clinch River breeder reactor project, along with the East Tennessee Energy Group. The movement seemed to be gathering more support and was becoming effective in the legal arena.

November 1975 brought the second Critical Mass antinuclear conference, with a candlelight vigil before the White House for Karen Silkwood. Ominous notes were sounded when South Africa announced its plans to construct a uranium-enrichment facility using the West German Becker jet nozzle process. And the NRC decided to allow the limited recycling of plutonium. But the following month, the National Council of Churches released a statement condemning the "plutonium economy," while the Federation of American Scientists released a poll of 10 percent of its members showing that a majority were opposed to the rapid development of nuclear power. The base of support for the antinuclear movement was broadening and becoming more inclusive of diverse segments of society.

1976: The Nuclear Showdown

The antinuclear movement intensified and sharpened its struggle in 1976 with a frontal attack on the nuclear establishment. Since 1976 was both the year of the American bicentennial and a presidential election, the movement's activities became even more significant.

The government seemed to be on the brink of finding some solutions to the nuclear-safeguards problem. An international accord was reached on nuclear exports—but then details were not announced. Nationally, the Natural Resources Defense Council appealed the NRC decision to allow the interim recycling of plutonium as a violation of the National Environmental Policy Act *and,* in a new precedent, as a violation of the Atomic Energy Act of 1954. After meeting with representatives from the National Organization for Women, Senator Lee Metcalf reopened the Karen Silkwood investigation. Stop Nuclear Power of Margate, New Jersey, intervened in hearings over proposed floating nuclear power plants off the Atlantic coast. An Iowa citizens' group petitioned the NRC to revoke operating licenses for plants that repeatedly violated existing regulations. Public Media Center of California filed a suit for fairness in radio time for antinuclear advertisements.

The first major political test for the movement was the Nuclear Safeguards Initiative on the California ballot, which would take the issue directly to the people of that populous state. Early in 1976, three engineers resigned their positions in the nuclear industry to participate in the antinuclear movement in California, and a few days later a fourth engineer resigned his position in New York to work for the Union of Concerned Scientists. The resignations gave the movement a tremendous impetus, for they captured the attention of the mass media.

While the media focused on the initiative and the upcoming presidential election, antinuclear groups continued to hammer away at every level of government. The Union of Concerned Scientists, the Sierra Club, and the Natural Resources Defense Council filed a suit asking the NRC to withdraw a nuclear-export license of Edlow International Company that allowed it to ship nuclear materials to the Tarapur nuclear power plant in India. (This was eventually agreed to by President Carter, who in turn was overruled by Congress in 1980, allowing shipment to resume.) This was the first time international controls were legally sanctioned by the NRC rather than by international accord among governments. In Washington, D.C., the Silkwood case was summarily closed again, and the Supporters of Silkwood organized to focus national attention on the case. Locally, legal petitions were directed to the problem of planning for a nuclear accident. Maine Public Interest Research Group filed a show-cause order for evacuation plans in the event of an accident at Maine Yankee, and a Pennsylvania antinuclear group demanded *immediate* emergency nuclear safeguards. Friends of the Earth attempted to have the Department of Transportation in New York City stop nuclear wastes from being transported through the city until an environmental impact statement was prepared.

As the stage was set for the confrontation in California, the National Council of Churches voted in favor of a nuclear moratorium, and the NRC released a study of terrorist and sabotage threats against nuclear installations, with the suggestion that an army unit be trained to act against terrorist groups in the event of an attack against a nuclear installation. At the site of the Indian Point reactors in New York, antinuclear activists were confronted by plant workers, who felt their jobs were being threatened by the demonstrators, prompting the formation of a group called Environmentalists for Full Employment. In April, *Time* magazine made the startling revelation that Israel had nuclear weapons at the secret Dimona installation in the Negev desert, and that the Israeli government had come within thirty minutes of using the weapons in the 1973 Yom Kippur war. *Time* also reported that in 1972 an American commercial airliner with 108 passengers aboard had been forced down by Israeli jets after it had strayed over the Dimona installation.

Utility companies throughout the nation massively infused funds into the pronuclear Citizens for Jobs and Energy organization. After a "red alert" scare to nuclear power plants on the eve of balloting day, the California Nuclear Safeguards Initiative was defeated by a two-to-one margin. The movement was not stopped; in the same month, Jimmy Carter was nominated as the Democratic presidential candidate, with a party platform supporting the development of alternatives to nuclear power. Frustrated by the failure of the tactics of legal intervention and voter referendums, however, antinuclear groups turned to direct action. The construction site of the Seabrook nuclear power plant in New Hampshire was occupied by members of the Clamshell Alliance, followed by a second demonstration with two hundred arrests. Presidential candidate Carter announced his support for civil disobedience on the part of the Seabrook activists *if* they were willing to take the consequences of their actions. These demonstrations were immediately successful: in a surprising victory for the movement, the NRC issued a temporary moratorium on new licenses until a study could be completed of nuclear-fuel reprocessing facilities and the handling of radioactive wastes. The suit had been filed by Consolidated National Intervenors, the Natural Resources Defense Council, and the New England Coalition on Nuclear Pollution.

Direct action means confrontation with authorities. Activists charged that the Federal Bureau of Investigation and the Central Intelligence Agency had monitored the activities of civilian antinuclear groups, and that the nuclear industry had funded background investigations into the Sierra Club, Friends of the Earth, Another Mother for Peace, the Union of Concerned Scientists, and Ralph Nader. In May 1976, disclosures were made that the FBI had cooperated with an informer, Jacque Srouji, in preparing a book with derogatory information about the sex and drug life of Karen Silkwood by showing the informer one thousand pages of FBI files on Silkwood. A few months later, the informer disappeared.[24]

National attention then focused on the presidential election. Antinuclear groups prepared for referendums on the ballots in six states. Internationally, Swedish Center party leader Thorbjorn Falldin defeated the Social Democratic party in a struggle in which his opposition to nuclear power was crucial to his victory. The parents of Karen Silkwood filed a suit against the Kerr-McGee Corporation, charging company responsibility in the death of their daughter. Shortly before the elections, the NRC dramatically issued shoot-to-kill orders in the event of any attempt to sabotage fourteen nuclear-weapons facilities. The referendums' results were less than dramatic; all were soundly defeated, and the antinuclear movement was at least temporarily routed.

During 1977, the antinuclear movement persisted by relying on the tactic of demonstrations.[25] These localized conflicts involved the nuclear power plant under construction at Seabrook, New Hampshire, and the arrest of ninety protestors at Diablo Canyon in California. The first inklings of a countermovement involving public participation came about a month after the Seabrook demonstrations, when more than three thousand construction workers and company employees who called themselves the New Hampshire Voice of Energy staged a counterdemonstration in support of nuclear power outside Seabrook, and in

Charlestown, Rhode Island, pronuclear supporters disrupted a talk by Ralph Nader.

The greatest escalation of the movement occurred in Europe. Thousands of helmeted demonstrators carrying communist flags fought a three-hour battle with the police at the nuclear-power-plant site at Grohnde, West Germany, injuring fifty demonstrators and forty policemen. A protest of thirty thousand people against the Super-Phenix breeder reactor at Creys-Malville in France left one person dead in a clash with the police, and in Italy, seven thousand persons demonstrated against two nuclear power plants proposed in Monalto d'Cristo. The high point of the year, however, was in November, when President Carter vetoed the $80 million appropriation for the Clinch River breeder reactor in Tennessee. This and other government action perhaps took some of the steam out of the movement by incorporating its goals into public policy.

Demonstrations continued at Seabrook in 1978, including one in which twenty thousand people participated. Daniel Ellsberg, veteran of the 1960s antiwar movement and the Pentagon Papers controversy, was one of nineteen persons arrested during a demonstration outside the military nuclear-waste dump at Rocky Flats, Colorado. The Potomac Alliance demonstrated outside the White House over the Karen Silkwood case, arrests were made outside the Trojan nuclear power plant in Oregon, and three hundred out of two thousand demonstrators of the Abalone Alliance were arrested at Diablo Canyon. The Ku Klux Klan organized a pronuclear demonstration outside Seabrook, while in the conservative South the first major demonstration took place outside the nuclear-fuel reprocessing plant in Barnwell, South Carolina, with over one thousand participants, who called themselves the Palmetto Alliance. But generally the movement was slowing down. The greatest successes were again in November: during the 1978 off-year elections, the voters of Hawaii and Montana passed limited antinuclear referenda.

On 28 March 1979, the world was abruptly awakened to the perils of nuclear power when a complex series of human and mechanical errors resulted in the release of radioactive gases into central Pennsylvania. When the cooling system of the nuclear reactor at Three Mile Island in Harrisburg malfunctioned, the reactor core began to overheat, raising the specter of a nuclear meltdown. Reverberations from this near-disaster were immediate. Shouting "We all live in Pennsylvania," 35,000 people attended an antinuclear rally in Hanover, West Germany, to oppose plans for an underground dump for nuclear wastes. In San Francisco, demonstrators "played dead" outside a utility office, and a "die-in" was held outside the office of the Philadelphia Electric Company.[26] Proposed bans on new nuclear power plants were introduced into state legislatures (although in Austin, Texas, voters approved a bond issue allowing the city to continue participation in a nuclear project).

The largest antinuclear rally so far took place in Washington, D.C., involving an estimated 65,000 people, following a demonstration of 20,000 people in San Francisco. According to the *New York Times* (7 May 1979) the demonstrators in Washington included representatives of the Communist party, the Socialist Worker's party, the Women's International League for Peace and Freedom, the Union of Concerned Scientists, the Grey Panthers, and the Gay Liberation Movement, among others. One month later there were more mass demonstrations throughout the world, as 5 June 1979 became designated as International Anti-Nuclear Day by movement groups. Demonstrators were arrested in Oklahoma, Arkansas, and Massachusetts. Twenty thousand Dutch citizens turned out for a rally. Six hundred protesters out of an estimated fifteen thousand were arrested outside the Shoreham, Long Island, nuclear power plant, and in Spain, one demonstrator was killed.[27]

The size of the demonstrations and the number of people arrested grew larger and larger. In October, at Battery Park, New York, over 300,000 people turned out for a demonstration in which many movement people of the 1960s, such as Jane Fonda, reappeared. A few weeks later, 1,045 persons were arrested at the New York Stock Exchange.

But then a new crisis diverted attention from the nuclear issue. The takeover of the American Embassy in Iran and the subsequent crisis over the hostage situation "preempted" the antinuclear movement from the national media, and demonstrations were small and sporadic all through the following year.

International Diffusion (1975–80)

Harrisburg became symbolic to antinuclear forces throughout the world. Initially, the diffusion of the antinuclear movement to Western Europe was facilitated by the activities of ecology organizations with international affiliates, particularly Friends of the Earth; criticisms of nuclear power published by the Union of Concerned Scientists; publicity given to controversial studies of the Atomic Energy Commission in the international media; and the activities of indigenous citizen groups in Europe that often looked to their American counterparts for strategic and tactical leadership.

The movement became strongest in West Germany, Sweden, France, Holland, and Britain. Legal interventions were also initiated in Denmark, Norway, Switzerland, and Austria. Italy and Spain joined the list of countries with strong opposition to nuclear power, and the movement even began to diffuse to Eastern Europe through Yugoslavia. Violence and bombings erupted in the French movement, while in West Germany the tactical action quickly escalated to sit-ins and demonstrations even before similar tactics were used at Seabrook. Violent resistance also emerged in Spain.

In 1975, nuclear power protests in West Germany centered on opposition to a plant under construction in Whyl, a small town of two thousand residents near the Rhine.[28] Farmers were among the staunchest opponents because they feared the nuclear power plant would damage their fruits, vegetables, and vineyards. A sit-in in which farmers and villagers virtually took over the plant site attracted conservationist groups, middle-class university students, and other citizens. These groups defined their tactics as "burgher initiatives," a form of citizen action embracing a wide variety of community issues. Radicals and procommunist students were usually excluded from burgher initiatives; nonetheless, government leaders in Stuttgart attempted to portray all the demonstrators as radicals.

In Germany and France, the antinuclear movement not only resulted in massive demonstrations, it provided electoral support for antinuclear candidates.[29] Violent demonstrations occurred in Grohnde and Brokdorf, West Germany; at the site of the Super-Phenix reactor in Fessenheim; and at the site of the Plogoff reactor in Quimper, France. Ecology parties—the Green movement—used the issue to gain small proportions of the vote in national and municipal elections. As Dorothy Nelkin and Michael Pollack indicate, opposition to nuclear power expressed popular anxieties over advanced industrial society such as the "industrialization of rural areas, the concentration of economic activities, the centralization of decision-making, and the incremental tendencies towards a tightening of police control."[30]

Nuclear policy in France is decided by the Council of Ministers under a shroud of secrecy, which inhibits opposition. Etienne Bauer describes the French nuclear opposition as "weakly organized ecologists who have almost no political power, and who can mobilize fewer people in France than in Scandinavia. They speak a passionate language, mixing serious arguments and apocalyptic delirium. To them, nuclear power appears to be more a symbol of a hateful form of civilization than a well-defined eco-technical and social problem."[31] Despite general public apathy, however, the antinuclear movement in France was the first to use violence.

In both France and Germany, radical left political parties and groups (but not the Communists) have been actively opposed to nuclear power, while socialist parties have been more ambivalent, supporting either a moratorium or a slower level of development of nuclear energy. Centrist parties, such as the Gaullists in France and the Christian Democrats in West Germany, have been the strongest advocates of nuclear energy and also the most responsive to the large companies, including the state-owned nuclear company in France, Framatome, and the Kraftwerks-union in West Germany.

Despite the growing strength of the antinuclear movement, France and Germany remain committed to nuclear power. This is particularly true of France, whose commitment to nuclear power was reaffirmed by President Giscard D'Estaing after Harrisburg. The commitment was made more palatable to the public by promising that people living near nuclear power plants would get a 15 percent reduction in their electricity bills.[32] With the socialist victory of Francois Mitterand rapid expansion of nuclear power has continued.

Swedish nuclear opposition includes the *Miljocentrum* ("environment center"), *Faltbiolergna* ("field biologists"), *Alternativ Stad* ("alternative earth"), and *Jordens Vanner* ("Friends of the Earth"). The Center party, along with the Communist party, introduced parliamentary opposition to nuclear power in 1974, after Arthur Tamplin and Dean Abrahamson (two American nuclear critics) and Amory Lovins, British representative of Friends of the Earth, gave speeches in the country. Pronuclear speeches were given in Sweden by Dixie Lee Ray and Edward Teller. The Conservative party, with support from the Social Democrats, was able to pass a bill through the Swedish Parliament expanding the nuclear power program, although a majority of the public supported the opposition.

Some of the major arguments against nuclear power have less impact in Sweden because its nuclear wastes are sent to England and because Sweden is not interested in nuclear-weapons development. Nevertheless, the controversy heated up when Thorbjorn Falldin, the Center party leader, credited Swedish physicist Hannes Alfven with having awakened him to the hazards of nuclear power.[33] The 1976 election became a virtual referendum on nuclear power and contributed to the defeat of the Social Democratic party for the first time in forty-four years.

However, the coalition that gave the Center party victory in 1976 collapsed two years later, again over the nuclear issue. This time the Liberal party gained power under the leadership of Ola Ulsten. Sweden has a very developed environmental consciousness, but most of the feasible hydroelectric sites have already been utilized. This accounts for the original commitment to nuclear power. The Center party had formerly been the Agrarian party, but it had broadened its rural orientation to a concern with the environment and the adverse effects of modernization, including centralization of government.[34] This predisposed them to opposition to nuclear energy.

The Swedish government adopted a report that called for neither phasing out nuclear power nor a binding commitment to it, and thereafter the issue began to die down. Falldin then compromised his position, infuriating his supporters in the Center party and leading to his resignation in 1978. However, after Harrisburg the leader of the Social Democratic party, Olaf Palme, announced his support for a referendum on nuclear power, and Liberal Prime Minister Ola Ulsten refused permission for two reactors to charge until after the referendum.[35] The referendum took place in March 1980 and was defeated, even though it would have allowed only *limited* expansion of nuclear power as a matter of public policy.[36]

Violent opposition to nuclear power also emerged in Spain, which depends heavily on hydroelectric power for electricity. There are three nuclear reactors operating in Spain and seven are under construction, but these have engendered opposition from local citizens as well as the Socialist and Communist parties.[37] Some of the difficulty occurred in the Basque region, where a demonstrator was killed in a clash with the police. But opposition also emerged in the rural western provinces of Badajoz and Cáceres, near Portugal. At one point, thirty thousand people defied a ban and demonstrated in the town of Villaneuva de la Serena. Mayors of seventeen towns declared opposition to starting up two new reactors at Almarez until safety guarantees were made.[38]

In other European nations, the antinuclear movement was somewhat muted. In 1979, Austrian voters refused to allow a $550 million reactor at Zwentendorf to be activated, and the Swiss now require parliamentary approval for building nuclear power stations. Of all the European nations, only Denmark, with its tremendous natural gas reserves, and Norway, an oil-rich nation, have no nuclear power programs. In Finland there has been little resistance to the construction of four nuclear power stations because they mean independence from Soviet oil.

The main reactor in Holland is at Borselles and is operated by a public corporation. A substantial minority of the Dutch public opposed nuclear power, including some scientists, doctors, and public-action groups. While the largest labor unions favored the development of alternative energy sources, the Protestant labor unions supported nuclear power. The Dutch government wanted a nuclear program in order to conserve the depleting natural gas fields at Groningen, while opponents of nuclear power argued that the North Sea deposits of oil and gas were sufficient for Dutch needs. In a controversy in Rotterdam, the Labor party rejected plans to build a large nuclear reactor near the city. Holland also participated in a fast breeder reactor, called the SNR-300, being built at Kalkar in the southern part of West Germany. The project involved both countries as well as Belgium. The Dutch were to help pay for their part by levying a 3 percent tax on all electric bills. This "Kalkar tax" was strongly opposed, and seventy municipalities refused to hand over revenues for the SNR-300. This forced a compromise, whereby the government allowed individuals to consign the 3 percent tax to alternative-energy programs.[39]

In Belgium, the mayor of Huy ordered a power station at Tihange to close down, although he was quickly overruled by the Belgian government. The Tihange reactor was shut down in 1980 by striking workers, who occupied the control room and threatened to reduce its output.

Britain has been moving ahead slowly with nuclear power. It relies on a British design that has produced public concern for safety but not enough pressure for a moratorium.[40] The main problem now is with the design, since it is similar to the pressurized water reactor at Harrisburg.

Finally, the antinuclear movement began to diffuse from Western to Eastern Europe. In Yugoslavia, a nation lacking in energy resources and a national power grid, the government planned to build the country's second nuclear reactor in the industrialized Dalmatian coast, but local citizens were concerned about pollution and the tourist trade. Yugoslavs who went to work in West Germany returned with ideas of antinuclear protest. Under public pressure, the government backed off from its plans to site a reactor near the beaches of Dalmatia.[41]

Significant opposition to nuclear power has not yet developed in Japan or in various South American and Asian countries with existing or proposed nuclear reactors. Japan, however, does have a substantial antinuclear movement that opposes nuclear weapons. In Canada, opposition is growing but is not on the same level as in the United States. There are twenty-one existing or planned reactors in Ontario, three in Quebec, and one in New Brunswick. Canada also has significant uranium reserves in Ontario and uses the unique CANDU reactor design, which uses heavy water as a moderator and burns natural rather than enriched uranium. The Canadian government is particularly concerned about occupational health hazards to uranium miners, and several commissions and inquiries have been officially made into a wide range of problems. However, as Robert Paehlke observes, "the various environmental—particularly antinuclear—groups in Canada are not yet so firmly established as a respectable part of the decision-making process in Canada as in the United States."[42]

The Antinuclear Movement in the 1980s

Jimmy Carter's defeat in the 1980 presidential election brought an end to the direct-action phase of the antinuclear movement (whose activists were branded as "modern day Luddites" by Ronald Reagan.)[43] Only small, isolated demonstrations continued at nuclear power plants, primarily at Seabrook and at Shoreham (where 138 people were arrested in 1983). Diablo Canyon, long the scene of demonstrations, began operations ten years behind schedule and at a cost of almost $5 billion, followed within a year by the resumption of Unit 1 at Three Mile Island. No new nuclear power plants were ordered, and some, such as Marble Hill in Indiana, were abandoned. In the early 1980s, as construction costs soared by almost ten times the original estimates, utilities, financing institutions, investors, and state utility commissions pressured to pass the costs on to rate payers.[44] The largest default in municipal bond history occurred when the Washington Public Power Supply System defaulted on $2.2 billion that had been borrowed to complete two nuclear power plants that were never finished.[45]

The "Reagan revolution" brought reversals of national policy so thorough in scope that antinuclear activists had to retrench to grasp the enormity of the changes. A blitz of fundamental changes in national policy brought a military buildup and deep cuts in domestic spending for social welfare programs.[46] Among the steps taken within only a few years were:

1. Two-thirds of the budget for alternative-energy resources, particularly solar energy and conservation, was eliminated, and funding for nuclear energy was

increased, including $240 million to continue work on the Clinch River breeder reactor.

2. Private companies were encouraged and given incentives—in the form of financial guarantees and relaxation of safety standards—to purchase the unfinished nuclear-fuels-reprocessing plant in Barnwell, South Carolina.

3. The production of nuclear weapons, such as warheads for the MX missile, was increased and much of that responsibility was placed with the Department of Energy.

4. Proposals were made to obtain plutonium for nuclear warheads by reprocessing the waste products of commercial nuclear power plants.

5. An official commitment was made to "streamlining" the licensing process to make it easier for nuclear power plants to be built without excessive government regulation.

6. Nuclear nonproliferation policies were relaxed to help U.S. companies become prime exporters of nuclear technology throughout the world.

7. Breeder-reactor research and the commercial reprocessing of nuclear fuels were encouraged in Europe.

8. James Edwards of South Carolina (location of the Barnwell plant and eight other nuclear power plants) was appointed secretary of energy, and W. Kenneth Davis, a former executive at Bechtel Corporation (the leading nuclear-construction firm) was appointed deputy secretary.

9. Caspar Weinberger, former president of Bechtel, was named secretary of defense, and George Shultz, former attorney for Bechtel, was named secretary of state.

These far-reaching policies and appointments did not crush the antinuclear movement but prompted it to create new tactics and strategies. The movement's focus shifted to confronting the renewed alliance between the nuclear industry and the federal government over the issues of radioactive wastes and emergency-evacuation plans for residents near nuclear power plants in the event of an accident similar to Three Mile Island. The Reagan administration sought to link the nuclear fuel cycle with the production of nuclear weapons and to overcome the last obstacles to a functional nuclear energy power system by advocating reprocessing of fuels and siting of wastes in specific states. Then an accident in the Soviet Union reawakened public opposition to nuclear power.

The Chernobyl nuclear-power-plant complex in the Ukraine, with its four operating reactors and two more under construction, is reminiscent of nuclear-energy parks once envisioned for the United States.[47] On 26 April 1986, during an experiment to test safety systems in Unit 4, a rapid decline in power prompted operators to withdraw graphite control rods to increase the power and at the same time shut down safety systems that would interfere with the experiment. A power surge occurred, and the operators could not insert the control rods in time. In seconds, the fuel overheated and caused several massive steam explosions that tore off a one-thousand-ton containment shelter and spewed radioactive elements from the reactor core into the atmosphere: iodine-131, cesium-137, plutonium, xenon, strontium, and krypton. Thirty fires ignited near the plant. Within two days, over 130,000 people were evacuated in a nineteen-mile radius of the plant, but the evacuation was not quick enough to prevent at least 24,000 people in the path of winds carrying the radioactive debris from being exposed to dangerous levels of radiation. Twenty-nine people died of thermal burns and acute radioactive poisoning, and two others died in the explosion itself.[48] Over three hundred people were hospitalized with serious injuries, and many received bone marrow transplants from a surgical team headed by an American, Dr. Robert Gale. Estimates of future fatalities range from a few thousand to several hundred thousand over the next several decades.[49]

Radioactive clouds from Chernobyl traveled across Europe and caused slight increases in radioactivity as far away as California.[50] Millions of dollars of fruit, vegetables, and milk were destroyed in Europe. (Much of this ended up in Third World countries.[51]) *Chernobyl* entered the vocabulary with a meaning as resonant as *Armageddon*. The political ramifications of Chernobyl were felt worldwide, but in the United States the Republican administration changed no policies. Rather, it promulgated the view that such an accident was unlikely to happen here because only one reactor in the United States was graphite-moderated—the N-reactor near Richland, Washington, used to produce plutonium for nuclear weapons. But this reactor was shut down late in 1986 for safety work following an evaluation prompted by Chernobyl. Unlike its Soviet counterpart, the N-reactor has no containment building and had already been operated beyond its expected life span of twenty years. Environmental groups initiated actions to keep the plant permanently closed.[52] This left the Savannah River facility in South Carolina as the only plant producing plutonium for nuclear weapons, but it has similar problems of aging and an inability to operate at full capacity.

The combined effect of Chernobyl and the strongly pronuclear policies of the Reagan era have set the stage for a vigorous antinuclear movement in the 1990s. The main issues are evacuation plans in the case of a nuclear accident, nuclear-waste dump sites, safety violations and cover-ups (often exposed by whistleblowers), drug abuse, the breeder reactor and nuclear-fuels reprocessing, and the production of plutonium for use in nuclear weapons. This last issue brings the antinuclear movement fully into the broader disarmament movement and creates the possibility of a merger of two seemingly disparate movements into one opposed to both nuclear energy *and* nuclear weapons.

Participating Groups

Three Mile Island and Chernobyl were critical events that intensified the movement after it met with powerful opposition in the Reagan era. The new issues, often produced by changes in government policies, are more salient to some groups than to others. Core groups in the movement have been remarkably persistent over at least a fifteen-year period, while other groups have gone on to pursue different goals with greater appeal to transitory public opinion until some new event brings nuclear energy again to the forefront.

Before the accident at Harrisburg that came to symbolize all that is wrong with nuclear power, the antinuclear movement had attracted perhaps no more than 1 percent of the American populace and a smaller percentage in Europe. Before the issue of nuclear energy was introduced into the 1976 presidential campaign, the most broad-based activity of the movement had been the obtaining of 400,000 signatures on a Clean Energy petition. This petition was circulated by the Task Force against Nuclear Pollution, based in Washington, D.C., using the good offices of Senator Mike Gravel of Alaska.[53] The Clean Energy petition simply called for a moratorium on nuclear power plants and the development of solar energy technology. Petitions were also circulated to put initiatives on nuclear energy before the voters in state elections.

Individuals who sign petitions are not necessarily active participants in a movement; signing a petition is only a minimal form of political expression. Membership in an organization or group is a higher threshold of participation, but the number of active individuals rarely exceeds 10 percent of the total membership and in most cases represents only a small nucleus of activities. Some organizations have a structure that enables members to vote on the strategy objectives of the group, such as Common Cause, while in other organizations local chapters may be intensively involved in specific conflicts, exemplified by the Sierra Club (although the Sierra Club is quite active at the national level). Many groups that became enmeshed in the nuclear controversy are actually voluntary associations, often aligned with the environmentalist movement. Numerically,

environmentalist and conservationist societies have the largest membership among voluntary associations in the antinuclear movement, with the
Sierra Club having the largest public following of all. Several large organizations, such as the National Wildlife Federation, have been involved
in the antinuclear movement only through a public proclamation against
nuclear power. But all these voluntary associations have played some
role in the antinuclear movement.

The mass base of the antinuclear movement in the United States consists not so much vast memberships in large organizations as of small
groups scattered throughout small towns and metropolitan areas. The
most active groups are found along the eastern seaboard and the West
Coast, but groups exist in every state. (The range of these groups is
indicated in Appendix D; local groups are the most numerous but not the
most influential.) After the accident at Three Mile Island, there was a
proliferation of new groups in the movement, although organizations
founded prior to Three Mile Island still formed the core of the movement.
Ecology and environmentalist voluntary associations such as the Sierra
Club, Friends of the Earth, and the Natural Resources Defense Council
are the most likely to have a national or international membership. (It
was through these groups with international chapters that the movement
diffused to European nations.)

Regional differences are significant. Some states seem to have political
cultures more supportive for movements than others. While activist
groups do exist in the larger cities of the South and the Midwest, they
have had less success than groups in California and New England in organizing large-scale opposition to nuclear power. Inspired by acts of civil
disobedience by the Clamshell Alliance at the Seabrook site, over three
dozen alliances with names such as Paddlewheel, Northern Sun, Bread-
basket, Catfish, Kudzu, Armadillo, Sunflower, Abalone, Cactus, and
Sagebrush flourished between 1977 and about 1980.[54] An effort to contact forty of these groups in 1988 netted only a half-dozen replies. Only
a few were still active, including Northern Sun Alliance in Minnesota, the
Sunflower Alliance in Missouri, and the Clamshell Alliance. Most of the
alliances appear to have broken up into smaller groups with unique em-
phases on peace or ecology, or to have dissipated altogether.

In Madison, Wisconsin, the Upper Great Lakes Green Network—
which has scheduled quarterly meetings—was formed in 1987 from seventeen different ecology, peace, and community-organizing groups in
Michigan, Wisconsin, and Minnesota.[55] Most of these groups are involved in ecology or "Green" issues local to their area, such as Styro-

foam, groundwater contamination, chemical-free food, and incineration. Further contact with these groups revealed strong antinuclear attitudes and earlier involvements in fighting the Department of Energy over the possible siting of a radioactive-waste dump site in Wisconsin. The Northern Sun Alliance in Minneapolis, although involved in the anti-incineration movement, still defines itself as an antinuclear group.[56] Many of the direct-action groups no longer exist in 1988, but the antinuclear movement is still strongly represented by such organizations as the Union of Concerned Scientists, the Natural Resources Defense Council, the Clamshell Alliance, and others with a mass base of activists available in any area where there is a specific nuclear issue.

Social-action theory is one of the main theoretical perspectives in sociology that I have used to analyze the antinuclear movement.[57] One axiom of this theory is that in order to understand social reality, we should look at the subjective orientations that individuals and groups have toward situations that are relevant to them.[58] What is their *frame of reference* when they react to events significant to the movement? When an antinuclear group responds to an event such as the nuclear accident at Three Mile Island, the social scientist must deal with the event as it appears from the point of view of the groups or individuals whose action is being analyzed. The report of the Kemeny Commission on Three Mile Island might appear to some to be a more objective analysis than that of antinuclear activists, but in a study of antinuclear groups, their reactions to and definitions of the situation must be reported.

The political actions taken by various antinuclear groups are guided by their own specific orientations, which include their beliefs about nuclear power, their social values, and the symbols that express their opposition. Group members have ideas about what they consider a desirable state of affairs to be. They may, for example, want an energy technology that is compatible with their ideas about ecology and the environment. These dominant value orientations are intertwined with individuals' motivations.

Four main types of social action have been defined, given the existence of specific social values and motives. These are intellectual, expressive, moral, and instrumental types of social action.[59] For the hundreds of groups involved in the antinuclear movement, this typology is a useful way of indicating the differences in how groups perceive nuclear power.

Antinuclear groups with *intellectual* patterns of social activism, such as the Union of Concerned Scientists, place an emphasis on their knowledge of nuclear technology. These scientists' groups are among the most influential antinuclear organizations, both within the movement and with the public, but they are also the smallest. The Union of Concerned Scientists has long been on the front line challenging the Nuclear Regulatory Commission. Publications by members of the UCS are utilized by movement groups throughout the world, since the technical knowledge in them is unsurpassed by any other antinuclear group.[60] Criticism of reactor safety by the Union of Concerned Scientists is often based on documents prepared by the Nuclear Regulatory Commission and as such directly confronts the government on technical issues. Some scientists' groups, such as the Committee on Nuclear Responsibility, are issue-specific, while others, such as the Federation of American Scientists, provide a forum for scientists from many disciplines to speak out and lobby on a variety of issues.

Other groups have a *moral* reaction to the social implications of nuclear technology, such as the National Council of Churches and the World Council of Churches. These organizations define and explore the ethical dilemmas of nuclear power for society. Should we accumulate large amounts of radioactive wastes that future generations must live with? Are we justified in selling nuclear technology to nations that might use it to develop nuclear weapons? Intellectual groups by comparison might be more concerned with the technological or economic merits of nuclear power relative to other sources of energy. In reality the types of social action overlap, but they do indicate something about the dominant orientations of groups.

The orientation of ecology and environmentalist organizations is generally that of *instrumental activism,* meaning that they wish to realize ideal values in our culture concerning self-reliance, appreciation of the natural environment, and efficient utilization of resources.[61] In the instrumental type of orientation, activists are motivated to attain desired states of affairs through rational means. Goals are specific but often related to a more general system of values. For example, the Black Lung Association in West Virginia helps afflicted coal miners receive benefits from the federal and state governments as well as other forms of compensation.[62] Many environmentalist groups in the antinuclear movement fit this pattern. The Sierra Club, for example, values the preservation of the natural environment and therefore has taken steps to block future nuclear power plants from being built.

The backbone of the antinuclear movement consists of organizations that have the nuclear issue as their raison d'être. Direct-action groups are the vanguard of the movement, a kind of elite whose status derives from its direct confrontations that garner significant mass-media attention. They lead the action against the nuclear establishment, that is, the federal government, the utility companies, oil corporations, and manufacturers of nuclear technology. These organizations usually have had strong regional support, such as the New England Coalition on Nuclear Pollution and the Clamshell Alliance in New England, and People for Proof, the Western Bloc, and the Abalone Alliance in the West. (Two organizations—the Task Force against Nuclear Pollution and the Consolidated National Intervenors—did attempt during the earlier part of the movement to coordinate it on a national scale from their offices in the national capital. Their efforts, however, were overshadowed by the regional alliances of antinuclear groups.)

The orientation of regional direct-action groups is frequently *expressive* in nature; that is, their opposition to nuclear power is also a means of realizing more general political or social objectives. These groups oppose nuclear power primarily because it represents an affront to larger social values that they hold. For example, in his study of the Campaign for Nuclear Disarmament (CND) in Great Britain, Francis Parkin found that the movement attracted individuals who were opposed to broader features of British life than simply nuclear weapons.[63] For example, CND activists were likely to reject the monarchy in favor of republicanism. Another example of this type of group is Supporters of Silkwood, a group that helped create a kind of martyrdom for Karen Silkwood. (Supporters of Silkwood was actually a spinoff group from the National Organization for Women, which had taken up the cause after Silkwood's mysterious death following her revelations of safety abuse at the plant where she worked.)

Most of the regional groups reflect the antibusiness tenor and objectives of the counterculture, which has survived since its emergence in the late 1960s. Other groups hope to merge with the antinuclear movement. The Environmentalists for Full Employment, for one, attempts to forge an ideological link between the labor and antinuclear movements.

Numerous other groups have been peripherally involved in the antinuclear movement. These include farmer organizations, the Piedmont Organic Movement, the Hudson River Sloop Restoration, the Women's Christian Temperance Union, and the 4-H Earthkeepers. Student organizations, labor union locals, and state political party organizations have also issued antinuclear proclamations to their constituencies.

Goals and Ideology

Because of the diverse kinds and degrees of involvement of groups in the antinuclear movement, there is no consistency in their specific goals. However, for the movement as a whole an ideology does exist that includes goals common to most groups. Goals are changed or redefined during the career of the movement, and they may vary according to their generality or specificity. Thus, the groups may seek change in the core values of society or in more peripheral values, but they always criticize existing conditions. The ideology of a movement incorporates its goals and provides a conception of alternative, "utopian" social orders.

The goal of a moratorium on the construction of nuclear power plants, and alternative emphasis on solar energy development, has been common to all organizations in the antinuclear movement, with variations in emphasis from group to group. One organization, the Consolidated National Intervenors, experienced a displacement of its antinuclear goals and became strictly an advocate of solar power. It now exists as a clearinghouse for information on solar energy. In fact, many groups have been more occupied with energy alternatives, such as solar power, than with the pitfalls of nuclear energy.

More commonly, the antinuclear goals of many organizations appear to be means to realize values not directly related to nuclear power. Voluntary associations such as the Wilderness Society are fundamentally more concerned with the preservation of the natural environment than with the economic and social implications of nuclear technology. The technical characteristics of nuclear power plants become salient only insofar as they threaten the basic values of the Wilderness Society.

The ideology of the movement reflects the heterogeneous doctrines of the peace, environmentalist, and labor movements. First, the ideology proclaims a danger of proliferation of nuclear weapons that accompanies the spread of nuclear power plants throughout the world. Scientists have argued particularly vocally that arms control involving nations embroiled in conflict—such as South Africa, Israel, Egypt, and South Korea—must extend to control of nuclear-technology and fuels exports. Second, the ideology warns of nuclear power plants' potential hazards to the natural and human environment. Environmentalist groups have been most activated by this dimension of antinuclear ideology. Third, the movement's ideology stresses doctrines of the labor movement. It charges the nuclear industry and the federal government with failures to provide for the safety of workers in nuclear facilities and to invest in energy systems that are labor intensive, thereby creating more employment and business opportunity for those not affiliated with large corporations.

Some of the assumptions that underlie the antinuclear ideology held by all groups are 1) that nations will acquire plutonium to produce nuclear weapons and will use those weapons; 2) that terrorists have the capability to divert nuclear materials for clandestine purposes; 3) that nuclear accidents are probable; 4) that radioactive wastes cannot be adequately disposed of; and 5) that alternative-energy technologies can meet the nation's energy needs.

Analytically, the ideology covers a complex time frame that is invested with social and political meaning. Nuclear power plants have been in operation for only two decades and were intended to be a peaceful application of an energy source that had brought unparalleled destruction in World War II. The reinterpretation of this time frame by antinuclear ideology is that nuclear technology is not inherently progressive, for it is potentially destructive.

There is also an awareness in this ideology that an imminent catastrophe will be precipitated by the rush to meet world energy shortages by building more nuclear power plants. A nuclear accident will bring havoc to the affected area and possibly cause a world disaster because of the accumulation of radioactive wastes. The ideology depicts the present as a sequence of irreversible steps toward a probable tragedy taken by a monolithic nuclear industry in collusion with the government.

Three generalized beliefs have diffused throughout the antinuclear movement. One is that nuclear technology is dangerous and cannot be entrusted to mankind for centuries to come. Another is the belief that solar energy and other energy alternatives are preferable to nuclear power. Finally, activists believe that social institutions cannot cope with the consequences of a nuclear infrastructure or a "plutonium economy." A conservative skepticism of human nature is often an intrinsic part of these beliefs, accompanied by a faith that alternative-energy technologies are perfectable and are not life-threatening. The ideology opposes large-scale technological systems with concentrated control and advocates decentralized and less complex systems that are more "appropriate" to the needs of individuals.

The conservative or at least parochial nature of aspects of the ideology is implied when activists frame a dilemma of whether the public interest will prevail over the private interests of the nuclear industry and the oil corporations and their defenders, elite academic scientists, federal bureaucrats, and to some extent the Republican party. But few groups have articulated substantial concern for the economic importance of nuclear power to the Third World. That the most disadvantaged minority groups and the masses of poor people in this nation and abroad suffer the most from energy shortages is not acknowledged. Antinuclear ideology depicts the conflict as between an elitist nuclear establishment and consumers. It is middle-class activism, not explicitly on behalf of the underprivileged.

The Pronuclear Countermovement

A countermovement is a response to an initial movement advocating social change.[64] The nuclear industry is the main source of the pronuclear countermovement, for its interests are those most threatened by the antinuclear movement. Two organizations promote the general interests of the nuclear industry on political issues: these are the Atomic Industrial Forum and the American Nuclear Society.

The Atomic Industrial Forum is an international association of 625 organizations. As early as 1974, the forum outlined its basic positions—that "sun worship" is not a solution to energy problems, and that as many as forty thousand workers had lost their jobs due to delays and cancellations in the construction of nuclear power plants as a result of "the backlash against authority and technology."[65] The American Nuclear Society functions as a professional, scientific, and educational organization and asserts that unemployment will result from conservation efforts, since industry and commerce are the major consumers of electrical energy.

These industry groups at first did not acknowledge the existence of an autonomous antinuclear movement but adhered to the idea that they were being unduly attacked by an obstructionist environmentalist movement. The president of a third major pronuclear organization representing the utilities, the Edison Electric Institute, said for example that "the precipitous rush to solve environmental problems through legislation and the ensuing process of legislative interpretation undertaken by the courts has brought our nation to the edge of a real crisis in electrical energy supply."[66]

Nuclear proponents believe that nuclear energy is a clean and safe energy source vital to our national welfare and national security. They have a greater faith in technological progress than do their opponents. The litany of nuclear energy's merits once ran as follows: nuclear power plants do not produce chemical air pollution; radioactivity is kept to minimal levels; uranium mining is safer than coal mining; no fatalities have occurred among the public as a result of the civilian nuclear power program; and nuclear accidents are improbable. Events in the 1980s such as Chernobyl have made proponents of nuclear energy qualify these arguments but not drop them.[67]

The pronuclear countermovement includes many groups other than those directly associated with the nuclear industry. Support has come from utilities and private corporations, as well as from construction workers, the Ku Klux Klan, and the John Birch Society. The role of the federal government is much more complex; both the proponents and the opponents often believe that the government is on the side of the opposite group.

The case of Save Maine Yankee, the countermovement group mobilized to defeat the first Maine nuclear referendum, illustrates how pronuclear groups operate. During the 1980 referendum battle, the organization raised over three-quarters of a million dollars to fight the Maine Nuclear Referendum Committee, which had raised only about $127,000. Donations to Save Maine Yankee came primarily from the pulp and paper industry in Maine, Stone and Webster (the Boston engineering firm that designed Maine Yankee), Procter and Gamble, Exxon Nuclear Corporation, General Electric, Maine Public Service, and Merrill, Lynch, Pierce, Fenner & Smith.[68] It also received a contribution from Winner/Wagner, the Los Angeles consultants who engineered the defeat of the 1976 California Nuclear Safeguards Initiative.[69] The objectives raised by Save Maine Yankee were strictly economic: shutting down Maine Yankee would mean higher electricity costs, dependence costs, and dependence on foreign oil.[70] With the pocketbook arguments on their side, Save Maine Yankee achieved a modest victory in the 1980 Maine nuclear referendum.

Conclusion

As the first major public referendum on the nuclear issue in the 1980s, the 1980 vote in Maine represented a more cautious approach to nuclear energy in the United States. This trend is also apparent in Western Europe.

The controversy over nuclear power is far from over. The movement has taken new directions in the late 1980s over the issues of nuclear-waste reprocessing and storage and emergency-evacuation plans in the event of a nuclear accident. The antinuclear movement has also become more international and less dependent on events occurring within the United States.

Subsequent chapters are concerned with the internal structure of the antinuclear movement, including the division of labor within the organizations, their available resources, types of leadership, and coordination of activities. They also consider the social values of the main groups in the movement and how their activities relate to the significant events in the career of the antinuclear movement.

Chapter Two

Environmentalist Antinuclear Groups

The antinuclear movement arose as a single-issue coalition of environmentalist groups before it evolved into a distinct movement incorporating other groups. Since the core values of antinuclear activists center on the environmental consequences of nuclear power generation, organizations such as the Sierra Club, the Wilderness Society, the Audubon Society, Friends of the Earth, the Natural Resources Defense Council, and the Public Interest Research Groups founded by Ralph Nader have been and remain an integral part of the movement. While perceptions of the issue vary greatly from one group to another, all are involved in the antinuclear movement primarily over the issue of radioactive wastes. During the late 1970s, direct-action groups were predominant in the antinuclear movement, but in the 1980s the movement continued through the activities of environmentalist organizations.

Environmentalists are often depicted by their opponents as obstructing economic and technological development. These opponents often view jobs and economic efficiency as tradeoffs for a polluted and hazardous environment. That environmentalists have battled over a diversity of energy-related issues is seized upon by opponents as evidence of their opposition to any mode of energy production. However, the environmentalist movement encompasses a broad range of groups with complex variations in the solutions they offer to ecological problems. All energy technologies have some negative environmental consequences, but opposition to damaging consequences is not opposition to energy production itself. Some environmentalists do call for zero population growth and

37

an end to economic expansion as the only way to prevent environmental catastrophe, but others advocate accelerated economic growth and environmental management as the safest way to achieve a mass-consumption society that provides for the basic needs of human populations.[1]

Antinuclear activists also believe that changes in the value systems of societies are as likely to produce positive results as purely technological changes are. Subtle ideological differences among environmentalist groups reflect the fact that all have unique ways of interpreting their ecological values and each chooses a different tactical style to bring about the preferred changes.

Participation in the antinuclear movement is usually a *means* to realize an interpretation of the ecology ideal, a form of activity sociologically defined as *instrumental activism.* The following examples of environmentalist involvement in the antinuclear movement illustrate these groups' unique role in the nuclear controversy.

Preservationist and Conservationist Groups: The Sierra Club and the Florida Audubon Society

In 1974, when the board of directors of the Sierra Club voted to oppose the construction of new nuclear power plants, the antinuclear movement gained an impressive endorsement—the Sierra Club is one of the oldest and probably the most prestigious of all conservationist societies. The initial reasons the board gave for its vote were the potential threats to public health from radioactive wastes, questions regarding the operating efficiency of nuclear power plants, and the ability of the government to prevent the theft or diversion of nuclear materials.

The Sierra Club did not, however, issue a blanket approval of antinuclear goals. It opposed nuclear power only in its present state of development. In other words, the Sierra Club feared an irreversible commitment to nuclear power before its technological problems were solved. The Sierra Club statement acknowledged that many environmentalists view nuclear power proponents as potential allies, for nuclear power reduces air pollution caused by the burning of fossil fuels and avoids the adverse consequences of strip mining for coal and of marine drilling for oil and natural gas. Since the preservation of natural beauty is a core value of the Sierra Club, nuclear-power-plant construction could end plans to dam and flood scenic canyons for hydroelectric power. Michael McCloskey, executive director of the club, wrote, nuclear power is now undergoing severe questioning because it was a technology that was prematurely overstimulated and was managed by a less than competent bureaucracy. The premature expansion of the nuclear power industry resulted in poor government decisions which actually hurt the development of the technology.[2]

Local units of the Sierra Club have considerable autonomy and command of resources. In California, they initiated many legal actions against nuclear power, sometimes with other organizations. The national organization of the Sierra Club (in conjunction with the Union of Concerned Scientists or the Natural Resources Defense Council) has on many occasions filed suit against federal agencies on issues such as the prohibition of nuclear-fuel sales to India and has favored litigation that would have required the NRC to consider the alternative sources of energy available in an area before it issued a construction permit for a nuclear power plant.

Strip mining of coal has always been anathema to Sierra Club members. Thus, its opposition to nuclear power has been tempered by its awareness that heavy dependence on coal is extremely detrimental to the aesthetic beauty of the environment as well as to the quality of air. A major victory of the Sierra Club was the defeat of the Kaiporowits project in southern Utah. Kaiporowits was to be the largest coal-fired electricity-generating plant in the world, supplying electricity for southern California. The success of the Sierra Club in defeating the multibillion-dollar project, an effort supported by some of the most powerful corporate and political leaders in the nation, is testimony to its power and prestige.

The Sierra Club is effective due to its large membership and its access to considerable resources. Since local units are autonomous, the Sierra Club has been a factor not only in the national struggle over nuclear energy but in innumerable local controversies. Without officially adopting a policy preference for solar energy or any other alternative energy source, the Sierra Club is quick to oppose any energy source that will alter the environment in a detrimental way. Preservationist and conservationist ideology tends to run contrary to the liberal conception of technological progress. But Sierra Club members have a distinctive orientation that is, in the terminology of classical sociological theorist Max Weber, *wertrational* ("value-rational"). Preserving the natural environment is imperative for Sierra Club members, and the pragmatic consideration of conflicting social needs is largely irrelevant in realizing this primary goal.

The Floating-Nuclear-Power-Plant Controversy

Another major conservationist group, the Audubon Society, is organized in much the same way as the Sierra Club. The Audubon Society has a smaller membership than the Sierra Club, but it has a greater number of local affiliates throughout the nation. These affiliates are autonomous, which frees them for local initiatives in the nuclear controversy.

In 1973, a significant controversy brought the Florida Audubon Society affiliate headlong into the antinuclear movement. A series of floating nuclear power plants were to be constructed in Florida and then towed by barge up the Atlantic coast. They were to be anchored and operated off the New Jersey shore. The plants were to be manufactured by the Westinghouse and Tenneco corporations at a site on Blount Island, in a marshy extension of the St. John's River, near Jacksonville.[3]

The $200 million project had been authorized by the Atomic Energy Commission before the commission had officially approved the concept of floating nuclear power plants or conducted environmental impact studies. Using this weakness as an opening, the Florida Audubon Society filed a complaint in federal district court against the Army Corps of Engineers to prevent the dredging and filling of the Blount Island marsh.

The society presented as evidence a study of the ecology of the St. John's estuary that had been conducted by Dr. Edward LaRoe. The study was based on a review of field observations, conservation measures taken, aerial photographs, and other available data. Dr. LaRoe found that the marshes formed an extremely rich and productive marine ecological system that

is very complex and depends for its fertility and continued viability on the interplay between the marshland and the river; the tides and fresh-salt water balance; water quality and runoff; the nutrient inflow and seasonal or cyclical migrations of fauna and flora. Dredging, filling, pollution, and water diversion all stress this system and decrease its productivity.[4]

The LaRoe study was not accepted as legitimate scientific evidence by the Army Corps of Engineers because, it said, LaRoe's observations were casual and based on hearsay evidence. Accusations of unethical behavior and countercharges quickly undermined the role of science in matter, and the conflict became purely political.

LaRoe then suggested that Westinghouse and the Army Corps of Engineers had deliberately kept the project a secret and then rammed it through reviews and agency approvals. Furthermore, the Florida Audubon Society argued, data that had been prepared by consultants in support of the project were not objective—the consultants had been hired by the Jacksonville Port Authority, which had a vested interest in the Blount Island project.

Since the feasibility of the concept was still open to question, and alternative sites—as the Florida Audubon Society argued—had not been given sufficient consideration by the Army Corps of Engineers, the federal court issued a restraining order.

The resource-mobilization theory of social movements states that the success of a movement often depends on how well contending groups utilize external resources. In particular, the mass media play an important role in forming public opinion on an issue. The controversy over Blount Island was the object of a study on mass-media manipulation by Sean Devereaux.[5] In the struggle, he wrote, economic and political elites in Jacksonville manipulated the media to support their views. Florida Seaboard Coastline Industries of Jacksonville would have been the recipient of railway business and land sales if Blount Island had become a reality. The company also owns a local newspaper, the *Florida Publico,* and publishes the *Times Union,* a newspaper with a circulation of over sixty thousand. A committee was formed to support Blount Island, and included on the committee were the Jacksonville Chamber of Commerce, the publisher of *Florida Publico,* and eleven of the thirteen members of Offshore Power Systems, the Westinghouse-Tenneco project management organization.

Initially, news concerning Offshore Power Systems was kept out of the Jacksonville newspapers, evidently to avoid news of any local conflict over the project from reaching Portsmouth, Virginia—another potential site. Then the newspapers began a blitz in support of Blount Island, with large advertisements, over 146 stories, and sixteen editorials. Either the environmental impact of the Blount Island project on the ecology of the estuary was overlooked, or the impact was discredited. The newspapers did not publish a UPI story on biological hazards until an opposing article had been written. A local environmentalist leader was only mentioned once in two and a half months, and pictures showed only supporters of the project.

Offshore Power Systems represented a probable gain of 120,000 additional jobs in the Jacksonville area. How did the Florida Audubon Society respond to this argument? There has always been a latent conflict between environmentalists and labor groups over this kind of question.

The Audubon Society proposed that the floating nuclear plants would benefit their community of destination rather than Jacksonville, which would gain economic benefits only from construction of the plants. If the plants operated off the coast, the Audubon Society argued, there would be no great employment opportunities, and New Jersey citizens would pay an even higher burden in taxes and utility bills to support the project. In addition, the Audubon Society questioned the military security of plants in open seas.

In the end, Westinghouse agreed to purchase one thousand acres of marshland and donate it to the public as compensation for the marshland lost in building a factory. This factory would mass-produce one floating nuclear power plant every twenty-seven months. However, the battle over these plants had still to be won in New Jersey.

The first four floating nuclear power plants were to be constructed for Public Service Electric and Gas Company of Newark, New Jersey. The first two were to be sited in the Atlantic Ocean off Little Egg Harbor by the mid-1980s. Significant local opposition was spearheaded by the twenty-nine members of the Women's Club of Linwood, New Jersey. After hearing a local physician speak on nuclear poisons, the women formed a nuclear-power study group, then adopted a resolution to keep nuclear power plants out of New Jersey.[6]

The tactics of the women were fourfold. They pressured the city council to pass an antinuclear resolution; they involved other organizations and the public in the opposition; they insured a negative vote in Linwood on an Atlantic County nuclear referendum; and they secured signatures for a Clean Energy petition that was then being circulated by the Task Force against Nuclear Pollution.

By showing up in full strength, the Linwood Women's Club was able to move the city council to officially oppose the siting of nuclear power plants off the New Jersey coast. The Women's Club produced literature focusing on the moral issues and the dangers of plutonium. This literature was mailed to seventy-five other groups and organizations in the area. Other local groups, such as Stop Nuclear Power of Margate, New Jersey, joined in the campaign to bring voters to oppose floating nuclear power plants in a referendum. The eventual outcome in Atlantic County was twenty-five thousand votes against nuclear power and fifteen thousand votes in favor.

Citizens' strength in local referendums does not alone decide the future of nuclear power; court maneuvers by the nuclear industry later negated the vote. When the Nuclear Regulatory Commission published a report that indicated that the risks associated with floating nuclear power plants were exceedingly small, citizens were helped by the state. The Department of Public Advocate intervened on behalf of the Atlantic County Citizens Council on the Environment because the federal agency had excluded them from hearings when an environmental impact statement was being made.

In this instance, the New Jersey Department of Public Advocate *funded* an independent study of the issue by the Center for Science in the Public Interest (CSPI) of Washington, D.C., an organization active in the antinuclear movement. The CSPI study concluded that in the event of a core meltdown, land-based nuclear plants could be surrounded by layers of sand, concrete, and gravel that would contain radioactive materials, but a floating nuclear power plant would be surrounded by water, which, through tidal action and ocean currents, would transport radioactive materials to the shore. Residents feared that even the possibility of such a catastrophe would destroy the tourist trade on the New Jersey shore.

A federal hearing was then held in Atlantic City. The citizens' group had a local physician testify on potential radiation hazards; Westinghouse found support from the Chamber of Commerce, the National Association of Industrial Parks, and the New Jersey Industrial Development Association. The hearings were emotional. An antinuclear spokesman, for example, argued that "plans for evacuation in the event of accidental release of radiation are very vague. How are we going to get out? It is our lives you are dealing with, and by God, it's our ocean."[7] A member of Stop Nuclear Power of Margate objected to citizens being guinea pigs. Israel Mossee, a black resident, added, "They plan to use the poor as guinea pigs in this highly experimental venture. They are saying to the poor and minorities: your lives have no value. I resent that!"

Human emotions and fears often drive citizens in local controversies, but residents of urban areas face the further question of whether they would be able to leave in time in the event of an accident because of the inadequacy of public transportation systems and emergency planning. In a state where years ago mass panic was created by the broadcast of Orson Welles's *War of the Worlds,* this might have been a legitimate concern. In fact, many opponents at these hearings believed that a nuclear accident might create a tidal wave that would devastate the New Jersey coast. Moreover, a list of over five thousand individuals who declared that they would not vacation in New Jersey if the floating plants were built was also presented at the hearings. A few months later, demonstrations were held outside the courthouse.

Despite the escalation of the conflict in Atlantic County, it was neither legal tactics nor demonstrations that succeeded in ending the project. New Jersey utility companies were participating owners of the plant at Three Mile Island. Almost a year and a half after the Three Mile Island accident, New Jersey residents had to pay higher utility rates to help pay for the damage. Renewed public opposition and lingering questions over the feasibility of the project forced the floating-nuclear-power-plant concept to finally be abandoned.

Friends of the Earth and Environmental Alert

Friends of the Earth represents a more politically aggressive approach to environmentalism. It retains environmental lobbyists in Washington who are experts in energy, wildlife, air and water pollution, and wilderness and public-lands issues. The organizational structure of Friends of the Earth is a key source of its strength. Field representatives in major cities direct activities on state issues, while sixty branches emphasize local issues and generate grassroots support for its state and national activities. There are parallel organizations in England, France, Australia, New Zealand, Germany, Sweden, Yugoslavia, Ireland, and Guam.[8] The British representative of Friends of the Earth is Amory Lovins, a leading critic of nuclear power and an advocate of a nonnuclear future. Friends of the Earth estimates its membership at twenty-three thousand. Moreover, it has an advisory council with such luminaries as Jacques Cousteau, Linus Pauling, Konrad Lorenz, George Plimpton, C. P. Snow, George Wald, and Pete Seeger.

A major effort of Friends of the Earth is the publication of conservationist literature. In its publications, photographic studies of the most remote wildernesses in the world are combined with technical studies of "earth island." *Not Man Apart* is a newsletter on environmental and nuclear issues, while *Earth Law Journal* analyzes legal responses to environmental issues in different nations, including the socialist countries.

The organization's emphasis on conservation reflects its origins. It was established in New York City in 1969 by David Brower as an alternative to the Sierra Club. Brower believed that traditional conservationist societies were not concerned about nuclear proliferation, the most serious environmental threat in both a military and an ecological sense. Neither did traditional organizations concern themselves with inflation, unemployment, and other inequities produced by environmental abuse. Eschatological elements appear in the ideology of Friends of the Earth in the group's depiction of a single, all-encompassing, accelerating crisis as the product of mindless technological and economic growth. The "California Tomorrow Plan" of Friends of the Earth envisages a utopian "California Two" that will be planned with intelligence in "post-industrial age earth." Yet the ideology is tinged with romantic nostalgia:

If you think back no more than fifteen years ago, you know the loss as you remember how enjoyable breathing used to be, the taste of water, the sound of birdsong, or the renewal that could come safely from a walk in the city evening with stars in it, or on a lonely trail in the wilderness that ages have made perfect[9]

Using often flamboyant tactics, Friends of the Earth has campaigned against the Boeing SST and the Concorde, the trans-Alaska pipeline, and the building of new towns on agricultural lands. Founded out of concern for nuclear proliferation, Friends of the Earth was largely responsible for diffusing the antinuclear movement to Europe. In one case, data it provided resulted in the British government rejecting nuclear reactors manufactured in the United States.

Together with Greenpeace, Friends of the Earth is one of the major organizations opposing nuclear power in Britain, where the Anti-Nuclear Campaign has been overshadowed by the Campaign for Nuclear Disarmament. Most of the British opposition centers on radioactive leaks at Sellafield, on a proposed nuclear reactor at Sizewell, and on a planned nuclear reprocessing plant at Dounreay. Generally, there has been less public support for the movement in Britain than in France and West Germany—although the efforts of groups such as Friends of the Earth bore fruit in Britain in 1985, when the Labour party voted to take an antinuclear line.

In the United States, working with Senator Edward Kennedy, Friends of the Earth attempted to block passage of the Price-Anderson Act extension bill while it was being debated by Congress. The 1957 Price-Anderson Act provided government insurance for owners and operators of nuclear reactors, and in 1977 it was due to expire. Defeat of Price-Anderson would have been a death blow to the nuclear industry, for without insurance the utilities could not afford nuclear energy.

Under pressure from antinuclear organizations such as Friends of the Earth, Congress attached an amendment to the extension bill that would have invalidated Price-Anderson if the Rasmussen report on reactor safety had produced disturbing results. This prompted President Ford to veto the extension, which was later passed again by Congress.

The insurance protects manufacturers and operators of nuclear power plants more than potential victims of a nuclear accident, but Congress has continued to support government-backed insurance until it can be gradually phased out and replaced by private insurance pools. When the Price-Anderson Act expired again in 1987, Congress responded to criticism that it was subsidizing the nuclear industry by proposing a $7 billion cap on liability for a nuclear accident, with each nuclear utility paying $10 million per reactor each year, retroactive to an accident, until the claims have been paid. Most antinuclear activists believe that the peril of nuclear energy is so great that no insurance can ever indemnify the human and environmental losses that an accident would cause.

Social movements often attract marginal "fringe groups" (sometimes derisively called the "lunatic fringe") whose doomsday prophecies seem to border on hysteria. Early in the evolution of the antinuclear movement, Environmental Alert Group of California published pamphlets that may have been less emotional overreaction than scare tactics. Much of their propaganda was written by Dr. Douglas DeNike, who was also the vice president of Zero Population Growth and the alleged author of "a forthcoming book of radioactive crime and banditry."

Environmental Alert Group depicted the fast breeder reactor as a commercial doomsday machine that would produce plutonium in ever-greater quantities. This raised the specter of the abridgment of civil liberties, since a federal security force would be needed to protect nuclear installations. Although the NRC is officially opposed to the creation of such a force, the fear exists that massive numbers of security clearances and investigators would eventually be needed. A newsletter of Environmental Alert Group reported that

the proliferation of nuclear materials opens wide the door to anarchy and chaos. Large regions, or any specific target within them, will be placed at the mercy of enemy spies, fanatic terrorists, criminal blackmailers, and deranged persons.[10]

Scare tactics, however, do not enter into the strategies of most antinuclear organizations, despite heightened awareness of the dangers of radioactive wastes and nuclear accidents.

Congresswatch and the Citizens
Movement against Nuclear Power

The prime mover for environmentalist opposition to nuclear power was Ralph Nader, the consumer advocate. Nader sponsored the convention of nuclear power critics in Washington, D.C. (Critical Mass '74), to co-ordinate antinuclear activities throughout the nation. Initially, Nader en-visioned that a garrison state would be necessary to protect plutonium. Only by abjuring the use of fission power could this possibility be avoided. (The energy program advocated by Congresswatch, the Nader organi-zation, in fact became federal policy during the administration of Jimmy Carter. Conservation and the use of coal, with environmental safeguards, were established as interim solutions, while in the latter part of the cen-tury solar, geothermal, and fusion power would be available.)

Nader developed a strategy for nuclear lobbying to be implemented by Congresswatch. The chief Congresswatch lobbyist was delegated the responsibility of meeting with other environmentalist groups to share information. Nader called for increased citizen intervention and joint ac-tivities among divergent groups, including those fighting utility rate struc-tures. In the *Critical Mass* handbook, Nader wrote that

social movements need all the tactics and strategies they can muster. Thus, a coalition of these two movements is essential if either is to succeed. Citizens fighting utilities as nuclear proliferators need to understand the strategy of cutting off the flow of money to utilities for nuclear expansion—by entering rate fights, stockholder and mismanagement suits, etc. [11]

In response to this attack, the Atomic Industrial Forum launched its countermovement, approving a budget increase of over a million dollars. Tahi L. Mottl of Harvard has argued that specific tactics of counter-movements are defined in response to tactics employed by the initial movement, even to the extent of adopting some of the initial movement's program. [12] The case of the Atomic Industrial Forum supports this argu-ment, for it copied Congresswatch by giving its own press conferences, sponsoring trips for reporters to nuclear facilities, taping messages for small-town radio stations, and ghost writing pronuclear articles on behalf of distinguished experts. The forum also encouraged petitions, staged events, and directed article placement to minimize filtration by editors.

The Atomic Industrial Forum counteroffensive was aimed at decision makers in both the federal and the state governments. Meanwhile, Congresswatch concentrated its lobbying efforts on blocking any legislation favorable to the nuclear industry, including the Price-Anderson extension bill and fast-breeder-reactor research appropriations. Utility rate hikes related to the construction of nuclear power plants were opposed, and citizens were encouraged to participate in licensing proceedings for new plants and in nuclear referendums.

Nader's organization established the *Critical Mass* newsletter, representing the Citizens Movement to Stop Nuclear Power; its themes centered on discrediting the nuclear industry. Powerful coalitions of financial and industrial interests, manipulation of the press, and biased government activity were exposed. One article, for example, uncovered alleged evidence that five banks—Morgan Guaranty, Chase Manhattan, Banker's Trust, Citibank, and Merrill Lynch—unduly influence promotion, purchasing, financing, and insurance for the nuclear industry. These banks were all members of the Atomic Industrial Forum, were among the top ten stockholders of 74 percent of all utility companies, owned almost 10 percent of General Electric and 11 percent of Westinghouse stock, and provided almost half of short-term loans to the nuclear industry. The inevitable conclusion: financial self-interest and government subsidies, rather than the stability of the nuclear industry, furthers the construction of nuclear power plants.

A second common theme of *Critical Mass* is that government agencies with functions of regulating the nuclear industry are staffed with persons who have a strong pronuclear bias. For example, chief lobbyist Jim Cubie wrote that

almost thirty years of propaganda by the Atomic Energy Commission had convinced much of the public that atomic power was safe, cheap, and dependable. Thirty years of pork barrel patronage had placed nuclear facilities in a large number of Congressional districts, anesthetising otherwise skeptical members.[13]

Cubie argued that the Joint Committee on Atomic energy refuses to listen to critics of safety regulations or to realistically assess the economic problems of the nuclear industry. Although the antinuclear movement was successful in getting Congress to abolish the Atomic Energy Commission and replace it with the NRC, no similar reorganization has been made for the Joint Committee on Atomic Energy.

A third theme of *Critical Mass* is that scientists cannot be objective on the nuclear issue because of their corporate affiliations. Ralph Nader reiterated this argument in 1974, pointing out that engineers who sign pronuclear statements work for organizations or corporations that have a vested interest in nuclear power. [14]

Student Activism.   The Ralph Nader consumer and environmentalist Public Interest Research Group (PIRG) adopted an antinuclear program that called for the Price-Anderson Act to include all segments of the nuclear fuel cycle; a moratorium on the recycling of plutonium; nonfunding for the breeder reactor; a ban on nuclear exports; and an end to government subsidies for the nuclear industry.

PIRG also introduced the tactic of show-cause suits. These suits were filed to force utilities to produce evacuation plans that could be used in the event of a nuclear accident. Often these plans were inadequate. PIRG found in 1973 in Maine, for example, that emergency-evacuation plans for Maine Yankee included the sounding of nonexistent sirens in nearby towns and the treatment of patients with radiation contamination in nonexistent hospital facilities. [15]

A similar petition was filed against Con Edison's inadequate emergency-evacuation plans for the Indian Point reactors, near New York City. The evacuation issue became the rallying point for antinuclear groups in the late 1980s. Both the Shoreham plant on Long Island and the Seabrook plant in New Hampshire were unable to get operating licenses from the NRC until their emergency-evacuation plans had been approved.

PIRG has affiliates among students in colleges and universities across the United States. Students in PIRGs research information needed to advocate a cause and then bring it to public attention through the organization. Ralph Nader conceived the PIRGs as a way for students to work within the system after the frustrating 1960s. Student PIRG organizations originated in Oregon and Minnesota, then spread to twenty-five states.

The PIRGs' organizational structure allows students to pool their monies and hire a full-time professional staff under their control. Newsletters tie them together with the national PIRG in the capital, and funding is provided by an optional fee after a general petition among student bodies. The groups are multiissue-oriented, but many sent representatives to the Critical Mass conferences in Washington.

New Jersey PIRGs provided good examples of PIRG structure. Major student PIRGs existed at Seton Hall and Rutgers University in the 1970s, and at one time New Jersey PIRG had twenty-thousand fee-paying constituents in all on eight campuses in the state. Its staff in 1976 received a basic salary of $5,200 and sometimes more, determined by need. Nine professional staff members filled the positions of director, staff attorney, coordinator, researchers, and issues coordinator. Six of the nine had college degrees, and two had graduate or law degrees. The common denominator of all was previous work for organizations like the National Organization for Women, the Movement for a New Congress, the American Civil Liberties Union, and the Sierra Club.[16]

New Jersey PIRG confronted a broad range of issues, including feminist concerns, tax reform, unemployment, and various higher education issues. Although the national PIRG coordinates activities that require federal and statewide action (such as a nuclear moratorium), New Jersey PIRG cooperated with state affiliates of Common Cause, the League of Women Voters, and the United Auto Workers, among others, to develop an effective strategy on nuclear issues. As a consequence of PIRG activities, the New Jersey Environmental Protection Agency prohibited the use of plutonium in nuclear power plants in the state and provided for the dismantling and restoration of the Hope Creek power plant in Salem County when its useful life was exhausted.[17]

An article in the *Portland Press Herald* depicted Maine PIRG members as romantics who, in the name of public interest, were actually causing the public more expense. William Clark, the author, went on to write that "we will all pay to prove to this small group of prejudiced people that the leading scientists of this country and the specialists in nuclear power know what they are talking about."[18] The acting director of Maine PIRG responded that Clark was "hoisted by his own petard," a conservative afraid to challenge the rising costs of electricity. Rob Burgess asked, "Where would we be if Ralph Nader and his public-spirited, public interest progeny were not with us?"[19]

The Maine students were ultimately successful with their show-cause suit. Central Maine Power Company was required to disseminate information on evacuation plans each year to all its customers within a forty-mile radius of Maine Yankee. Along with other groups (such as Safe Power for Maine in Stockton Springs), students blocked the proposed nuclear power plant at Sears Island and obtained the forty thousand signatures necessary to put a seven-year moratorium on nuclear power on the ballot.

Utilitarian Environmentalists: BPI and NRDC

Public sentiment often views professionals and businesspeople as being concerned only with their own interests and not at all with the public good. A Chicago-based organization, Businessmen and Professional People in the Public Interest (BPI), attempted to reverse that image by becoming a public advocate in the 1970s. Its directors included the presidents of several Chicago-based corporations, lawyers, and college professors. Organized as a law firm and research center in 1969, BPI was defined as

a legal-oriented instrument for investigating and instituting action on behalf of the general public in such matters as safety and health, housing and discrimination, police procedures and public administration, favoritism in taxation, and conflict of interest in government.[20]

The environmental director of BPI became a national figure in the antinuclear movement. David Comey was originally a specialist in Soviet studies at Cornell University and was involved in the controversy over the proposed nuclear power plant at Cayuga Lake. For his efforts to improve the safety of nuclear reactors, Comey received an Environmental Quality Award from the U.S. Environmental Projection Agency.

Comey argued that nuclear power plants have serious human-error problems, for operators are poorly trained and often careless. His research was aimed at showing that nuclear power plants are more expensive than coal-fired plants because of their low efficiency. They have less efficiency because nuclear power plants operate at low percentages of their capacity and are often shut down as a result of human error, malfunction, or refueling.

With an annual budget exceeding a quarter of a million dollars and with volunteer assistance from lawyers in private practice and law students, BPI effectively confronted federal regulatory agencies for their failures to abide by their own rules. In 1975, when a fire closed down the Brown's Ferry reactors in Alabama, BPI petitioned the Nuclear Regulatory Commission to order the immediate closing of all nuclear power plants that did not meet electrical safety standards established by the Institute for Electrical and Electronic Engineering. BPI also struggled against the Zion reactor, owned by Commonwealth Edison, located only forty-five miles north of Chicago. This reactor had one of the poorest safety records of all nuclear facilities, despite its location near a major metropolitan area.

Together with the Izaak Walton League (one of the oldest conservationist societies), BPI initiated a court battle to halt construction of a nuclear reactor in Bailly, Indiana, one mile from the city of Portage on the southern shore of Lake Michigan. The court action was successful—

the federal panel ruled that the Atomic Energy Commission had violated its own regulations by building the plant too close to a densely populated area. The utility company was ordered to fill in its excavation of the site. It was the first time that a federal district court had blocked the construction of a nuclear power plant. However, several months later the Supreme Court reversed the decision.

A second organization that is issue-specific and that uses legal tactics after carefully researching technical problems is the Natural Resources Defense Council (NRDC), a nonprofit corporation with offices in Palo Alto (California), New York, and Washington, D.C. The NRDC, with over twenty thousand members, promotes the intelligent management of natural resources. To accomplish this goal, it monitors the activities of federal and state agencies. It attempts to improve agency decisions that affect the environment by participating in administrative proceedings and by litigation. The NRDC frequently provides legal and technical assistance to individuals and organizations that are involved in confrontations with government agencies.

NRDC has a high-powered core staff that includes Arthur Tamplin, the biophysicist who was a key figure in the antinuclear episodes of the 1960s; Thomas Cochran, a nuclear physicist; Terry Lash, a microbiologist; Dean Abrahamson, a former reactor designer at Babcock and Wilcox; and attorney Gus Speth. Along with the Sierra Club, the NRDC attempted to block the export of nuclear fuel to India by Edlow International Company. Two of the most important issues the organization has been involved in are radioactive-waste disposal and the fast breeder reactor.

In June 1973 the NRDC won a decision before the court of appeals in Washington requiring that the Atomic Energy Commission prepare an environmental impact study of the liquid-metal fast breeder reactor. One major reason for the NRDC's opposition to the breeder is that double systems failures are possible, for the emergency-shutdown system would have to operate in a few seconds. Human error under pressure might be sufficient to produce a core meltdown and possible core disassembly. The economics of the fast breeder reactor fare no better under NRDC scrutiny. It argued that learning curves, or decreasing costs per unit due to experience in manufacturing efficiency, would not actually occur because of unforeseen safety problems and increased construction costs. The NRDC argues that only solar energy can benefit from a learning curve, and that hidden costs of the fast breeder reactor include safeguarding the plants.[21]

Conventional nuclear power plants cannot explode, although they may experience loss-of-coolant accidents. Breeder reactors, however, are susceptible to core disassembly if the sodium coolant is blocked from the core. If this happened, the breeder would reach a stage of "autocatalytic criticality," in which the fuel would be compressed and collected on the walls of the reactor core, allowing a spontaneous and uncontrolled nuclear accident to take place. Dispersion of plutonium into the atmosphere would have far more serious consequences than a core meltdown in a conventional plant. The probabilities of core disassembly and the amount of property damage or number of fatalities that could result have not even been calculated by a government agency.

The NRDC reports that 0.0000001 ounce of plutonium causes cancers in dogs when inhaled as fine particles. Thus plutonium and other radioactive wastes are "the more fearsome products ever handled in quantity by man."[22] Fuel assemblies have begun to accumulate, for the West Valley, New York, reprocessing plant has been closed and federal funds have been provided for decommissioning the facility. The Barnwell nuclear-fuels-reprocessing plant in South Carolina was forbidden to operate by executive order of President Carter in 1978. Wastes are being stored at the site of nuclear power plants. The arguments made by NRDC years ago have been borne out: no satisfactory plan yet exists for even the interim storage of high-level radioactive wastes.

Military Wastes.   Since Chernobyl, the NRDC, Greenpeace, and the local Snake River Alliance in Idaho have focused some of their efforts on the issue of the radioactive wastes that are produced or utilized in the manufacture of nuclear weapons. The controversy is centered both in Washington and in Idaho. N-reactor at Hanford, Washington, is a graphite-moderated reactor whose design is similar to that of the Chernobyl reactor. It was built to produce plutonium for the U.S. thermonuclear defense program. Substantial damage occurred at the reactor in 1984 as a result of neutron bombardment of the graphite core, and in 1986 the plant was closed following an evaluation initiated by the Chernobyl accident.

The only other reactor producing plutonium for military use is the Savannah River plant near Aiken, South Carolina.[23] The Savannah River complex produces tritium for use in nuclear weapons and was itself closed down in 1988 owing to safety concerns after an unexplained power surge at P-reactor. The three plants at Savannah River were scheduled to be reopened in 1989, but they are known to lie in an earthquake zone.

At the same time in 1988, the plutonium-reprocessing plant at Rocky Flats, near Golden, Colorado, was closed due to radioactive contamination. These closures temporarily halted U.S. production of nuclear weapons.

The Hanford Reservation provides 6,400 jobs, and environmentalism is at odds with employment in this controversy. Vigils in favor of keeping Hanford open have clashed with NRDC and Greenpeace efforts to keep it closed. The cleanup of Hanford alone could take over fifty years and cost between $40 billion and $70 billion.[24] Since N-reactor is unlikely to reopen and since the Savannah River plants rarely operate at full capacity due to technical and safety problems or inadequate containment domes, the Department of Energy has planned a new facility at Idaho Falls, Idaho, to be ready in the 1990s. Laser technology will be used there to enrich plutonium wastes from commercial nuclear power plants into weapons-grade material. By using the wastes from commercial plants, the Special Isotope Separation plant would defuse efforts to close the nuclear fuel cycle with the breeder reader.

Local business and labor groups support the Special Isotope Separation plant because of the economic benefits it would bring to Idaho Falls. But the NRDC and Greenpeace have argued that there is already an oversupply of plutonium in the United States and that much of the plutonium available for nuclear weapons comes from the redesign of existing weapons. In addition, they argue, the nuclear arms race shows positive signs of slowing down. In 1989, Congressman Albert Bustamente, a Democrat from Texas, was to offer an amendment to the Defense Authorization bill to delete this plant.[25]

Ironically, utilizing high-level radioactive wastes from commercial nuclear power plants has been proposed as a solution to the problem of radioactive-waste disposal (although in reality only a small portion of commercial wastes could be diverted for this purpose). Since the United States no longer has an operating nuclear-fuel-reprocessing plant, high-level wastes must be recycled for use either in a breeder reactor (for which the technology has not been successfully demonstrated) or in nuclear weapons. A third solution is long-term storage of the wastes. Since the Department of Energy does not have the same restraints of public opposition placed on it for the disposal of military wastes, an underground repository for these wastes is being built in the salt caverns of New Mexico—and water has already been discovered seeping into it.

By 1989 production of tritium for the nuclear weapons program had ceased in the United States as cracks were discovered in the cooling systems of the Savannah River complex. At a fuel assembly plant in Fernald, Ohio, workers went on strike. The secrecy was being broken over potential hazards in the military nuclear fuel cycle to sixty-seven thousand workers and to citizens with continued revelations of releases of radioactive materials at these plants. Idaho Governor Cecil Andrus blocked the transportation of radioactive wastes from Savannah River to Idaho. The problem of military wastes is as serious as the problem of disposing of commercial radioactive wastes.

Local Environmentalist Opposition

In the mid-1980s, the Department of Energy began hearings in eastern and western states that had been selected as possible sites for regional nuclear-waste dumps. The states chosen were for the most part rural ones, with geological formations thought safe for the long-term storage of wastes, such as the granite beds of New Hampshire. The public hearings were among the most emotional in the nuclear controversy: citizens of small communities and elected state officials of both political parties united to oppose the selection of their state as a dump site.

In Maine, for example, DOE officials were confronted by statewide resistance to selection of a site near Sebago Lake, a popular recreational area and source of the water supply for the city of Portland. The entire Maine delegation to Congress spoke out against the DOE plans, and hundreds of residents displayed "no" placards at a public meeting.[26] Similar hearings took place in New Hampshire, Wisconsin, and other states. The DOE quelled this swelling opposition by announcing that only one site, Yucca Mountain, in a remote part of Nevada, had been chosen as the future burial site for high-level radioactive wastes from commercial nuclear power plants.

Surging antinuclear sentiment in Maine set the stage for the third referendum since 1980 on Maine Yankee. This 1987 referendum would have closed any facility producing radioactive wastes. Fueling the argument was the fact that the Nuclear Waste Policy Act, which was responsible for the initial search for a high-level radioactive-waste disposal site, also mandates that each state take title to the low-level wastes produced by nuclear power plants in their states by 1993. The Maine Nuclear Referendum Committee (MNRC) argued that even though half the electricity produced by Maine Yankee was sent out of state, Maine would have to dispose of the nuclear wastes. The MNRC compared the costs of handling these wastes with the costs of the hydro power and conservation alternatives. People for Maine Yankee's Electricity, a pronuclear group, stressed that the plant was reliable and safe, that jobs were involved, and that the costs of replacing the inexpensive electricity with foreign oil would be high. The pronuclear group also pointed out that if coal were to replace nuclear power, the potential hazard of acid rain and the acceleration of the "greenhouse effect" could result. Moreover, it said, earlier efforts in Maine to block hydro projects and a coal plant for environmental reasons had been successful. This use of environmentalist arguments against environmentalists, as well as the employment and economic arguments, once again resulted in the defeat of the MNRC—at a cost of $4.7 million to the pronuclear group and $600,000 to the MNRC.

Similar referendums have been defeated in Oregon and California, but in 1988 the Massachusetts Citizens for Safe Energy got an initiative on the ballot that would have mandated the closing of the Rowe and Pilgrim nuclear reactors for the same reason—that is, because they are facilities producing nuclear wastes.[27] Local opposition to nuclear power in the 1980s was not confined to New England. Ninety miles southwest of Houston, Texas, the Southwest Texas Nuclear Project was running eight years behind schedule at a $4 billion cost overrun. The project met with strong resistance from local groups, including a new constituency of whistleblowers. Over sixty whistleblowers are affiliated with the opposition, and their argument is that workers have been harassed and fired for filing complaints about hundreds of safety violations and construction errors in the building of the nuclear power plants.[28]

In the Dallas–Fort Worth area, the Comanche Peak Citizens Audit took a new approach in the mid-1980s by circulating petitions to demand an independent audit of the management and construction costs of Comanche Peak and a review of the options to replace the plant. The group also wanted a hearing to assess the environmental impact of Comanche Peak and exclusion of the plant from the utilities' customer rate base until the audit and hearings took place.[29] The Comanche Peak Citizens Audit raised questions about plans to entomb the wastes at the plant site in layers of concrete after its thirty-year lifespan (a step already under serious consideration at Maine Yankee).

One effect of the Nuclear Waste Policy Act that requires states to take possession of low-level wastes in 1993 is that nuclear power plants may never be decommissioned (as Hope Creek in New Jersey was in the 1970s), but rather they may become the permanent tombs of radioactive wastes. Since the NRC allows nuclear power plants to store high-level wastes for no more than five years onsite, the possibility of these wastes also being entombed is not unlikely.

The issue of the onsite storage of wastes was raised in 1988 by the Northern Sun Alliance in Minnesota, a "volunteer based membership organization formed in 1977 to halt the spread of nuclear power plants and weapons." Group members released helium balloons at the Prairie Island plant to illustrate dangers posed by Northern State Power's plans to double the density of its waste storage for "spent fuel rod consolidation." The balloons were intended to show how radioactive gases and debris would be carried by the wind.

The Irradiation Controversy

The environmental impact of radiation is not limited to potential cancers and leukemias from low-level radioactive wastes and the lethal effects of high-level military and commercial nuclear wastes. The irradiation of people, food, and water are other environmental impacts. The National Association of Radiation Survivors (NARS), headed by Dr. Dorothy Legaretta; the Nevada Test Site Widows; and the Atomic Veterans are groups promoting the rights of people who have actually been affected by radiation. NARS lobbies on behalf of nuclear laboratory workers, Nevada test site victims, uranium miners, and others who need medical diagnosis and legal assistance. The National Coalition to Stop Food Irradiation cites testimony that increasing the shelf life of foods and controlling bacteria by bombarding the food with cobalt-60, cesium-137, or X rays may be related to cancer, reproductive failure, and other health problems.[30] The sale of irradiated food is banned only in Maine and in England. Similarly, the Health and Energy Institute argues that there is a correlation between the incidence of birth defects, such as cleft lip and mongolism, and irradiated water.

Organized Labor and Environmentalists

Internal division or uncertainty within a movement may necessitate the formulation of ideological doctrine. This usually comes at a time when the conflict becomes more focused, and growth of the movement may suffer as a result. The only group in the antinuclear movement to have developed an incipient theoretical doctrine was Environmentalists for Full Employment. This organization was created in response to conflict between environmentalist and labor factions within the movement (or to forestall such conflicts), and confrontations between antinuclear activists and workers in nuclear power plants. At the site of the Indian Point reactors in New York, Representative Bella Abzug was jeered by construction workers after speaking in favor of the antinuclear groups demonstrating outside the plant. At Seabrook, construction workers participated in counterdemonstrations that supported nuclear power. Out of such conflicts, ideological rationalizations of a movement's goals are born. When Environmentalists for Full Employment was formed in 1976, it appealed to Leonard Woodcock, president of the AFL-CIO, to unite the two factions, arguing that "both the environmentalist and the labor movement must keep in mind the ecological principle that there can be no division between the natural and social environment."[31]

Organized labor in general and construction unions in particular support nuclear power. Both the Teamsters and the United Mine Workers are pronuclear, the latter in order to protect the coal industry. Unions that support the construction of nuclear power plants worked with utilities to help defeat the 1976 California Nuclear Safeguards Initiative and to mobilize pronuclear demonstrations at Seabrook. But gradually, labor union locals have increasingly sided with antinuclear groups. They have opposed nuclear power projects at Barnwell, South Carolina; at Bailly, Indiana; and the Clinch River breeder reactor project in Tennessee.[32] Groups such as the Clamshell Alliance have endorsed resolutions that express their solidarity with the labor movement.[33]

Antinuclear groups have been open to the issue of worker safety in nuclear facilities, but they have not overtly adopted left-wing views on capitalism in general. That groups such as the Clamshell Alliance refuse to condemn capitalism is a strategic consideration, as well as the result of competing points of view among the affinity groups. Most activists had no desire to broaden the nuclear issue to an attack on corporate capitalism by advocating socialism, as this would alienate the public and the government.[34]

Environmentalist or ecology-oriented groups tend not to recruit from the working class. They appeal instead to the college-educated and upper-middle-class social stratum.[35] Ironically, the U.S. Labor party, a Marxist-Leninist group, views "Naderism" as the ideological enemy in the nuclear controversy. In its publication *Stop Ralph Nader, The Nuclear Saboteur*, the U.S. Labor party asserted that banks are trying to increase the cost of raw materials and energy in order to generate capital to amortize debts. These banks are supposedly funding the environmentalist movement in order to hold back technological progress and economic growth, including the denial of nuclear power plants and technical assistance to the Third World.[36]

The U.S. Labor party may not accurately reflect the views of the American left wing, but it has been one of the more visible leftist groups in the controversy. At one time, travelers at major airports were often urged by members of the Fusion Energy Foundation to subscribe to a magazine entitled *Fusion,* at an extraordinarily high price. This group seems to be ideologically affiliated with the U.S. Labor party and propounds a view that nuclear fission power is a necessary transition to nuclear fusion power and a growth economy. Radical left groups as such have not gained prominence in the antinuclear movement, although it has attracted many individuals with radical left views.

An irony in the nuclear controversy is the contention that the federal government is actually a major funder of antinuclear and antiutility direct-action groups. In two articles entitled "Where Do the Antis Get Their Money?" H. A. Cavanaugh asserts that public-interest groups that attack investor-owned electric utilities, nuclear power, oil companies, banks, and corporations have been funded by government grants that total over $2.5 billion.[37] Cavanaugh claims that one of the three major antinuclear intervenors in the Seabrook controversy, the National Consumer Law Center, was supported by grants from both the Department of Energy and the Federal Trade Commission. Some of the success of the antinuclear movement must therefore be attributed to its access to external resources from within the political elite. According to Cavanaugh, many government administrators are actually recruits from Nader and other environmental or antinuclear organizations.[38]

The Future of Environmentalism

When a nuclear power plant is proposed for construction, the Nuclear Regulatory Commission must prepare a draft environmental impact statement. After comments are received on the draft, a final environmental statement is prepared. The 1971 *Calvert Cliffs* v. *Atomic Energy Commission* decision required that the 1969 National Environmental Policy Act (NEPA) be complied with to the fullest extent possible. And in 1976 in *Natural Resources Defense Council* v. *Nuclear Regulatory Commission,* a federal district court judge agreed with the NRDC that the

Vermont Yankee nuclear plant could not be granted an operating license until the environmental impacts of reprocessing spent fuel and disposing of nuclear wastes had been considered.[39]

These rulings were hailed as major victories, both for the antinuclear movement and for environmentalism. But two years later, the Supreme Court decided all the issues in favor of the Nuclear Regulatory Commission. The conservative Burger court viewed environmental impact statements covering all phases of the nuclear fuel cycle as speculative, and it reasoned that it would be better to prepare a study while reprocessing and waste-disposal facilities were being considered for licensing. In addition, the court ruled that courts may not demand procedures such as cross-examination in the informal rule-making process of the NRC.

This 1978 decision has been damaging to the environmentalist strategy of pursuing litigation against utilities and nuclear power corporations under NEPA. It has had the effect of excluding public-action groups from participating in proceedings to challenge NRC findings in environmental impact studies, because the decision indicates that agencies will not be required to comply strictly with the act. As James F. Raymond concluded in his study of the Burger court decisions, "by minimizing NEPA's role in restraining agencies, and by holding sacrosanct agency discretion, the Court has dealt environmental law a severe blow."[40] Environmentalist groups increasingly find that higher court decisions neutralize their lower-court successes in changing government policy and protecting environmental quality.

Future success for the environmentalist movement may well depend on the development of broader social consciousness in the movement itself. Although the problem of environmental toxins affects entire populations, epidemiologists have discovered patterns that suggest that specific class strata and age groups are more affected than others by toxins.[41] Certain blue-collar workers are more likely to be victims of cancer than the general population, and the poor often receive inadequate medical treatment. Other pollutants affect particular age groups more than others, such as the respiratory diseases of the very young and the elderly.

Conclusion

Environmentalists have long emphasized the dangers of radioactive wastes as the prime reason for their opposition to nuclear energy. More than anything, the unresolved problem of what to do with nuclear wastes has made environmentalists fundamentally opposed to nuclear power. But since radioactive wastes pose a hazard to human health no matter what their source, environmentalists are slowly broadening the scope of their arguments to include the military use of nuclear energy. Nuclear-waste reprocessing, the breeder reactor, and the manufacture of nuclear weapons are all linked to commercial nuclear power as a means to close the nuclear fuel cycle, lacking a real solution to the problem of storing radioactive wastes. From the early issues of fish kills and floating nuclear power plants, the conflict has escalated to issues of national defense policy, which would dispose of high-level wastes by making more nuclear warheads, and of federal policy to store low-level wastes on the sites of nuclear power plants, where they may contribute to the cancer risk for generations to come. This is one of the most significant developments in the antinuclear movement going into the 1990s.

Ecologists' attempts to function in a judicial and regulatory system often hostile to their goals have made them keenly aware of scientists' important role in the movement in supplying criticism of the NRC and addressing the safety problems of nuclear power plants.

Chapter Three

Scientist and Moralist Activists

Many environmental associations such as the Natural Resources Defense Council have competent scientists on their staffs (although the recognition given to scientists who conduct environmental impact studies, especially in nonacademic settings, is eclipsed by that given to those who remain in the American scientific establishment). The most influential groups in the antinuclear movement count among their members individuals who are a part of the scientific ultraelite, including several Nobel laureates and many nuclear physicists.[1]

Elite scientists sympathetic to the goals of the antinuclear movement have belonged primarily to three groups: the Union of Concerned Scientists in Cambridge, Massachusetts; the Federation of American Scientists; and the Committee for Nuclear Responsibility. The last organization is typical of several other ad hoc committees in which prestigious scientists and relatively well-known public servants articulate their views. Some of these scientists have been involved in major policy decisions and have achieved recognition as "scientist statesmen," both in government and within their disciplines.[2] That they represent a higher echelon in science means their authority and opinion on matters of national policy and science affairs is respected and influential.

The normative structure of scientific institutions accords scientists the opportunity to engage in the disinterested and universalistic pursuit of truth. The products of their efforts are evaluated by their peers, who determine the originality and significance of the research for the advancement of human knowledge. Scientific institutions, however, are interdependent with the larger society. Thus, demands made on them by society external to scientific institutions may lead them to be involved in political affairs.

For example, nuclear physicists became deeply involved in policy decisions regarding the uses of atomic energy during World War II. The federal government created roles of researcher, adviser, administrator, and diplomat for many scientists.[3] These scientists were not an apolitical elite; indeed, their power in government policy decisions was increased when political leaders were indecisive or divided over how to control the awesome power of nuclear technology. Although the scientific achievements of nuclear physicists gives them authority to speak on matters of nuclear energy, their views and assumptions on nonscientific matters can be integrated into the formulation of government policy. This presents a dilemma because the institutional nexus within which scientists operate and the norms of science are markedly different from the institutional nexus and norms of politics.

During the 1950s, the scientist Edward Teller was an important influence on President Truman, who decided to proceed with the development of the hydrogen bomb—an innovation in atomic warfare that to a large extent had been based on the technical breakthroughs of Teller himself. While Teller received a sympathetic hearing at the highest level of government, his opponents in the Federation of Atomic Scientists were able to express their opinions only at the lower levels of the Truman administration. For this reason, one observer asserts that "the brief history of American nuclear policy does not encourage one to believe that depending upon a restricted intellectual elite is a sound practice in democracy."[4]

Don K. Price believes that the threat to democracy comes not from the secrecy of scientific advice to political leaders or from an excess of centralized authority, but from scientists who promise technological miracles when lobbying for research funds. Price claims that powerful, eminent scientists who are *insiders* accept the subordination of science to government authority, while the independent critics who are *outsiders* see no need for science to be subordinated to a system of organized authority based on traditional views.[5] Caustically, Price argues that scientists are capable of supporting any kind of authoritarian political theory, so that their attempts to guide political action are "little more than a rationalization of the will to power than a valid intellectual discipline."[6]

Scientists must also fear espionage trials, security-clearance hearings, and other manifestations of the national phobias that have occurred in the past.[7] Daniel Bell has estimated the actual number of persons in the scientific elite at about thirty thousand; over half are in the physical sciences and most are concentrated in elite universities.[8] However, these scientists divide ideologically on issues or align themselves with other elites. Modern technological systems have contributed to the centralization of political functions in society, but the division of labor in science has tended to diffuse rather than concentrate authority.[9] The political elite depends on scientists because of their expertise in increasingly complex areas. Although scientists are competent in these areas, we must ask if this assures their competence in making decisions that affect the lives of all members of society.

Scientists involved in the antinuclear movement have not accepted government authority as irreproachable on matters of atomic energy. Some of this opposition such as the Federation of American Scientists, is a continuation of the past, while other efforts represent a new breed of scientists willing to advocate the public interest. The technical objections to nuclear power raised by antinuclear scientists are paralleled by their concern about the arms race and the proliferation of nuclear weapons. Scientists' participation in the political arena is perhaps more significant than their criticisms of technology and energy policy.

The Federation of American Scientists

The Federation of American Scientists was formed in 1945, although it was then called the Federation of Atomic Scientists. It was a lobby to facilitate the civilian control of atomic energy. Its efforts are epitomized by the struggles of J. Robert Oppenheimer with the government and the top military brass. Despite the tragic consequences of security-clearance hearings for some of its members, the federation successfully opened an office in the national capital for the purpose of educating the public on nuclear issues. Membership dropped from three thousand in 1949 to a low of about a thousand, but revived when the organization broadened the scope of its activities in 1969.

The new, renamed Federation of American Scientists grew from 1,500 members in 1970 to 2,300 in 1971 and gained prestigious sponsors. Among its supporters were Nobel laureates Hans Bethe and Harold Urey, ex-presidential science advisers George Kistiakowsky and Jerome Wiesner, and economist and former ambassador to India John Kenneth Galbraith. Many scientists in the organization have at one time or another been involved in the government of science or in secret defense-policy committees. Their first goals after the reorganization were to defeat the development of the supersonic transporter (SST), to fight congressional approval of the antiballistic missile (ABM), and generally to work to stop the strategic arms race and to prevent the unemployment of scientists.

When President Nixon abolished the White House Office of Science and Technology, the Federation of American Scientists fought unsuccessfully to have the decision reversed. The federation also urged the Nixon administration to require cutbacks in the operating levels of nuclear reactors, to reorganize the federal government for management of the energy crisis, and to separate the promotional and the regulatory functions of the Atomic Energy Commission.

The Federation of American Scientists never officially supported a moratorium on nuclear energy; it includes pronuclear scientists, including Hans Bethe, who won a Nobel prize in physics for his work on nuclear reactions and energy production in stars. The federation has published newsletters discussing both pronuclear and antinuclear arguments. However, many individual sponsors of the federation are also members of antinuclear organizations or have signed petitions indicating their support for a moratorium. Among these are Carl Cori (Nobel laureate in medicine), Christian Afinsen (Nobel laureate in chemistry), John Edsall, Paul Ehrlich, Mark Kac (a refugee from Poland during World War II), George Kistiakowsky, S. E. Luria (Nobel laureate in medicine), Roy Menninger, Severo Ochoa (Novel laureate in medicine), Robert Merton (social theorist), Harold Urey (Nobel laureate in chemistry), Linus Pauling (Nobel laureate in chemistry), David Riesman (sociologist at Harvard University), Albert Szent-Gyorgyi (Nobel laureate in medicine), Victor Weisskopf (Nobel laureate in physics), and Jerome Wiesner.

The membership of the federation consists of approximately 20 percent physicists, 16 percent medical scientists, 15 percent chemists, 15 percent biologists, and 7 percent engineers. The remaining 20 percent is distributed among other disciplines. The influence and prestige of its membership on a wide range of social and scientific controversies has given a halo effect to its antinuclear activities. The federation has some prominence in the antinuclear movement, despite its relatively low rate of participation on nuclear-power-plant issues in comparison with issues surrounding the strategic arms race.[10]

The Union of Concerned Scientists

The Union of Concerned Scientists (UCS) is a coalition of about a hundred scientists, engineers, and other professionals concerned with the impact of advanced technology on society. This association, based in

Cambridge, Massachusetts, is the most influential of all scientist antinuclear groups. Twenty to 30 percent of its membership is nontechnical; the internal organization is made up of small study groups that hold loosely structured ad hoc meetings. Only twelve to fifteen people work on the nuclear issue. Its activities are funded by members, by the Sierra Club, and by other antinuclear groups when it intervenes in federal hearings on nuclear power plants.

During the 1970s, UCS scientists conducted research on nuclear technology and government regulations of plant safety. They have concluded that nuclear technology poses a serious threat to the nation's safety, environment, and national security. The UCS is both an advocacy and a research organization. Its technical studies encompass the strategic arms race, air and water pollution, pesticide use, liquefied natural gas transport and storage hazards, and energy-policy alternatives. It has published numerous volumes on the technical inadequacies of the United States nuclear-power program.

The UCS began in 1969 as an informal faculty group at the Massachusetts Institute of Technology, growing out of the radical "March 4th" movement the previous year among MIT graduate students. The goal of the March 4th movement was to stop all research activities at MIT and to pressure the U.S. government to end the Vietnam war. A joint faculty-student committee was formed, and 4 March 1969 was chosen for a symbolic one-day research stoppage.

Students and faculty formed two distinct organizations; the faculty organization became known as the Union of Concerned Scientists, and the student group was the Scientists and Engineers for Social and Political Action. Some of the major planks of the UCS's program were opposition to the antiballistic-missile program and the promotion of civilian control of science. The student organization was more interested in direct confrontation with the political establishment than in the consensus politics of the UCS, but despite disagreements on tactics and strategy, the research stoppage was held on the day scheduled.

Eventually, the more radical Scientists and Engineers for Social and Political Action denounced the UCS. The student organization went on to indict those who committed "crimes of science against the people" (which prompted Glenn Seaborg, the discoverer of plutonium and then-chairman of the Atomic Energy Commission, to provide himself with five bodyguards). Edward Teller, who had been crucial to the development of the hydrogen bomb, was given a "Dr. Strangelove Award" for being a "war criminal." The UCS responded to the extremism of the radicals by affiliating with the Federation of American Scientists, stating that its goals were similar to those of that organization.[11]

The Union of Concerned Scientists has contributed to the antinuclear movement by providing technical analyses of the dangers of the nuclear fuel cycle, and on numerous occasions it has intervened in federal hearings on nuclear power plants and initiated a variety of legal actions to control nuclear energy in concert with other antinuclear groups. Three of their concerns are mining hazards in obtaining uranium for nuclear fuel, the safety of emergency core-cooling systems in nuclear power plants, and the export of nuclear fuels.

Uranium-Mining Hazards. It was the Union of Concerned Scientists that brought the issue of uranium-mining hazards to the attention of antinuclear groups.

Until 1949, uranium for American nuclear weapons came from a single mine in the Belgian Congo. When the AEC realized that depending on a single source of uranium made the United States vulnerable, domestic production of uranium was initiated (with government price supports).

In Europe, it had long been established that mining radioactive materials is dangerous without proper ventilation.[12] European radium and pitchblende miners suffered from epidemics of lung cancer because of poor ventilation in the mines. Airborne radon gas changes into radon daughters, which are responsible for the cancer. As far back as 1879, a researcher named Hesse had discovered that radium miners employed between 1869 and 1877 in Schneeberg, Germany, had an average life expectancy of less than twenty years after entering the mines.[13] Hesse diagnosed the cause of death as lung cancer in 75 percent of the cases. In 1939, a scientist by the name of Peller found that radon entering fluorospar mines in groundwater had contributed to the deaths of twenty-six out of twenty-nine miners. Pitchblende miners in Germany also died early after working in mines for more than two years from what was then called *Bergkrankheit* ("mountain sickness"). Excess cancer risk was also demonstrated in studies off British coal miners, American potash miners, and Russian manganese miners.

Although the AEC was apparently aware of high levels of radioactivity in uranium mines as early as 1947, no steps were taken to protect miners from radiation hazards. During the first period of intensive uranium mining in the southwestern United States, over six thousand miners were exposed to airborne radioactive gases in underground mines. The UCS reported in 1974 that among white uranium miners, there had been an

excess of sixty-seven deaths over the normally expected rate of malig-
nancies. The accumulated total of excess deaths among the six thousand
miners was estimated at between one and two hundred deaths. (American Indian males had a significantly lower risk than white males.)[14]

Between 1930 and 1946, uranium mines had been excavated for vana-
dium in the southwestern United States, but emissions and ventilation
were not monitored until 1961. A U.S. Public Health Service study predicted that there would be a significant mortality rate from lung cancer
among miners, and a 1962 follow-up study found that deaths from respiratory cancer were occurring at five times the normal rate. But uniform
standards were still not adopted until 1967, and even then responsibility
fell under state authority.

The ECCS Controversy. The 1975 fire at Browns Ferry and the
1979 accident at the Three Mile Island ingrained in public consciousness
the fear that a catastrophic accident could release large amounts of lethal
radioactivity into the atmosphere. Such an accident actually could occur
if a reactor's emergency core cooling system (ECCS) functioned incor-
rectly during an emergency, such as if a pipe rupture caused a loss of
normal cooling water. Emergency backup systems do work, as Three
Mile Island demonstrated, but there is always the possibility that a nuclear reactor could overheat, melt through its containment structure, and
release radioactive poisons. In other near-catastrophes in the history of
nuclear power plants, the ECCS systems tested by the AEC had all
failed.[15]

This issue had previously been a major focus of concern for the Union
of Concerned Scientists. The UCS had become involved after discover-
ing a 1957 Atomic Energy Commission report (WASH-740) that had predicted that if an ECCS failure should occur, an area as large as
Pennsylvania could be affected. (Ironically, Three Mile Island is located
in Pennsylvania. Released just before the accident was the popular film
The China Syndrome, in which a similar accident was depicted.)

Conducting its own studies, the UCS concluded that emergency core
cooling systems have design defects that may cause them to fail in emergencies (although it believed this would more likely occur from a pipe
rupture than from human error, as at Three Mile Island). Scientists
working within the government had also complained of suppression of
information on emergency core cooling systems.

The efforts of the UCS had no measurable impact on the U.S. government, but the Reactor Safety Committee of the West German govern-

ment recommended a moratorium on nuclear power until more research had been completed on emergency core-cooling systems. Both the Federation of American Scientists and the RAND Corporation advised against further construction of nuclear power plants until the effectiveness of emergency core cooling systems could be resolved. Even the Atomic Energy Commission's Advisory Committee on Reactor Safeguards listed ECCS reliability as an unsolved reactor-safety problem, and a working research group at the 1973 Pugwash Conference and government scientists in Sweden both reached similar conclusions.

The original 1957 report, WASH-740, had estimated that an upper limit of 3,400 persons would be killed in a nuclear accident and over 43,000 persons injured.[16] A 1965 update of WASH-740 was withheld from the public after these estimates were revised upward. A major step forward for the antinuclear movement came when the UCS provided technical and scientific support for a coalition of citizens' groups that was intervening in federal hearings on the effectiveness of emergency core-cooling systems. Its technical studies suggested that radioactive gases released from a nuclear power plant could be lethal at a distance of a hundred miles, and that health injuries could occur hundreds of miles away. As the Union of Concerned Scientists pointed out, the Indian Point nuclear reactors are located only twenty-four miles from New York City. A temperature inversion at Indian Point could expose more than 100,000 persons to lethal or near-lethal radiation in just a two-mile-wide strip.

The WASH-740 update predicted 45,000 fatalities and tens of billions of dollars' worth of damage in an accident. Conducted in 1965, the update was released in June 1973 only after the UCS threatened to obtain it under the Freedom of Information Act. The update indicated that a pipe rupture could cause a core meltdown in a nuclear reactor and that it would overcome all manmade structures. The UCS estimated that a pipe rupture would occur approximately every seven years, although this did not mean that the emergency core-cooling system would fail in every case. (No deaths among the general population were recorded as a result of the operation of a nuclear power plant until Chernobyl. Many accidents have occurred, often involving fatalities to plant workers.[18] The main casualties after Three Mile Island were local residents who experienced severe psychological distress.)

Pressure-vessel ruptures are the most serious problem, because the ECCS would be rendered ineffective. If bolts that hold the main pressure vessel together ruptured, steam lines would be destroyed and would disable the emergency core-cooling system. Even minor accidents, however, can have devastating consequences. For example, the March 1975 fire at Browns Ferry was caused when an electrician working for the Tennessee Valley Authority held a lighted candle near insulation to determine the source of an air leak under the control room. The fire decommissioned the reactor for several months and destroyed the ECCS control cables; they would have been inoperative if the system had been needed.

Containment structures in nuclear reactors are capable of withstanding powerful impacts. If a plant reaches supercriticality, it cannot explode like an atomic bomb, as some environmentalists once presumed. Bernard Cohen, a nuclear physicist at Stanford University, points out that there is a fail-safe mode in nuclear-reactor operation—the control rods automatically go into the reactor core to stop the fission reaction if anything goes wrong. This process is enhanced by the "Doppler effect": a rise in temperature as water is converted into steam may cause a reactor to shut down as more neutrons are absorbed and the reaction becomes supercritical for a few thousandths of a second. [19]

A loss-of-coolant accident (known in the industry as a LOCA) could be precipitated by a leak in the cooling system or a rupture in the reactor vessel. Pipes—thirty inches in diameter and made from two-inch-thick stainless steel—are monitored by radiographic, ultrasonic, and magnetic-particle techniques. In an accident, the fuel pins would rise to a temperature of 2,700 degrees Fahrenheit for four to five seconds in the pressurized-water-reactor type and in two to five minutes in the boiling-water-reactor type. Coolant would be useless at this point. Complete melting of the fuel would occur in thirty minutes in the pressurized-water reactor and in two hours for the boiling-water reactor. The reactor core would melt into the earth: this is "the China syndrome."

The failure of ECCS tests in Idaho prompted the Union of Concerned Scientists to challenge the AEC in federal court. Three workers died at the government test station in Idaho in 1961 when the experimental reactor went out of control. More tests were scheduled using a small fifty-five-megawatt reactor known as LOFT, but the results of these tests have not been publicized by the NRC.

After the Atomic Energy Commission was forced to disclose the WASH-740 update, a $3 million study headed by Professor Norman Rasmussen was conducted at the Massachusetts Institute of Technology. The Rasmussen report, released in 1974, calculated that there is a one-in-17,000 chance of a core meltdown each reactor year, and that one such accident would occur every 175 years. The probability of an accident with more than a thousand fatalities was one in a million years—the same probability of a large meteorite hitting a large city and causing a thousand fatalities. The maximum damage would be $4–6 billion, and only one in ten meltdowns would have measurable health effects; that is, one disastrous accident in seventeen and a half centuries.

The Rasmussen report (WASH-1400) estimated that in the worst case, an accident would cause 3,300 early fatalities, 45,000 cases of early illness, and $14 billion in property damage. The long-term health effects were estimated at 1,500 latent cancer fatalities per year, 8,000 thyroid nodules per year, and 170 genetic effects per year. The report did not analyze the risks of breeder reactors, catastrophes from sabotage or acts of war, or the risks involved in other parts of the nuclear fuel cycle.

The UCS criticized the Rasmussen estimates of deaths as being at least sixteen times too low, primarily because the assumption had been made that evacuation procedures could move people out of the way of airborne radiation. Critics of the Rasmussen report also asserted that its methodology—adapted from the Apollo space and ballistic-missile programs—was inadequate for the purpose of evaluating nuclear power plant accidents. One failure per ten thousand missions has been predicted for the Apollo program, but the lives of three American astronauts were lost during a fire in an Apollo spacecraft. Nuclear physicist David Inglis used the same methodology to calculate the chances of a chain of seven safety circuits and two backup circuits failing simultaneously—one in a billion trillion; nevertheless, human error accounted for such a failure in a Virginia nuclear power plant (which is now being considered for conversion to coal).[20] The barrage of criticisms of the Rasmussen report eventually resulted in its repudiation by the Nuclear Regulatory Commission.

Export of Nuclear Fuels: The Tarapur Case.   New tactical ground was broken in 1976 when the UCS, in conjunction with the Sierra Club and the Natural Resources Defense Council, intervened in the Edlow International Company's application for a license to export nuclear fuel to the Tarapur atomic power station in India. This was the first time antinuclear groups had employed legal tactics to control the international diffusion of nuclear technology. Among the more than 175,000 persons who are members of the Sierra Club and Natural Resources Defense Council are citizens in India and Pakistan. Because such legal cases usually require that the petitioners themselves be threatened by specific actions, the organizations contended that some of their members who travel to India could be exposed to radioactive risks. Without a review of the case by the NRC, the ability of the petitioners to carry out their function (of disseminating information to the public concerning the environment and nuclear power) would be impaired.

The real issue was that India—not a party to the Nuclear Nonproliferation Treaty—had detonated a nuclear weapon in 1974 using nuclear fuel supplied to them by Canada. This fuel was to have been used only for peaceful purposes. The United States failed to require India to meet safeguards and radioactive-waste agreements. If the United States allowed the export of nuclear fuel to India, other nations might also be encouraged to ignore the prohibition against developing nuclear weapons. Therefore, the export of nuclear fuels to India was a risk to the common defense and national security, as defined by the Atomic Energy Act of 1954, and inconsistent with the health and safety regulations of the National Environmental Policy Act of 1969.

General Electric manufactured the nuclear reactors at Tarapur, the largest nuclear complex in Asia. Paul Jacobs, an antinuclear activist until his death (from cancer, perhaps the result of having been forced to witness atomic bomb tests while in the military), reported that workers at Tarapur had been seen using bamboo poles to operate the reactors' radioactive-waste disposal system. Jacobs investigated Tarapur after being informed of the situation by a disgruntled employee from the Bechtel Corporation. Writing in *Mother Jones,* Jacobs argued that the nuclear community had long been aware of the situation at Tarapur but had said and done nothing because

the nuclear fraternity is a close one. Born so recently, shrouded for so long in military secrecy, this elite now numbers only a few thousand physicists and technicians. It has been likened to an "old boy" network of elite colleagues and, like other fraternities, it has bred close bonds of support and mutual protectiveness.[20]

Jacobs argued that these bonds develop into symbiotic relationships between the nuclear industry and government. To support his contention that a closed elite chose to ignore Tarapur, Jacobs pointed out that the Bechtel Corporation had employed at one time or another the former secretary of the treasury under President Nixon, George Shultz; the former secretary of health, education, and welfare, Caspar Weinberger (the secretary of defense in the Reagan administration); and former AEC general manager R. Hollingsworth.

Some of Jacob's contentions regarding a closed elite are supported by a study of stratification in American science by Harriet Zuckerman, a sociologist at Columbia University. Zuckerman found that elite scientists are close to being a gerontocracy, in the sense that they have shared many common experiences in laboratories and in World War II. Long associations have created a strong sense of social solidarity in the group, as well as similar commitments and interests.[21] However, no evidence is presented that suggests scientists would not be concerned with the misuse of nuclear technology. The existence of scientists' groups such as the Union of Concerned Scientists contradicts the notion that government has total control over the scientific establishment. In the specific case of Tarapur, their efforts were largely unsuccessful because Congress voted to continue the shipment of nuclear fuel to India in 1980, overruling a decision by the NRC to prohibit such sales.

Conflict with the NRC. One of the most important ongoing activities of the Union of Concerned Scientists is its criticism of the Nuclear Regulatory Commission. The UCS believes that the NRC is now a promotional voice for nuclear power and that it fails to regulate the nuclear industry adequately. For example, the NRC itself has admitted that there is a 90 percent chance that Mark I containment shelters, used in twenty-four General Electric reactors, could fail if there were a core meltdown, but it nonetheless continues to license operation of the reactors.[22]

In 1985, a near-meltdown of the Davis-Besse plant near Toledo, Ohio, was only narrowly avoided, resulting in a $900,000 fine levied on Toledo Edison by the NRC. Also in 1985, all five of the nuclear reactors in the TVA system were shut down after widespread management and safety enforcement breakdowns were discovered, including allegations that the manager of the Watts Bar plant near Knoxville had deliberately made false statements to the NRC about the reactor's safety.[23] Workers at the Dothan, Alabama, plant testified that managers repeatedly falsified radiation readings at the plant to prevent a shutdown and were dismissed if they raised safety questions. In 1987, the Peach Bottom nuclear power plant near Philadelphia was ordered closed when it was discovered that control-room operators regularly slept on the job.[24] A Justice Department attorney investigating these cases testified before the Senate Committee on Governmental Affairs that the NRC appeared to deliberately "hamper the investigation and prosecution of individuals and companies in the industry the agency regulates."[25] But as one observer points out, "Contrary to public perception, the NRC has neither the authority nor the resources to comprehensively regulate the nuclear power industry: it cannot check and monitor every nuclear power plant in detail to assure reasonable reactor safety."[26]

A UCS study of the NRC and safety at nuclear power plants focused criticism on four main issues: the NRC does not deal with generic safety issues; the NRC tries to circumvent public participation in decision making; the NRC disregards its own rules and regulations; and the NRC is not independent of the industry it regulates.[27]

Generic safety issues are "possible deficiencies in the design, construction, or operation of several or a class of nuclear power plants such that the protection of the public from radiation may be inadequate."[28] These deficiencies include fire protection, equipment design, cracking of pipes, and inadequacy of containment shelters. The UCS argued that the NRC avoids grappling with serious safety issues by labeling them generic and instead concentrates on less serious "unresolved safety issues."

For example, the Grand Gulf I reactor in Mississippi, the largest nuclear power plant in the world built on a standardized design (thereby escaping new review and approval), was found to have serious design errors in safety systems, and training records of operators who were later found to be unqualified had been falsified.[29] The UCS depicted the NRC as arbitrarily enforcing regulations, since its basic allegiance to the nuclear industry results in important rules, such as those regarding emergency-evacuation plans, being circumvented. Its allegiance to the nuclear industry makes the NRC discourage public contributions to safety and environmental protection, despite over two hundred documented "precursors" to core melt accidents.[30]

In its 1988 voter-information paper, UCS proposed that acutely dangerous reactors be closed and that the NRC undergo reform. The UCS argued that energy policy should resolve the issues of radioactive wastes and emergency planning and redirect energy strategy for the future by focusing on conservation, clean coal and gas technologies, small-scale independent power producers, and other long-term options so that nuclear reactors may be eventually phased out.[31] Generally, reactor safety has been upgraded as a result of UCS actions, but serious problems remain. Unlike many of the environmentalist antinuclear groups, the UCS is also an opponent of the Strategic Defense Initiative ("Star Wars") and supports the INF treaty to eliminate all intermediate-range nuclear missiles from Europe.

The Committee for Nuclear Responsibility

Founded in California by Lenore Marshall, the Committee for Nuclear Responsibility (CNR) included on its board of directors several of the same scientists active in the Federation of American Scientists and other ad hoc antinuclear groups. Four of these scientists were Nobel laureates: James D. Watson (for his work on DNA), George Wald (for work on chemical and physiological processes in the eye), Harold Urey (the discoverer of deuterium), and Linus Pauling (for his work on the forces that hold matter together).[32] The other scientists were Paul Ehrlich (biology), John Edsall (biochemistry), John Gofman (medical physics), and Robert Bellman (mathematics). The board of directors also included writer Lewis Mumford, former U.S. Attorney General Ramsey Clark, architect Ian MacHarg, and Richard Max McCarthy, a former congressman from New York state.

Of these scientists, Linus Pauling was an important figure in the antinuclear movement of the 1950s, when he was active in trying to stop atomic-bomb testing because of the dangers of radioactive fallout. John Gofman was one of the early critics of commercial nuclear power in the antinuclear episodes of the 1960s. Paul Ehrlich gained a reputation as something of a doomsday prophet by popularizing an alarmist version of the Malthusian thesis of overpopulation. Ramsey Clark, George Wald, and James Watson were all critics of U.S. involvement in the Vietnam War.

The Committee for Nuclear Responsibility was formed as a political and educational organization to disseminate antinuclear views and information to the public. Its goals were a moratorium on nuclear power and the development of alternative-energy resources. Actor Jack Lemmon endorsed the goals of the CNR with the statement that

nuclear power plants will introduce the age of private atom bombs. Nuclear power plants will put so much plutonium into commercial circulation that, sooner or later, terrorists will get hold of enough to make their own atom bombs. The moment they demonstrate their first explosion here, we can kiss our civil liberties goodbye. We can expect panic, and then martial law . . . indefinitely.[33]

The official spokesperson for the CNR, Egan O'Connor, had even more direct views. Before a group of religious leaders in Washington, D.C., she said,

Ph.D.'s and other nuclear engineers have no special expertise in either common sense or morality. They are the wrong kind of experts to be making our country's energy policy—to be making a decision which will affect all men for all time.[34]

According to O'Connor, both advocates and opponents of nuclear energy agree that it is an inherently dangerous technology, and that cancer and genetic mutations might someday nullify all the lifesaving efforts of modern medicine and social work. She quoted former President Nixon, who once said:

all this business about breeder reactors and nuclear is over my head. That was one of my poorest subjects, science. . . . But it has always been fascinating to me that if a people are to be a great people, we must always explore the unknown.[35]

O'Connor called the notion of safe nuclear power a fantasy, claiming that "a rapidly growing number of middle Americans are ready to revolt before they will make the habitability of this planet dependent on miracles in the nuclear power industry."[36] She argued that a "sunshine economy" instead of a radioactive one would have good effects for millennia.

The Moralists

Scientists active in social causes justify overstepping their scientific neutrality by citing their moral responsibility to humanity. The moralist outlook holds that the problem of nuclear technology on future generations and on less developed societies must be resolved by referring to moral standards.

Political-action and religious organizations that raise moral arguments in the antinuclear movement include Common Cause, the National Council of Churches, and the World Council of Churches. These organizations' arguments are not encumbered by analyses of the technical or economic efficiency of nuclear technology.

Common Cause, for example, attempts to redirect government policy on the basis of political and moral principles fundamental to the American system. It was founded in 1970 by John Gardner, former secretary of health, education, and welfare, and grew into a national citizens' organization with over 300,000 members. With an active core of about 30,000 persons and a professional staff of seventy in Washington, D.C., Common Cause lobbies federal and state governments for reforms. Its ideology is nonpartisan. Since its members ranked the energy crisis as one of their major concerns, Common Cause approved a statement in 1975 advocating a reduction in research commitments to nuclear fission power and an increase in funding for solar and geothermal energy projects, including the creation of a Solar Energy Research Institute.[37]

Another moralist organization is the National Council of churches. Its Church and Society division, in response to requests from its members, commissioned anthropologists Margaret Mead and René Dubos to produce a report on nuclear power and plutonium wastes. (Nuclear supporters were not asked to participate in the research committee because it was felt that a "balanced" report based on the principle of neutrality would be viewed as a tacit acceptance of nuclear power.) The research group felt that a lack of consensus on the nuclear power plant issue exists because the issues are really moral and ethical rather than scientific and technological.

The moral dilemma is whether our descendants should be bequeathed with nuclear wastes that potentially cause cancers and genetic defects through exposure to plutonium. To end dependency on nuclear power, we must be willing to accept necessary changes in our material standard of living by redistributing resources and technology according to the principle of equity. The 1975 National Council of Churches statement warned that "the more a society relies on complex technology, the more vulnerable it becomes to pathological behavior of a few, and to human errors which are bound to occur."[38] The statement was endorsed by the Reverend David Eaton of All Souls Church in Washington, D.C., and by a number of well-known liberal social scientists, including sociologists Robert Merton and David Riesman, economist Robert Heilbroner, ecologist Barry Commoner (who founded the Citizens Party and ran for president of the United States in 1980), historian Barbara Ward, and environmental activist Amory Lovins. Many scientists active in other antinuclear organizations also endorsed the statement.

The moralist perspective does not always fully support the views of the antinuclear movement, but it certainly raises questions that scientists alone cannot answer. But the criticisms of nuclear energy by scientists and environmentalists all come into play when we consider the direct-action groups on the front lines. These are the groups that have mobilized mass support for the antinuclear cause and have directly confronted the nuclear establishment through the organization of referendums on nuclear power, demonstrations outside nuclear power plants, legal tactics, and the integration of other movements into the antinuclear movement. In this sense, they are the real movement elite.

Chapter Four

The Movement Elite:
Direct-Action Groups

Social movements differ from voluntary associations or public-interest groups most often in their tactics. The sit-in, the mobilization of people for demonstrations and mass protest, and similar tactics are usually characteristic of a social movement. At the vanguard of the antinuclear movement are the regionally based direct-action organizations such as the Clamshell Alliance in New England. Such groups may intervene legally in nuclear issues, but they do not confine themselves to the courthouse or federal agency hearings. They take their cause directly to the people—in the streets, if necessary.

Some organizations have attempted to coordinate the antinuclear movement on a national scale, in much the same way that the Nader organizations did. The Task Force against Nuclear Pollution, Consolidated National Intervenors, and the Energy Action Committee tried to transcend the often singular and disparate activities of antinuclear groups. Their efforts were mostly symbolic, however, for most discrete groups that make up the antinuclear movement rarely join in common action.

Regional direct-action groups have generally been more successful in creating coalitions and alliances among antinuclear groups. For example, the Environmentalists for Full Employment attempted to link the antinuclear cause to the labor movement. Many antinuclear direct-action groups represent linkages of diverse social movements that have been an important aspect of the American political system since the 1960s. These alliances and coalitions forged the social values of the movement as a whole, and they integrated the movement on an ideological level. As a struggle becomes more intense, theoretical and ideological doctrines evolve to justify the movement's goals and to provide a constant reference point from which to view changes in the career and direction of the movement.

It is unusual that each of the antinuclear movement's various organizations seems to fulfill a specific function for the movement as a whole. This is a primary advantage of a loosely structured movement with many organizations that do not compete with one another either for ideological leadership or for power over the movement. Division over ideological leadership has always fragmented the socialist movement, preventing the cooperation of competing factions or a consensus on the goals of the movement. The synthesis of varied organization goals in the antinuclear movement is one of its most distinctive features.

Expressive symbolization emerges in a social movement as a result of direct action. Seabrook became a symbol for the antinuclear movement across the country as the Clamshell Alliance persistently confronted the nuclear industry and the federal government with mass demonstrations outside the construction site of a nuclear power plant in this New Hampshire town. Seabrook created a collective identity for the antinuclear movement as a whole. An even more powerful collective form of expressive symbolization is created by martyrdom, for personal identification with a martyr merges the self with the community of the movement. Mass meetings in New York City and Washington brought attention to the 1974 death of Karen Silkwood. The National Organization for Women and a spinoff group, the Supporters of Silkwood, helped fuse individuals from diverse organizations into a collective cause by focusing on Silkwood's struggles and death. Since Silkwood was a labor activist, the issue brought both the women's movement and the labor movement into the antinuclear movement.

National Coordination of the Movement

When the antinuclear movement was in its infancy in the early 1970s, the Task Force against Nuclear Pollution (TFNP) was instrumental in helping to coordinate the activities of emerging antinuclear groups. It did so by focusing efforts on a specific task, the collection of signatures for the Clean Energy Petition. The petition states:

I, the undersigned, petition my representative in Government to sponsor and actively support legislation to: (1) develop safe, cost-competitive solar electricity and solar fuels within ten years or less, and (2) phase out the operation of nuclear power plants as quickly as possible.[1]

Collecting signatures for a petition facilitates group formation. It can command national attention without offending or shocking the public. Tables set up near shopping centers or other busy pedestrian intersections attract signatures because influencing congressional leaders is an accepted form of democratic political participation. When I observed a group, mostly women, obtaining signatures for the Clean Energy Petition across the street from Princeton University, I found that few if any persons refused to sign the petition after reading it. None of the petitioners were shabbily dressed, and none could be identified by appearance as a counterculture adherent. All took the petition seriously and believed that it was going to be effective. Speaking with the group, I found that they stressed being polite but persistent and did not argue with those who refused to sign.

After the petitions were signed, they were forwarded to the TFNP in Washington. There, volunteers sorted the petitions by congressional district and added the names to a computerized mailing list. The petitions were then shown to members of Congress or were used to influence state and local officials. By June 1974, the TFNP had collected 80,527 signatures, which grew to 200,324 by May 1975, then to 306,241 by October 1975, and to 401,223 by June 1976.[2]

The success of the petition is partly due to its sponsorship in the political elite. Senator Mike Gravel of Alaska worked closely with the TFNP, allowing it to take advantage of some of the resources available to a U.S. Senator. (Gravel also introduced the first nuclear-moratorium bill in Congress after his involvement in the controversy over nuclear-weapons testing on Amchitka Island.) The strategy of the TFNP was to show the public the link between the peaceful and the military uses of nuclear power. Senator Gravel perceptively outlined six reasons why he felt the nuclear issue would be a major focus in the 1976 presidential campaign:

(1) the local nature of the nuclear opposition would pressure Congress; (2) the exchange of antinuclear information was becoming more effective; (3) the issues and choices were becoming well defined, particularly with introduction of a five year moratorium bill into Congress; (4) the potential following of the antinuclear movement would be larger as more information was disseminated; (5) energy growth had begun to decline in the United States; and (6) the costs of nuclear power made it increasingly unattractive.[3]

Petitioning subsided as more groups became involved in the antinuclear movement, and the strategy and tactics of the movement were changed. In the House of Representatives, the five-year moratorium bill was introduced by Hamilton Fish of New York, a Republican. The bill— entitled the Nuclear Energy Reappraisal bill (H.R. 4971)—would have directed the NRC to grant no construction licenses for new nuclear power plants pending a five-year independent study of the entire nuclear fuel cycle by the Office of Technology Assessment. The bill provided for the independent assessment of the effectiveness of all safety systems in fission power plants; a determination that radioactive wastes can be stored or disposed of despite earthquakes, theft, sabotage, acts of war, or governmental and social instabilities; a demonstration of the effectiveness of security systems throughout the nuclear fuel cycle; and an analysis of all the safety, environmental, and economic consequences of nuclear energy to prove its superiority to other energy sources. The Office of Technology Assessment would have been required to study the short- and long-term genetic effects of low-level radiation, the economic implications of a plutonium economy (including the availability of raw materials and the potential for foreign uranium cartels), the cost of frequent shutdowns of nuclear plants, the hidden costs of government subsidies, and the question of nuclear-weapons proliferation. Virtually none of the controversial questions surrounding nuclear energy as a source of electricity was left untouched. The authorization of funds would be $15 million for each of the five years the moratorium would be in effect. Representative Fish argued that three tablespoons of plutonium was enough poison to give nine billion people lung cancer and that a "plutonium economy could instantly wipe out all the advances made in the field of human health in the last quarter of a century."[4]

H.R. 4971 became the focal point of the TFNP. It gained many sponsors in Congress but fell far short of the number of supporters required to pass it. The influence of the TFNP in the antinuclear movement waned thereafter, but Senator Gravel and the TFNP were the first influential opponents of nuclear power to define that opposition as "the antinuclear movement." The label was taken up by the press in articles on the controversy.

Senator Gravel asserted that the antinuclear movement was not a response to technical or economic issues but to moral concerns. He said,

the most dedicated nuclear opponents see atomic energy as a fundamental anti-human technology, one that requires of mankind a perfection which he simply does not possess. In nuclear energy, the kinds of mistakes that we know we make—including mistakes of irrationality and malice—can lead to the most disastrous consequences. Nuclear supporters have acknowledged the danger when they have referred to atomic energy as a "Faustian bargain."[5]

Consolidated National Intervenors further articulated national goals for the antinuclear movement. While the TFNP clarified the criticisms of nuclear power, Consolidated National Intervenors refined the ideas of the antinuclear movement on alternative-energy sources. (The antinuclear movement is unique in this sense, for many social movements are sharply critical of the social order without offering viable alternatives, while others simply become absorbed in their utopian goals.)

Consolidated National Intervenors, a coalition of nearly 150 environmentalist, consumer, and labor groups, began as a means to concentrate resources and talent in interventions during nuclear-power-plant licensing proceedings. But the organization gradually changed its goals and became almost exclusively concerned with generating support for solar energy legislation in Congress. Specifically, Consolidated National Intervenors supported solar-energy legislation to provide a solar tax incentive, along with low-interest loans for solar-energy systems by the Small Business Administration, the expansion of solar-energy research funds, and the prohibition of construction that blocked sunlight necessary for heating and cooling systems. Other major goals were to require that buildings constructed with federal funds be equipped with solar-energy systems where possible, and that a special administrative office be created for Solar and Geothermal Energy within ERDA (now the Department of Energy). The organization was remarkably successful, for Congress was amenable to all these goals and went on to implement them in a number of legislative proposals.

The transformation of its goals also had the effect of removing Consolidated National Intervenors from the mainstream of the antinuclear movement. Its main function became the dissemination of information on solar energy, including guides to all state laws dealing with solar energy, test facilities, and information sources. However, the activities of the Consolidated National Intervenors were in large part duplicated by organizations such as the International Solar Energy Society in Maryland and by publications such as *Solar Times, Sun Times, Solar Life, Solar Energy Intelligence Report, Solar Energy News, Solar Energy Report,* and many more.[6] Organizations and research groups that advocate solar energy were so numerous that one could argue that the solar energy movement actually developed independently of the antinuclear movement, which simultaneously attracted the participation of many social-movement groups.

Since oil corporations are actually energy corporations with growing control over phases of the nuclear fuel cycle (for example, Exxon Nuclear), as well as over coal resources and solar energy companies, the antinuclear movement must challenge the oil industry along with the nuclear industry. Resentment against the large oil corporations emerged particularly after the energy crisis of 1973–74, a crisis that many believed had in part been engineered by the major oil companies. The radical left in the United States has long criticized the imperialistic and monopolistic practices of international oil companies, but hostility to the companies now surfaced among the public and among more elite groups. For example, the Energy Action Committee tapped public sentiment on energy issues. Its central goal was to challenge the oil lobby. James Flug, an attorney who advised Senator Edward Kennedy for several years, stated that the Energy Action Committee would have "energy policy made in Washington instead of the Houston Oil Club."[7]

The Energy Action Committee was formed by four wealthy Californians who each contributed $600,000 to fund its initial efforts: Harold Willen, national chairman of the Businessmen's Educational Fund; Leo Wyler, chairman of the TRE Corporation; Miles Rubin, chairman of the board of Optical Systems Corporation; and actor Paul Newman. Two coordinators were hired: John Cabusi, a former campaign worker for Morris Udall, and Tom Girard, a former employee of Westinghouse. A staff of twelve persons was created and given a suite of four offices in Washington.

The specific goals of the committee were the divestiture of oil corporations, placing each phase of production (transportation, refining, and marketing) in the hands of a different company, and the retention of regulations on natural gas. The committee launched a head-on attack on the monopolistic practices of oil companies in order to make the industry more competitive. Its slogan was "Get Mad." As Newman said in an appeal for funds,

the giant oil monopolies are the most powerful corporations in the history of the world. To enter into the battle with them is no easy task. Their influence over our government and others is mighty. And to keep their power, they will continue to bribe and deceive just as they have bribed and deceived for three-quarters of a century to obtain that power.[8]

Kenneth Curtis, former governor of Maine and later U.S. Ambassador to Canada, gave support to the group.

The Task Force against Nuclear Pollution, Consolidated National Intervenors, and the Energy Action Committee engaged in activities that reflect the overall evolution of the ideology of the antinuclear movement. After initial controversies over the safety and safeguards of nuclear power, groups went on to advocate that solar energy replace nuclear energy; as the struggle intensified, the latent hostility to American business and industry in general that has always been a part of our political tradition began to surface. The most dramatic and significant confrontations occurred in New England and California.

Regional Direct Action in the Movement

When Vermont Yankee was first proposed, most people in Vernon, Vermont, a small town of about a thousand residents, were generally indifferent to the proposal. But in nearby Brattleboro, Beatrice Brown, a former probate judge, wrote letters to the *Brattleboro Reformer* warning of the hazards of radioactivity:

As a result of her efforts, a small informal antinuclear group grew up which sponsored a debate between two officials from Vermont Yankee and Larry Bogart, a one-man crusader against nuclear power from New Jersey.

Bogart had been director of Publications and Advertising for Allied Chemical but had no formal qualifications in the field of nuclear energy. He was branded in the Brattleboro newspaper as an "out of state propagandist" by a letter writer from Vernon, and the rumor circulated that he was an agent for the coal industry.

In August 1967, just a few weeks after the Bogart-Vermont Yankee debate, Mrs. Brown and five other area residents founded the Anti-Pollution League of the Connecticut River Valley.

The League's first order of business was to arouse public interest in nuclear power through meetings, letters to the editor, and conversations. Their enthusiasm for this work was so great that many readers of the Brattleboro newspapers soon tired of reading their letters. League members became thought of as well-intentioned but misguided do-gooders in the community.

Nevertheless, they raised enough unsettling questions that the Windham Regional Planning and Development Commission (WRC), composed of two representatives from most towns in southeastern Vermont, appointed a study group to investigate whether Vermont Yankee was in fact a hazard to the region as claimed by the Anti-Pollution League. The study group included a forester, a real estate salesman, a laboratory technician, the Director of WRC, two members of the Anti-Pollution League and three local scientists.

The report was accepted by the entire group except for the two members of the Anti-Pollution League. It was adopted by the full WRC in January 1968 without discussion and without a dissenting vote.

Rather than opening up a complex problem, the WRC report seemed to settle the issue in favor of nuclear power. Opinion leaders in the community who previously had given the appearance of neutrality could now climb off the fence on the pronuclear side.

The matter might have rested there except for Peter Strong, president of the Conservation Society of Southern Vermont (CSSV), who was disturbed by what he considered to be a gross oversimplification of a complex issue in Brattleboro. On his initiative, the CSSV sponsored a conference entitled "Nuclear Power and the Environment: An Inquiry," held at Stratton, Vermont, in September 1968.

Unlike the WRC group, the CSSV went beyond Vermont for expertise and brought to Vermont knowledgeable critics of nuclear power from the Scientists' Institute for Public Information.

An attempt was made to get the AEC to send debators, but the chairman of the AEC, Glenn Seaborg, declined, asking Strong on the phone if he was against progress and telling him that the meeting sponsors and participants were being investigated. Finally, the late Dr. Theos J. Thompson came to Vermont from the Nuclear Engineering Department of MIT to represent the utility point of view.

The locus of the controversy now shifted from Brattleboro to Montpelier.[9]

In many ways, this account of the Vermont Yankee controversy tells the story of the entire movement against nuclear power. A nuclear power plant is scheduled for construction in a remote, rural area, whose residents accept it without question. A few individuals voice opposition and are labeled "propagandists" or "do-gooders." Nevertheless, local officials listen to the criticisms and then reject them, producing a reaction from other people concerned about the issue. An outside expert is brought in, while the AEC chairman (if we accept the validity of this account) suggests that the sponsors of the debate are against progress (because of rural ignorance?) and are being investigated (as disloyal Americans?). But more people become interested, and the issue turns into a controversy.

The New England Coalition on Nuclear Pollution and the Clamshell Alliance.　Small groups of scientists and citizens from southern Vermont and western Massachusetts formed the New England Coalition on Nuclear Pollution (NECNP) to intervene in the operating-license proceedings for the Vermont Yankee plant, relying on public donations for legal retainer fees. This was the beginning of the regional direct-action group that eventually became the Clamshell Alliance—perhaps the most publicized of all antinuclear organizations. The scientists of the NECNP, affiliated with nearby universities, reviewed documents, wrote interrogatories, assisted in policy formation, and educated activists on the technical problems of nuclear power plants. Despite their intervention, Vermont Yankee received an operating license.

The NECNP persisted, gaining the cooperation of the Natural Resources Defense Council. It brought a lawsuit before a court of appeals, asking for a second review of Vermont Yankee on the grounds that plans for the transportation and permanent disposal of radioactive wastes had been excluded from the initial review. The outcome of this case was a court order requiring that Vermont Yankee construct cooling towers to prevent thermal pollution, but the order circumvented the issue of radioactive-waste disposal.

The New England Coalition on Nuclear Pollution incorporated in 1971 as a voluntary, nonprofit organization with more than four hundred individual members and with support from fifteen organizations in the New England area. It was governed by a twenty-seven-member board of trustees that met every month to establish policy and to decide what actions to take to challenge nuclear power. The strength of the organization was its ability to get expert help from scientific advisers and legal counsel from specialists in nuclear-power-plant-hearings and environmental law.

Later, the NECNP joined Consolidated National Intervenors to participate in AEC hearings on the safety of the emergency core-cooling systems of nuclear power plants. This major shift in the strategy and tactics coincided with an increase in its membership. It made more sophisticated use of experts in intervention proceedings, and it used energy-conservation lectures, public-education seminars, debates, radio and television appearances, and energy conferences to broaden the attack on nuclear power. Its office, with a library and part-time staff, was maintained in Brattleboro, Vermont.

The coalition called for a moratorium on further construction and licensing of nuclear power plants, a gradual phasing out of all existing plants, and a national effort to develop nonradioactive and renewable-energy options. One president of the coalition, Diana Sidebotham, observed, "This was an early and aggressive action in the national moratorium movement."[10] New Hampshire became the arena for the next confrontation with the AEC. The Public Service Company of New Hampshire, a utility company, proposed in 1971 to construct two large nuclear power plants on an estuary along the seacost area at Seabrook, near Hampton. The NECNP initiated an intervention in the construction-permit hearings for the proposed reactors. Its case was strengthened by the poor financial condition of the utility company, the seismic history of the area, and the summer resort nature of Hampton Beach, which lay only two miles from the proposed site. (The NECNP also intervened in Massachusetts, where two plants were being proposed for construction in Montague, near Amherst. Sam Lovejoy, an environmental activist, received considerable publicity when he blew up a tower in protest of these plants.)

By 1976, Seabrook was the primary interest of the organization. Nathaniel Smith, another former NECNP president argued, "Powerful vested interests—the 'uranium lobby,' the reactor manufacturers, including General Electric and Westinghouse, the multibillion-dollar utility industry—are pushing the country toward an almost all-electric and almost all-nuclear energy economy."[11] For the Seabrook intervention, help came from the Audubon Society of New Hampshire, the Forest Society of New Hampshire, and the Seacoast Anti-Pollution League. Dr. James Nelson, an economics professor at Amherst College, testified that the utility industry could not generate enough capital internally to finance the construction of large nuclear power plants. Other expert witnesses on behalf of the intervenors were Carl Stein, an architect from New York City; Dr. Gordon J. MacDonald, a professor of environmental policy at Dartmouth College; Dr. Alvin O. Converse, an engineering professor at Dartmouth (who testified on the uses of solar energy); and Dr. Myrick Freeman, chairman of the economics department at Bowdoin College in Maine. The NECNP also enlisted the help of Dr. George Field, director of the Center of Astrophysics at Harvard University.[12]

Despite this highly credentialed expert testimony, the NRC issued the construction permit for the nuclear reactors at Seabrook. Shortly thereafter, the Clamshell Alliance was formed to take direct action against building the reactors. A new stage of the antinuclear movement began, and civil disobedience became the major tactic. For the next three years, arrests and mass demonstrations were commonplace at Seabrook, although the demonstrations remained nonviolent.[13] The nonviolent tactics were tacitly accepted by Jimmy Carter, who was then campaigning in nearby Manchester. When asked about civil disobedience and nuclear power, Carter replied,

I've always felt that anybody who disagrees with the civil law in a matter of conscience has a right to openly express that disobedience. At the same time, under our societal structure it's necessary that they be willing to take the consequences of their disobedience.[14]

During a 1979 demonstration at Seabrook, when the nuclear reactor core was being transported to the plant site, protestors were again arrested. The resource-mobilization perspective on social movements directs our attention to the importance of outside support and internal resources available to movement groups, but internal bonds of "positive solidarity" among members of movement groups are also important. These bonds of solidarity allow members to attempt acts that they would never contemplate as individuals. As Mark Traugott explains,

In the case of failure, they enjoy a relative impunity that is no mere illusion because, acting as a collectivity, participants can neutralize the efficacy of social control by concentrating equal or superior forces. Similarly their sense of power is realistic, based both on the strength of numbers and the opportunity to coordinate efforts of individuals joined by a sense of common destiny.[15]

Without this sense of positive solidarity, the hold of the movement on the individual is weakened.

The Clamshell Alliance consists of small groups from throughout New England called "affinity groups," each of which has autonomy. Maine groups, for example, include the Downeast Alliance in Franklin, the Island Energy Coalition in Bar Harbor, and the Bluehill Mussels in Bluehill. The Clamshell Alliance itself has a coordinating committee, and representatives from these small groups attend "Clam Congresses."[16]

The Maine groups later coalesced as MAGIC (Maine Affinity Group

Information Committee). According to Jeanne Christie, MAGIC groups were aware that many people are interested in affinity groups but associate them with left-wing radicalism. To appeal to these people, MAGIC established a task force to look into "creative strategizing," or minimal-commitment activities such as adding a dollar to your utility bill to be used for solar-energy research.[17]

Emergency Evacuation. By 1986, Seabrook's Unit 1 was complete and ready to begin low-power testing. As part of the aftermath of Three Mile Island, the Nuclear Regulatory Commission was prohibited from granting a nuclear power plant a license until an evacuation plan for the ten-mile radius around it had been approved. Six Massachusetts towns, with the support of Governor Michael Dukakis, refused to cooperate in emergency planning, believing that any emergency-evacuation plan would be inadequate. Even the Chernobyl nuclear reactor had been at low power when that accident occurred, but upward of 100,000 people visit Hampton Beach, near Seabrook, in the summer, and over 130,000 year-round residents live in the emergency-planning zone. The Shoreham nuclear power plant in Long Island (also the scene of demonstrations in the 1970s), was faced with the identical situation, as Suffolk County officials and Governor Mario Cuomo of New York refused to cooperate in emergency planning, thinking it an impossible task.

In 1987, the NRC voted 5 to 0 to relax its own rules and to allow plants such as Seabrook and Shoreham to be licensed even in the face of a state veto if the utilities had made a good-faith effort to involve local and state governments and had drawn up a plan likely to work. The Atomic Safety and Licensing Board scheduled hearings in Concord, New Hampshire, to hear the New Hampshire part of the evacuation plans. President Reagan met with New Hampshire's all-Republican congressional delegation to discuss the possibility of an executive order allowing the Federal Emergency Management Agency (FEMA) to draft evacuation plans if local governments refuse and even to assume all functions in an actual evacuation. Ironically, FEMA twice rejected the Seabrook evacuation plans and found serious deficiencies during a mock evacuation. In late 1988, however, President Reagan issued an executive order for federal officials to implement evacuation plans when state and local governments refuse to cooperate.

The NRC asserts that the construction of Seabrook was unusually safe,[18] but a report released by Representative Edward J. Markey (D-Mass.) questions this, partly because between 1976 and 1986 289 con-

struction workers at Seabrook were discharged for drug and alcohol
abuse, and in 1986 136 were discharged after mandatory urine testing
by New Hampshire Yankee revealed similar abuse.

Public Service Company of New Hampshire filed for bankruptcy in
1988 and later petitioned the Public Utilities Commission for rate increases. However, a state law bars utilities from charging ratepayers for
power plants before they generate power. These requested rate increases were over 20 percent above current rates, indicating the cost of
nuclear power. The Long Island Lighting Company (LILCO) has agreed
to abandon the Shoreham plant in return for tax breaks, rate increases,
and the right to continue operating as a public company. Ironically, a jury
found LILCO guilty of fraud in December 1988 for making false projections of Shoreham's completion date in rate hearings in 1978 and 1984.
Public Service of New Hampshire has not ruled out a similar agreement
for abandonment of Seabrook. Seabrook's future could have been decided
by the outcome of the 1988 presidential race, as candidate Michael Dukakis opposed the plant.

When a small group of activists marked the tenth anniversary of the
large demonstrations at Seabrook, they argued for its conversion to nonnuclear uses. Depending on the direction of energy policy in the 1990s,
such conversion could be the fate of some newly constructed nuclear
power plants, while others may become permanent repositories of nuclear wastes when they are decommissioned. Seabrook has been given
a low-power operating permit but faces further legal and political
challenges.

People for Proof, the Western Bloc, and the Abalone Alliance.
In the 1980s, antinuclear referendums in Maine, Oregon, and California
were all defeated. The experiences of antinuclear groups in the West are
similar to those of groups in the New England area, but nuclear power
plants in California that were the object of social protest in the 1970s are
now operating.

Nevertheless, the 1976 Nuclear Safeguards Initiative (Proposition 15)
struggle illuminates dimensions of the nuclear conflict in California. People for Proof, based in San Francisco, coordinated the drive for the initiative, which would have mandated a public review of the safety of
nuclear power plants by shifting the burden of proof to the nuclear industry. Full compensation would have been given to all affected members
of the public in the event of a nuclear accident, thereby removing federal
liability limits on nuclear insurance. The initiative would also have re-

quired that the effectiveness of radioactive-waste disposal systems be demonstrated. Although the initiative did not explicitly call for a moratorium on nuclear power, its passage would have prevented the construction of new nuclear power plants in California.

People for Proof obtained the 500,000 signatures necessary to have the initiative placed on the June 1976 California ballot. Supporters of the initiative included Ralph Nader, Jack Lemmon, Friends of the Earth, and various local citizens' groups. A highlight of the controversy was a debate between actor Robert Redford and former Governor Pat Brown, who argued that the initiative was a step backward because it would replace clean-burning nuclear fuels with polluting fossil fuels. Brown's attitude might not be accepted in West Virginia or eastern Kentucky by the United Mine Workers, but his argument appeared legitimate.

On the other side of the coin, former Governor Brown was deeply involved with the pronuclear group Citizens for Jobs and Energy. The organization hired three public-relations firms and received campaign funding from Pacific Gas and Electric, operator of the Humboldt nuclear reactor; from Southern California Edison, operator of the controversial San Onofre reactor; and from Westinghouse and Bechtel (the latter company was involved in the Tarapur case). Over $2 million was invested by opponents of the initiative, including Exxon Nuclear, Atlantic Richfield, and more than thirty utility companies from all over the United States.[19]

A regional organization was formed, the Western Bloc, a coalition of independent and local community groups that helped coordinate initiative drives in nineteen states—particularly Oregon, Colorado, Montana, and Maine. The founder of Western Bloc was Edwin Koupal (who had attended the Critical Mass '74 antinuclear conference sponsored by Ralph Nader). Koupal and his wife Joyce contributed $17,000 to the Western Bloc. Koupal died of cancer in 1976, but before his death, he wrote a masterful document entitled, "The Nuclear Web," illustrating the quasi-conspiracies between government officials and private industry leaders in the pronuclear countermovement.[20] His document supports what many sociologists have observed about the leadership of countermovements. For example, Tahi Mottl writes:

Countermovement leaders are elites within existing institutions who strongly oppose change; they perceive their power as threatened by change or augmented by their resistance to change. . . . Countermovements are frequently mobilized by elected officials and other elites in the name of their constituencies, whose prerogatives are superseded by the success of the initial movement.[21]

As the initiative vote loomed closer, the California State Assembly considered bills that would impose a one-year moratorium on the construction of new plants, pending a study of the feasibility of locating the plants underground and development by the federal government of reprocessing and waste-disposal systems for the California reactors to the satisfaction of the California legislature. This move to forestall possible defeat by incorporating some of the goals of the antinuclear movement into legislation was supported by Governor Jerry Brown (who was then running as a candidate for President of the United States in the Maryland primary).

Edwin Koupal asserted that the nuclear web (which included Citizens for Jobs and Energy) was created not by design but "merely by the circumstances of finance and employment, and in some cases, marital and nepotistic ties."[22] The California web included many persons in a governmental system that had "become contemptuous of the voters and disdainful of the public at large."[23] Campaign contributions, friendships, and party affiliations all might determine who is part of the web of influence that makes government seem inpenetrable to ordinary citizens. Koupal presented impressive evidence that government agencies and officials in California worked in concert to discredit People for Power. He concluded that

all it took was a simple phone call from a government official to get several agencies involved in an effort to discredit a citizens organization that challenged the way the business of government was being conducted.[24]

The California Nuclear Safeguards Initiative was defeated by a margin of two to one. The result of both this initiative and the Maine nuclear referendums seem to bear out Koupal's warning to activists that "chances are that you have your own nuclear web, and it reaches all the way to the White House, just like ours does. Many of the same corporate characters will be in it."[25]

An interesting event in the history of the antinuclear movement was the resignation early in 1976 of three middle-management engineers, responsible for monitoring the performance of GE nuclear reactors, in order to participate in the antinuclear movement. These resignations brought the antinuclear movement to the center stage in the mass media. Dale Bridenbaugh, Gregory Minor, and Richard Hubbard had all had well-paying positions and had families to support. All three expressed concern over government plans to sell nuclear reactors to Egypt, Israel, and South Africa. Minor said, "Nuclear reactors and nuclear weapons present a serious danger to the future of all life on the planet,"[27] and stated that the fire at the Brown's Ferry nuclear plant in Alabama had been influential in his decision. Bridenbaugh cited the possibility of human error and the potential genetic effects of radiation as reasons for his resignation. Hubbard stated, "You cannot continue to build plants and operate them without having an accident."

The movement-recruitment process is not just a matter of the appeal a movement's goals have for individuals (who may be psychologically predisposed to joining a movement). Individuals are also drawn into a movement through their associations with friends or other persons who are already in the movement.[27] These preexisting social networks provide an interpersonal tie for outsiders of a particular movement.[28] All three engineers had been members of the Creative Initiative Foundation, a two-thousand-member organization in California with the goal of exploring ethical and philosophical values. (At a meeting only a few days before the three resignations, a group leader concluded a discussion of nuclear energy by saying, "God did not create plutonium and therefore it is evil."[29]) The Creative Initiative Foundation, in turn, had close ties with Project Survival, an antinuclear organization of approximately seven thousand members. This social network of the three engineers apparently helped create the motives for their dramatic resignations from General Electric.

We may assume that the membership of these engineers in the Creative Initiative Foundation provided social support for their entrance into the antinuclear movement. But we may also assume that they are rational men whose decision was facilitated by socially constructed motives in a group that offered an alternative view of reality. Sociology is replete with possible theoretical explanations of why and how people join social movements. The engineers might just as well have been experiencing midlife crises involving alienation from their work. Gregory Minor reported having a subjective experience, almost like an experience prior to a conversion to a different view of reality. Minor reported that just before his resignation he saw blue radiation given off by some plutonium in a tank of water at a government facility in Hanford, Washington:

I looked through that ten or fifteen feet of water, the life-saving shield between me and that fuel, and I knew that if any one of those elements were to come up and hit me, that I was dead, just like that. And I got the feeling right there of the precarious balance we have between radioactive materials in a safe state and radioactive materials in an unsafe state, and the dangers to life are that close.[30]

We cannot dismiss the testimony of an intelligent person who reacts to an advanced technology and a dangerous substance such as plutonium as merely the product of differential social experiences. Nor can we exclude the possibility that the engineers would *seek out* groups such as the Creative Initiative Foundation as a means to express a perspective on life or, in this case, on advanced nuclear technology. Appearing before the Joint Committee on Atomic Energy, Minor observed that "the nuclear industry has developed to become an industry of narrow specialists, each promoting and refining a fragment of the technology, with little comprehension of the total impact of our world system."[31] Again, he was reflecting on his occupational rather than his personal experiences.

Only a few days after the three resignations, Robert Pollard, a federal safety engineer for nuclear reactors at Indian Point and a project manager for the NRC, also resigned because he believed that the plants were unsafe and posed the danger of a major catastrophe. The Union of Concerned Scientists hired him as its Washington, D.C., representative at a salary of $20,000 a year. In his statement before the Joint Committee on Atomic Energy, Pollard said,

the Indian Point nuclear station constitutes an unconscionable threat to the health and safety of the millions of people who live in the metropolitan New York City area. The Indian Point plants have been badly designed and constructed and are susceptible to accidents that could cause large-scale loss of life and other radiation injuries, such as cancers and birth defects. The magnitude of these hazards associated with these plants have been suppressed by the government because the release of such information might cause great public opposition to their operation.[32]

The symbolic impact of defections from the nuclear establishment cannot be underestimated, nor can the personal courage of the engineers be denied. At a time when the nuclear issue was being coopted by the Democratic party in the presidential campaign of Jimmy Carter, these resignations signified that opposition to nuclear power was deep enough for three individuals to risk their financial security and substantial careers to bring changes to energy policy that they believed to be in serious error.

Expressive Symbolization: The Silkwood Case

Karen Silkwood attained the status of martyr for the antinuclear movement, leaving her supporters with a memory that helps to explain why the antinuclear movement continues to struggle.

Martyrdom is an important feature of social movements. Martyrs create solidarity within the movement and reinforce commitment to a movement's goals. Movement members identify with an individual who has experienced intensive suffering as a consequence of his or her beliefs and activities. Identifying with those who made a great sacrifice, even of their lives, as Silkwood did, allows individuals in the movement to feel that the sacrifices they are making are small in contrast to that made by the martyr. Mythological consciousness arises, as powerful as religious sentiment, and it often plays an essential role in eliciting mass commitment to a faith, as martyrdom did for the Catholic Church.

Feelings toward martyrs, however, may also be ambiguous, for their actions may be viewed as suicidal, as an escape, leaving the survivors to cope with problems. The human foibles and weaknesses of martyrs become acutely significant, for the opposition can point to those weaknesses to discredit the martyr. But a character defect only shows followers that the martyr was redeemed by sacrifice.

Karen Silkwood became a martyr for the antinuclear movement, even though her death may have been accidental. It occurred in the midst of an important labor struggle involving the safety of workers at a plutonium-reprocessing plant in Oklahoma. Silkwood had obtained a position at the Kerr-McGee plant as a laboratory assistant. Soon she was on the picket line with strikers. She was exposed to plutonium on three occasions within the next two years as a result of what appeared to be company negligence, prompting her to become a part of the steering committee of the local unit of the Oil, Chemical, and Atomic Workers International Union. In November 1974 she was documenting grievances on safety abuses for the union when she discovered that she had been exposed to high levels of plutonium and that her apartment—including food in a refrigerator—was also contaminated. After undergoing decontamination in Los Alamos, New Mexico, she arranged a meeting with a reporter from the *New York Times* and a labor union official to deliver evidence of safety infractions that her investigation had uncovered.

While driving to the meeting on 13 March 1974, Silkwood had a fatal automobile accident. The police report indicated that she had fallen asleep at the wheel, but a private investigation firm hired by the union found evidence that the car had been struck from behind by another vehicle. The safety-abuse documents were missing from the car. The Federal Bureau of Investigation collaborated in the police report but did not release its own report. A few months later, *Time* magazine (24 May 1976) revealed that an informer for the FBI, Jacque Srouji, had been given access to over a thousand pages of bureau documents on the Silkwood case in exchange for information about radical groups. The documents gave an unflattering view of Silkwood's drug habits and sexual life.[33]

The cause of Karen Silkwood was taken up by the National Organization for Women (NOW). NOW president Karen DeCrow headed a delegation that met with Justice Department officials to discuss the circumstances of her death. The organization awarded Silkwood honorary membership, and on 13 November 1975, one year after her death, NOW observed a Silkwood Memorial Day. Four nights later, following the Critical Mass '75 antinuclear conference, a candlelight vigil was held at the national capital, and Representative Bella Abzug of New York called for a congressional investigation of the case. Bella Abzug illustrated the mood of Silkwood supporters when she remarked at vigil that "as society grows larger and more impersonal, we must depend on courageous individuals . . . to expose and challenge unsafe conditions. These issues often seem technical and complex, but become very concrete when viewed through the life of Karen Silkwood."[34] *Critical Mass* quoted Abzug and commented that

the activities and reactions of the Kerr-McGee company in the Karen Silkwood case exposed many of the deficiencies of the nuclear power industry: careless safety procedures; violent corporate reaction to critical appraisal; worker harassment; intimidation of dissenters; ruthless support of corporate goals; arrogant corporate indifference toward neighboring communities; extreme secrecy and coverup of federal and state law violations.[35]

In 1976, a second delegation—headed by NOW, with representatives from the Coalition of Labor Union Women, the Environmental Policy Center, Critical Mass, and the United Auto Workers, as well as Karen Silkwood's parents—presented a petition of seven thousand signatures asking Senator Lee Metcalf (with the consent of Senator Abraham Ribicoff) to reopen the investigation of her death. National Public Radio had already filed suit against the Justice Department seeking details of its investigation under the Freedom of Information Act.

In the months that followed, Kerr-McGee was unable to account for at least forty pounds of plutonium. It shut down the plant in order to administer lie-detector tests, with questions reportedly designed to determine management loyalty. Two of Silkwood's co-workers who had aided in her investigation of safety procedures were either transferred or fired. A spinoff group from NOW, the Supporters of Silkwood, emerged with a NOW coordinator and a staff of five that handled communications, community organizing, legal issues, and financing. The Supporters of Silkwood concentrated on the labor issues that pitted the Oil, Chemical, and Atomic Workers International Union against the management of Kerr-McGee. Along with the traditional labor issues like scab labor, health and safety conditions, and management intimidation, several mishaps at Kerr-McGee had resulted in worker-contamination. Soon after Karen Silkwood was contaminated with plutonium, Kerr-McGee was accused of falsifying quality-control and health records. Since the documents of safety violations that Silkwood had complied were missing after her fatal automobile accident, one NOW member went so far as to say in the Supporters of Silkwood newsletter that "Karen's allegiance was to her sisters and brothers in the plant and to the American people, not to bulging bank accounts and/or corporate power at any price. Karen was silenced because she was an effective fighter for her constituency and a standard bearer of all women."[36]

In April 1976, the congressional investigation into the death of Karen Silkwood ended. Senator Metcalf was reported to have said, according to a Supporters of Silkwood newsletter, that the Oil, Chemical, and Atomic Workers International Union had been satisfied with the original Oklahoma police report, although the union president denied this. The Supporters of Silkwood argued that political pressure from the president of Kerr-McGee and other members of the Senate had abrogated the investigation.[37] Three years later, an Oklahoma City jury awarded the estate of Karen Silkwood $10.5 million in damages, and the judge ruled that the doctrine of "absolute liability" applied to Kerr-McGee Corporation— that is, that the company was fully responsible for radiation damages even to people outside the plant, whether or not government safety standards had been met.[38]

The spirit of martyrdom was best expressed in an essay entitled "Who is Karen Silkwood?" published in the first newsletter of the Supporters of Silkwood. The essay reveals the personal meaning that the death of Silkwood had for social activists:

Who was Karen Silkwood? What is her relevance to us as women? As union members? Karen Silkwood was a working woman, a union member, a rank and file union activist, a believer, a fighter. She was made of the raw material that built the American labor movement. Our history, that of the labor movement and women's contribution to it, is not the story of a few charismatic leaders; it is rather the history of thousands of quiet, responsible, committed union members, and Karen Silkwood was one of these.

Karen's story was most like those of other unionists who over the past two hundred years have fought to preserve the dignity of the worker by seeking to achieve decent hours, fair wages, and humane working conditions. These gains have been made, not by the hotheaded orator of the soapbox, but by thousands of individual workers and their families. They committed themselves not to personal gain, not to their own pleasure, but to struggle, self-sacrifice, and sometimes physical danger, imprisonment, and even death. So many of the martyrs who fought for the eight-hour day, for a fair day's wage for a fair day's work, to end the oppression of child labor have gone unmourned and unsung by their sisters and brothers. These women and men whose lifeblood gave us the legal rights to have a voice on workplace issues affecting our health and well-being were the building blocks of the growing labor movement.

Karen Silkwood is such a martyr. She saw the problem—saw the dangerous working conditions she and her fellow workers faced daily. She struggled and fought, she organized other union activists to overcome these threats to their health. Karen didn't lead a demonstration; she kept scrupulous records. She didn't seek personal notoriety; she worked to develop a strong, courageous shop committee. The very last meeting Karen had was with her fellow union members to map out last-minute strategy exposing the hazards and unsafe working conditions at Kerr-McGee facility. Then she was off, to meet with a representative from her International and a *New York Times* reporter. Karen Silkwood's work ended that night as her car went off the road. Yet she left us—women and trade unionists—a burden and a legacy.

Karen left us the burden of finishing the work she set out to do—the work of securing the rights of workers who deal with radioactive substances to rigorous job safety controls; the work of assuring that workers fighting for health and safety conditions on the job need never again fear the harassment Karen suffered; the work of investigating the conditions surrounding Karen Silkwood's contamination with radioactive materials during the last few days of her life and the "mysterious" accident which caused her death.

Her legacy is one of conviction, courage, and heroic determination; the legacy of one human life invested in the battle to defend the rights of all workers to work in dignity; the legacy of a woman who took the cause of worker safety and health forward and made it a rally cry for her survivors.

This is who Karen Silkwood is to us—the sisters and brothers who never knew her in life—who in her death must carry the burden of her work and preserve the legacy of her life for those who follow us.[39]

Sociological Profiles of Antinuclear Activists

Several interesting studies of the antinuclear movement shed further light onto who the activists are and what they believe in. Two 1979 demonstrations during the peak of the "direct-action phase" of the movement took place in San Francisco and Washington, D.C. Social scientists used the opportunity to collect 696 usable questionnaires.

One analysis of the data concludes that "participants in both demonstrations tend to be young, well-educated, politically liberal, and evenly split between the sexes."[40] More specifically, over half were college educated, and half of these held an advanced degree. No more than 4 percent identified themselves as Republicans, and well over 80 percent were under the age of thirty-five. Both demonstrations sought to strengthen the link between the antinuclear-energy and the antinuclear-weapons movements.

A second study of the Washington, D.C., demonstrators focused on ideological themes. These were found to center on the threat of war posed by nuclear weapons, the health and safety hazards associated with radiation throughout the nuclear fuel cycle, environmental destruction, and the bureaucratization and centralization of power production.[41] The last theme relates to activists' view that citizens rather than bureaucratic and institutional elites should participate in deciding what mode of energy production society should have. The elites prevent alternative forms of energy from being utilized, in the interests of the large corporations that dominate energy production.

However, the most important reasons the demonstrators gave for being there were the perceived problems of radioactive-waste disposal, reactor safety, and the danger of accidents. Ninety percent believed there should be either an immediate shutdown or a gradual phase-out of nuclear power plants, and support for solar power was nearly unanimous.[42]

The relatively high degree of consensus found among antinuclear groups was itself a goal of the Clamshell Alliance. An ethnographic study of the Clamshell Alliance found that although its emergence as a nonviolent direct-action group was inspired by the protests at Whyl in West Germany, the strategy of civil disobedience was also an important means to realize an identity based upon egalitarian ideological beliefs.[43] The Clamshell Alliance centered as much on the participatory and nonhierarchical democratic process within the affinity groups as on antinuclear goals and actions. Its attempts at "creative consensus" were often marred by political and personal differences, as the organization was leaderless except for group facilitators. Its meetings attacked an atomic-industrial establishment that used the technology of nuclear power as an instrument of domination of ordinary citizens.[44] Activists were also fighting this structure of domination.

In a third study, a group of French social scientists arranged discussions between activists and representatives of the political and industrial groups in the nuclear controversy in France. The purpose was to get antinuclear groups to define their adversary on a level more abstract than the nuclear industry, escalating the conflict to a larger movement against technocratic power. This "sociological intervention" became mired in its attempts.[45]

Conclusion

The antinuclear movement has remained loosely organized with diverse local and regional groups, despite the efforts of a few national organizations to coordinate its activities. Regional direct-action organizations provided the movement with symbols, especially in the struggle against the siting of nuclear reactors at Seabrook. The Karen Silkwood case offered the movement a martyr and widened the spectrum of the movement's ideology to include issues important to the women's and labor movements. As conflict intensified, antinuclear movement groups turned to civil disobedience.

But this lasted only a few years. In the 1980s one activist, Paul Schaefer, wrote regarding the Sunflower Alliance,

At present there are individuals and groups too numerous to mention, working to restore what can best be described or summed up as the *natural balance*.
This methodology allows folks to work in a manner appropriate to them while informally working with others when desirable. This is a very functional approach

to encouraging participation and developing solutions. This prevents everyone from being gathered together and becoming frustrated by being allowed only a very narrow boundary to work within which can easily be disrupted, managed, or controlled by the FBI, et al. [47]

An activist in the North Woods Alliance in Wisconsin emphasized that he was a "worn out radical" and spent most of his time with his wife running a surplus store, but that they still retained their activist outlook. A lone voice in Natchez, Mississippi, Kathy Moody, wrote that

there is no continuing public opposition to the local nuclear power plants (Grand Gulf and River Bend). Our area of the country is still so impoverished that any job at all is appealing to local residents as well as local governments. For the moment, construction has stopped on the 2nd unit of Grand Gulf—let's hope it never starts up again. [47]

The role of the federal and state governments has been critical in defining both the successes and the failures of the antinuclear movement. Eight years of Republican backlash against the movement effectively suppressed large-scale involvement. But even in this era of fragmentation the governors of New York and Massachusetts helped at Shoreham and Seabrook in what could be the most important victories of the movement.

Chapter Five

Consequences of the Antinuclear Movement

The success of a social movement is defined by the outcome of the controversy. A complete moratorium on nuclear power development would have signified total success for the antinuclear movement, but this has not occurred. Among the theoretical schools of thought on social movements, the resource-mobilization theory is most concerned with how and why a movement succeeds or fails:

The resource mobilization approach emphasizes both societal support and constraint of social movement phenomena. It examines the variety of resources that must be mobilized, the linkages of social movements to other groups, the dependence of the movement on third parties for success, and the tactics used by authorities to control or incorporate the movement.[1]

In practice, resource-mobilization theory assumes that a movement obtains resources and leadership from political elites. But division among political elites must also be assumed, for while some elites may help sponsor a movement, others may attempt to suppress it or neutralize it by incorporating some of its goals into government policy. The antinuclear movement has had significant effects on government policy in the allocation of energy resources and in the problems of nuclear proliferation and nuclear terrorism. It has also had dramatic effects on public opinion.

However, it would be misleading to overstate how much power the antinuclear movement has. We must keep in mind the keen observation of David Lilienthal, the first chairman of the Atomic Energy Commission:

> It is a formidable army that marches under the banner of *status quo atomicus*. If the controversy over the future of nuclear power were to be decided by a trial of political strength, there would be no contest. The pronuclear interests are immeasurably the more powerful. The protest marches, sit-ins, and environmental lawsuits are a nuisance to them, but once they rally their forces, there will be little doubt as to the outcome. [2]

But in actual fact, the major outcome of the movement in the United States has been that no new nuclear power plants have been ordered since the 1970s, and that as many reactor orders—108—have been canceled as presently exist or are in the final stages of construction. These reactors have better safety systems as a result of antinuclear pressure and opposition. On the other hand, nuclear power has grown substantially in France, West Germany, Japan, and the Soviet Union. And in the United States, nuclear reactors are not being phased out, nor have fundamental issues such as radioactive-waste disposal been resolved.

I have discerned four key areas in which the antinuclear movement has had an impact on attitudes or policies. The first area of impact is *presidential politics*. During the 1976 presidential campaign, nuclear energy was the most important issue on which Democrats capitalized to regain the presidency. The policies of the Carter administration initiated profound changes with respect to the recycling of plutonium and the fast breeder reactor; it gave new priority to alternative-energy technologies and the more general problem of nuclear proliferation in a worldwide arms race. The antinuclear movement had a lesser but still discernible effect on the 1980 presidential campaign that put Ronald Reagan into the White House. The Republicans from 1980 to 1988 pursued a reactionary reversal of Carter policies and buttressed the status quo rather than setting a new agenda. Still, the actual policies of the Carter administration will set the tone for the debate over nuclear power in the 1990s.

A second area of concern to the antinuclear movement is *international nuclear proliferation*, the worldwide expansion of nuclear power and therefore nuclear-weapons capability. The energy policy of the United States is intrinsically tied to this international expansion, which has made it difficult to separate policies concerning commercial nuclear power from those concerning nuclear weapons and national security.

The third area of impact of the antinuclear movement is also important to the pronuclear movement: *nuclear terror.* The potential threat of terrorists "going nuclear" increases with the growth of commercial nuclear power.

The fourth area of impact is *public opinion.* The antinuclear movement, like all movements, attempts to influence public opinion as well as the government elite. As a result of the movement, more voters have opposed nuclear power development in various initiatives and referendums, more people have participated in mass demonstrations and protests, public opposition has been diffused to larger political arenas as in Europe, and safety conditions at nuclear power plants as a result of public hearings have been improved. The impact of the movement on political parties, public opinion, and government policy is an important measure of its success.

Presidential Politics

The success of a social movement in the United States is intrinsically related to its impact on the major political parties.[3] Traditionally, the Democratic party has been more receptive to the demands of aggrieved groups and social movements. However, which political party is in power affects this receptiveness. The antinuclear movement began to attract national attention at a time when the Republican party controlled the White House, while the Democrats had control of the legislative branch. This classic situation in American politics frequently immobilizes the executive branch of government. During the 1970s, the Republicans did attempt to respond to the crisis in energy resources, but their response was not very flexible.

Project Independence, developed by the Federal Energy Administration and the Energy Policy Project of the Ford Foundation, provided the framework for a national energy policy that emphasized nuclear fission as a source of electricity. Project Independence analyzed alternative courses of action according to three different scenarios of energy growth (see Table 1).[4]

The first scenario, that of *historical growth,* assumed that the increase in energy use would continue at the rate of 7 percent a year. High oil prices and the OPEC cartel would necessitate a deemphasis on environmental problems in order to stimulate offshore oil and gas exploration, the commercial operation of the liquid-metal fast breeder reactor, the development of synthetic fuels, and the channelling of public funds to assist industry in the capital-formation problems that it would have.

Table 1. Project Independence Scenarios

Historical Growth

1. High oil prices
2. Less emphasis on environmental concerns
3. Stockpiling of resources
4. Offshore oil and gas exploration
5. Fast breeder reactor
6. Production of synthetic fuel from coal and oil shale
7. Capital-formation problem (25% of all plant and capital equipment for energy)

Technical Fix

1. Less capital requirement
2. Minimize demand on environmentally controversial sources of energy
3. Change rail regulations to promote recycling
4. More efficient automobiles
5. More efficient heating and cooling systems
6. More efficiency in steam generation
7. Restrict nuclear exports

Zero Energy Growth

1. Land-use problems
2. Offshore oil and gas drilling
3. Mining of western coal and oil shale
4. Change public attitudes on value of growth
5. Decentralize technology
6. Energy sales tax, reduction of tax for low-income groups
7. No nuclear expansion
8. Increase energy efficiency
9. Import natural gas from Canada

Source: Adapted from *A Time to Choose,* final report of the Energy Policy Project of the Ford Foundation, 1974.

The second scenario, the *technical fix,* emphasized research into energy conservation, such as more efficient automobiles, heating and cooling systems, recycling of resources, and co-generation. Less capital investment would be required, and nuclear power growth would be minimized, in part through a restriction on nuclear exports.

The third scenario, *zero energy growth,* stressed no nuclear expansion, the decentralization of energy technology, changed public attitudes on the value of growth, and resolutions of problems of efficient land use. Social-policy measures would reduce the impact of energy shortages on the populace.

Of these options, the historical-growth scenario has been accepted by the Republican leadership. It has been largely rejected by Democrats, who have proposed a plethora of politics based on combined aspects of the technical-fix and zero-energy-growth scenarios.

The historical-growth scenario required that if energy self-sufficiency were to be obtained, up to 25 percent of all capital formation in the United States would have to go to investment into energy industries. In the 1970s, the Republicans championed the proposal of Nelson Rockefeller that an Energy Independence Authority be created to make $100 billion of public funds available for energy loans to private industry. The proposal was never implemented, but the budget for ERDA (the agency that briefly preceded the Department of Energy), clearly indicated the Republican administration's priorities in energy policy. Fifty-four percent of the 1976 energy budget went for nuclear fission and fusion development, 11 percent for fossil fuels, 1 percent for energy conservation, and less than 4 percent for solar, geothermal, and advanced-energy-systems research. If defense and space nuclear systems are included, the sum actually budgeted to nuclear energy was absolutely enormous for even larger amounts were spent on these programs.

From the outset of the energy crisis, the Democratic party leadership was fundamentally opposed to the Republican program, believing that it was neither an equitable nor a comprehensive energy policy. Some Democrats supported the emphasis on nuclear power, but most favored increasing research expenditures for alternative-energy technologies and redistributing income to compensate poor families for the increased burden of energy costs. Two contenders for the Democratic presidential nomination pledged support for a moratorium on nuclear power and divestiture of the holdings of oil corporations but neither Senator Fred Harris of Oklahoma nor Representative Morris Udall of Arizona could mount a sustained campaign for the nomination. Governor Jimmy Carter of Georgia, on the other hand, made a more moderate appraisal of policy changes that would be needed for energy security.

Carter chose the nuclear power controversy as the topic for his first major policy speech, given before a United Nations conference on Nuclear Energy and World Order in New York City in May 1976. Carter emphasized his background in nuclear engineering and his work on Admiral Rickover's nuclear submarine program after his graduation from the Naval Academy. Before this speech, he had told the Washington Press Club that a disastrous nuclear accident would be more devastating than a total Middle East oil embargo and would necessitate the underground location of nuclear power plants. Now he proposed that the United States shift from oil to coal as its main source of energy, maintain strict energy conservation, derive renewable energy from the sun, and keep dependence on nuclear power to a minimum. Specifically, this would involve a voluntary moratorium on the sale of uranium-enrichment facilities and nuclear-fuels-reprocessing plants, and a world energy conference to control the spread of a dangerous technology.

Carter kept these promises when he went to the White House, and his ideas reflected the sentiment of the antinuclear movement:

Power reactors may malfunction and cause widespread radiological damage unless stringent safety requirements are met. Radioactive wastes may be a menace to future generations and civilizations unless they are effectively isolated in the biosphere forever. And terrorists or other criminals may steal plutonium and make weapons to threaten society or its political leaders with nuclear violence unless strict security measures are developed and implemented to prevent nuclear theft. By 1999, the developing nations alone will produce enough plutonium to build 3,000 Hiroshima-size bombs a year.[5]

With Carter's election in November 1976, it seemed as if the goals of the antinuclear movement had been realized, despite the simultaneous defeat of six antinuclear initiatives and referendums. Carter made a national commitment to energy conservation, the development of coal resources, and research into solar energy. The liquid-metal fast-breeder-reactor demonstration project at Clinch River was cut back when Carter vetoed its appropriations (but Congress attached a rider to a different bill to continue funding of the project).

Never was there any indication that Carter supported abandoning conventional light-water nuclear reactors. Rather, his policies actually facilitated their construction by blocking antinuclear groups' access to the legal system that they had successfully used to forestall the licensing and construction of nuclear power plants in the past. Specifically, Carter supported standardized designs for nuclear power plants that required only one hearing each.

In a televised address to the nation on 18 April 1977, Carter outlined a comprehensive energy policy that he termed the "moral equivalent of war."[6] The short-term goal of this policy was to reduce dependence on foreign oil by implementing a conservation program and by converting industries and utilities from oil and natural gas to coal. The long-term goal was to develop alternative sources of energy, including solar, geothermal, and hydroelectric power. Carter made good his campaign promise to avoid a "plutonium economy" by abandoning the Clinch River fast breeder reactor and by deferring opening the nuclear-fuels-reprocessing plant in Barnwell, South Carolina. However, the conventional light-water nuclear-fission plants would still be built, if on a lesser scale than suggested by Gerald Ford.

Generally, the Carter plan maintained centralization in both the private and the public sectors. The Carter administration avoided the horizontal or vertical divestiture of holdings of large oil corporations, and it did not require corporations to share the expense of research and development from which they would gain large profits. It created a superagency, the Department of Energy. These changes in energy policy were supported by Congress and were followed by a windfall-profits tax on the oil corporations to be used for research into synthetic-fuels development, a crash program to produce "synfuel" from coal liquids and gases and oil-shale. The move to synthetic fuels marked a major shift in energy policy. Congress responded by creating the Synthetic Fuels Corporation in June 1980.

In contrast to the heavy expenditures for nuclear energy in the energy budget for fiscal year 1976 (54 percent), only 34.6 percent of the 1979 energy budget went to nuclear energy (if expenditures for the strategic petroleum reserve are excluded), and an additional 6.6 percent for the administrative expenses of the NRC. Authorizations for solar- and alternative-energy sources rose enormously: together they accounted for over one-fifth of the 1979 energy budget, compared with less than 4 percent in 1976. Energy conservation experienced the greatest increase, from 1 percent in 1976 to over 12 percent in 1979. The proportion spent on fossil fuels was only slightly changed, from 11 to 15 percent. These figures, summarized in Table 2, indicate the shift in government energy priorities during the Carter administration.

The major shift to coal and synthetic fuels may have been a victory for the antinuclear movement, but its environmentalist segment did not completely regard it as such. Coal mining had been estimated to cost the lives of 250 miners each year, and air pollution from coal-fired electric-generating plants was once estimated to contribute to the deaths of twenty thousand Americans each year.[7] In addition, there are problems with coal involving reclamation of land after strip mining, acid rain, black-lung disease, sludge byproducts, and railway transportation. The Sierra Club had filed suit to force a better environmental review of the impact of shipping coal from the Wyoming reserves,[8] and it had previously been instrumental in preventing the multibillion-dollar Kaiporowits coal-fired plant in southern Utah from being built.

The environmentalist problems with coal, it must be noted, do not preclude its use as an energy source. Advanced clean-coal technology can resolve the problems of miner safety, acid rain, and the greenhouse effect with research and government support. The long-term trend has been to fewer fatalities and more advanced technology—but this too depends on political pressure.[9]

The federal government actually owns half of all potential energy resources in the United States. With the exception of the Tennessee Valley Authority, the government itself does not develop these resources but leases federal lands to private industry. The government's role in land-use decisions is extremely controversial, considering that energy costs consume about 15 percent of a poor family's budget, and that the energy crisis of 1973–74 contributed to the unemployment of 535,000 persons.[10] To what extent should federal lands and national resources be used for profit-making by private industry? Even without nationalizing the energy corporations, public lands could be used to provide cheaper energy for the populace as a whole rather than to subsidize large corporations.

In 1980, public sentiment was forcible enough for the Democratic party to officially adopt the position of a phaseout of nuclear power (a position accepted by President Carter despite his own pronuclear stance). But the Republican platform advocated increased use of nuclear power, storage of radioactive wastes in underground sites, and the reprocessing of spent nuclear reactor fuel.[11] Ronald Reagan also opposed the windfall-profits tax on oil companies that was being used to develop synthetic fuels, and he advocated abolishing the Department of Energy. Thus, the ascendancy of the Republican party to political power brought dramatic changes in energy policy.

Table 2. 1979 Federal Energy Budget

Program	Authorization (in Millions of Dollars)	Percent of Total*
Energy Research and Development		
Solar	514	10.4
Other renewable sources	541	11.0
Fossil	784	15.9
Nuclear fission	1218	24.7
Other nuclear technology	490	9.9
Total	3547	71.9
Energy Conservation		
Technology development	229	4.6
Conservation grants	377	7.6
Public information	5	.1
Total	611	12.3

Strategic Petroleum Reserves	3008	n.a.
Energy Information and Policy	82	1.7
Administrative and Regulatory Expenses		
Department of Energy	215	4.4
Nuclear Regulatory Commission	327	6.6
Other	153	3.1
Total	695	14.1
Grand Total	7,382†	100.0

*Excludes deductions made for offsetting receipts from direct energy production and expenditures for the strategic petroleum reserve in order to get a better comparison.

†Includes adjustment for offsetting receipts as well as expenditures for the strategic petroleum reserve. Percentages are based on total of $4.935 billion.

Source: *The Budget for Fiscal Year 1981* (Washington D.C.: U.S. Government Printing Office). Since the 1981 budget included a controversial temporary deficit of $17 billion for synthetic fuels and 1980 figures were only estimated expenses, the 1979 budget was used for a comparison of research and development on alternative-energy technologies.

Changes during the Reagan Era. The decidedly pronuclear Republican policies of the 1980s were in sharp contrast to those of the Carter years. Military goals took priority in the Department of Energy—over 60 percent of its $11.8 billion budget for fiscal year 1984 was for nuclear weapons, with dramatic cuts in solar energy, conservation, and fossil-fuel development. Solar-energy research received a mere $19 million, while the fast breeder reactor received the lion's share of funding for energy research and development. Through the power of appointment, pronuclear conservatives took control of regulatory agencies.[12] These changes (summarized in chapter 1) stymied any real progress toward the implementation of alternative energy, and at every conceivable level government regulations were bent and relaxed in favor of industry. With the military buildup and the escalated arms race, conservation and solar energy were sidelined, replaced by "Star Wars" and other military projects. The expansion of nuclear power occurred primarily outside the United States, and its international ramifications gave new meaning to the issues of nuclear-fuels reprocessing, the fast breeder reactor, and nuclear-weapons proliferation.

International Nuclear Proliferation

Former Secretary of State Henry Kissinger once called the transfer of nuclear technology the greatest single danger of unrestrained nuclear proliferation. International nuclear proliferation is a second area of impact of the antinuclear movement.

The issue of placing safeguards on nuclear materials to prevent further proliferation of nuclear weapons was as important to the antinuclear movement in the 1970s as the issues of nuclear-reactor safety and radioactive-waste disposal. Several events had made the safeguards issue acute: India detonated a nuclear device in 1974 that had been built with plutonium supplied by Canada in the 1950s, and West Germany sold an entire nuclear fuel cycle to Brazil.

The most specific success of the antinuclear movement in affecting government policy was the passage of the 1978 Nuclear Nonproliferation Act by Congress. Although Gerald Ford supported private control of uranium-enrichment facilities in the United States, the major nuclear suppliers met in conference and agreed to prevent nuclear materials from being used for weapons development. This agreement among the London Suppliers Group became in part the basis for the 1978 act. The act gave the NRC the power to prohibit the export of nuclear fuel to nations that are suspected of using that material for nuclear weapons, and it mandated a ban on nuclear exports to nations that aided others in nuclear-weapons development.

But Argentina, Brazil, China, Egypt, France, India, Israel, Pakistan, South Africa, and Spain had not signed or ratified the 1968 Nuclear Nonproliferation Treaty, in which nations that did not have nuclear weapons pledged never to develop them. Some of these nations, such as Brazil and Argentina, publicly stated that they intended to manufacture nuclear weapons.[13] Others have engaged in clandestine activities that suggest they will soon possess nuclear weapons. In the coming decade, it is likely that Brazil, Taiwan, South Korea, South Africa, Pakistan, and Argentina may all have nuclear weapons.[14]

Intrigue and clandestine activities characterize the international uranium and nuclear-reactor markets. A patent was filed in West Germany by two Israeli scientists who claimed that they could hypothetically enrich seven grams of uranium to weapons-grade material in twenty-four hours, according to the CIA. South Africa developed an enrichment process with secret technical assistance from the West German government–owned Gesellschaft für Kernforschung, which illegally cooperated with South African scientists (a discovery that came from documents stolen from the South African embassy in Bonn by the opposition African National Congress).[15] Among other possibilities, South Africa could conceivably use low-yield nuclear weapons against black insurgents to preserve its apartheid policies.

A second scandal rocked West Germany in the 1980s, when it was discovered that Nukem, a nuclear-fuels manufacturer, and its subsidiary Transnuklear had sent waste drums that were labeled "low-level" from a reprocessing plant in Belgium back to West Germany—drums that actually contained plutonium. After the revelation, the chief of Transnuklear's nuclear-waste department was arrested and committed suicide. This event coincided with the publication of a poll indicating that 63 percent of West Germans want a gradual or immediate shutdown of the nuclear industry.[16]

Other nations that have not signed the Nuclear Nonproliferation Treaty have similar reasons for joining the nuclear club. Italy provided Iraq with two nuclear laboratories (which were destroyed in a 1981 Israeli raid). Israel was long thought to possess nuclear weapons, developed with French technical assistance.[17] In September 1986, Mordechai Vanunu, a former employee at the Negev Nuclear Research Center in Dimona, revealed that Israel had parts for one to two hundred nuclear bombs. He was kidnapped and smuggled back to Israel for an espionage and treason trial. Among others, scientists Noam Chomsky, George Wald, and Linus Pauling co-sponsored a committee to help defend him.[28]

  Pakistan, a rival of India, has been the subject of much controversy, including speculation that it planted a spy in a Dutch nuclear project and was the recipient of stolen nuclear material from India. Trials have been held in West Germany, Holland, and Canada over illegal exports to Pakistan's classified Kahuta uranium-enrichment plant, which may be able to produce weapons-grade uranium.[19]

The Reagan administration deliberately relaxed the restrictions imposed by the 1978 Nuclear Nonproliferation Act on U.S. companies in an effort to make the United States a supplier nation of nuclear technology to "trustworthy" nations. For example, Taiwan was assisted in building two nuclear power plants through U.S. Export-Import Bank financing. The administration reportedly even discussed the possibility of shipments to the Koeberg nuclear station in South Africa.[20]

Diffusion to Europe and Japan.   The Carter administration had attempted to control the diffusion of nuclear technology with the 1978 Nonproliferation Act, but the worldwide failure to control nuclear proliferation must be attributed to factors not completely in the control of the U.S. government. (Even if agreement had existed among the United States and its Western European and Japanese allies to halt the diffusion of the nuclear fuel cycle, clandestine proliferation of nuclear technology into nations such as Pakistan and South Africa would most likely have continued.)

The nuclear industry believes that policies of nonproliferation harm the export market for nuclear materials and enable West Germany, France, Britain, and Japan to control the international market. But the idea that there is international competition is misleading; for example, American companies frequently have licensing agreements with foreign companies to provide them with steam-supply systems or electric turbines or even to invest in foreign companies or participate in consortiums with them. This participation enables the foreign companies to gain experience with the technology and later build their own nuclear reactors without having to depend on American corporations.

Europe and Japan depend on nuclear power more than the United States does. Nuclear power now accounts for approximately 35 percent of all electricity generated in Europe, compared with 18 percent in the United States. France is the world's paradigmatic nuclear state. Its fifty-three reactors produce 73 percent of its electricity, and that figure is projected to increase. In a nation the size of Texas with no coal or gas reserves, nuclear power is regarded as the solution to energy production. France has a national electrical utility (EDF), a single vendor of nuclear power plants (Framatome), and a powerful French Atomic Energy Commission (CEA). All its nuclear power plants are built on a standardized design, so there are no public-licensing hearings in which the public can participate. The courts normally defend the state. Demonstrations when François Mitterand came to power did result in the abandonment of the Plogoff nuclear plant, but the socialist government did not change the large-scale commitment to nuclear power. The Green movement in France has been inconsequential. [21]

But Europe's heavy use of nuclear power means that Europe now has a nuclear-waste disposal problem. The originally proposed solution was to reprocess wastes and use them in the fast breeder reactor, thereby closing the nuclear fuel cycle.

A sixty-nation, two-year conference called the International Nuclear Fuel Cycle Evaluation, initiated by Carter, revealed deep international rifts over the question of nuclear power. But ultimately, the conference gave international support to the development of the fast breeder reactor and to the international reprocessing of nuclear fuel. [22] Closing the nuclear fuel cycle in this manner would eliminate dependence on imported uranium (although large finds of uranium in the 1980s glutted the market). [23] These nations are also prepared to take a sizable share of the world nuclear-reactor export market.

In 1984, Britain, France, West Germany, Belgium, and Italy signed an agreement to pool their efforts to develop the fast breeder. West Germany, France, Great Britain, the Soviet Union, and Japan all have or will have fast breeder reactors in operation. Britain has a prototype breeder at Dounreay, and West Germany developed the SNR-300 breeder reactor at Kalkar with the help of Belgium and the Netherlands. The breeder reactor was also intended to close the nuclear fuel cycle in France—the Super-Phenix breeder went critical in 1985.

Nuclear-fuels-reprocessing technology, which enables a nation to obtain weapons-grade nuclear material, was once a monopoly of the United States. But both Great Britain and France now have operating nuclear-fuels-reprocessing plants—the world's largest reprocessing plant is La Hague in Normandy—and Japan will soon have facilities available. A West German reprocessing plant is being built at Wackersdorf. (The world market for nuclear-fuels-reprocessing technology will probably mean further diffusion of nuclear weapons potential to countries like Brazil, India, Pakistan, and South Africa.)[24]

The Reagan administration supported fast-breeder-reactor development and nuclear-fuels reprocessing in Europe, perhaps out of recognition that little control can be exerted over the energy policy of foreign nations.

France and other European nations are now backing away from the breeder as a result of technical, political, and economic problems as well as the discovery of large new uranium reserves. Six that were planned in France alone have been abandoned. Without the breeder, the problem of how to dispose of large amounts of nuclear wastes emerges—wastes added to the total amount of plutonium in the world.

All the major issues remain unresolved. But the antinuclear movement has been a major factor in the stalemate in today's nuclear-technology market, and it has had an effect on foreign governments. The West German plant being built at Wackersdorf has been the scene of continued demonstrations and opposition by the Green party, and its opening has been suspended owing to their pressure.

The most influential event for Europe in this regard was the 1986 accident at Chernobyl, from which a cloud of radioactive debris swept over the Continent.[25] Political fallout from this accident contributed to cancellations of plants proposed in the Netherlands, Greece, and Italy. The nuclear power plant in Italy at Monalto d'Cristo may be converted to one producing gas. In Sweden, a planned phaseout of nuclear power is to be accelerated and two plants decommissioned in the 1990s. Austria is dismantling its only reactor at Zwentendorf. Other nations with operating plants such as Finland and Switzerland plan to build no more, and in the Philippines President Corazon Aquino ordered the newly completed Bataan nuclear plant dismantled after Chernobyl. Spain is completing two plants but has canceled three and mothballed two others. In the Soviet Union, two plants were canceled after Chernobyl, but eleven others are under construction—the same number as Japan, where thirty-three plants now operate.

Diffusion to the Third World.   Energy shortages are particularly acute in the Third World. These nations invest considerable proportions of their gross national income in oil exports. As Dennis Goulet observes, in many of these nations intermediate-energy technologies would be more useful in helping alleviate unemployment and poverty, but investments are being made into nuclear technology for the military and political status that it may give them.[26]

The export of nuclear technology to developing nations involves far more than only a problem of nuclear proliferation. On the one hand, developing nations lack the technological infrastructure to support nuclear power systems, and the need for technological elites and nuclear materials might mean further domination by the advanced nations. Nuclear accidents might also be more likely. But on the other hand, it is discriminatory to developing nations to prohibit nuclear exports to them. The high cost of oil has dealt a severe blow to the economies of the developing nations as well as to the industrialized world.

Third World nations such as Colombia, Egypt, Hong Kong, Indonesia, Iran, Portugal, Thailand, Venezuela, and China all have incipient nuclear-power-development plans.[27] These nations have large potential markets, as most of their rural dwellers do not have electricity. But there are also many problems with nuclear power in these nations. They lack the electricity grids for the transmission of power. Although foreign oil is expensive, nuclear plants are capital intensive and demand many technical resources. Developing nations that lack the open political systems that allow for opposition and public hearings would have a heightened probability of accidents. Therefore, no large increase in nuclear-power-plant capacity is projected for the near future in these areas of the world. A commitment by the advanced industrial nations of the world to safer, more intermediate, and more decentralized energy technology would have more export potential in developing nations than would nuclear power. Global cooperation must involve consideration for the needs of nations for which a major investment in nuclear power is neither wise nor necessary.

The Bottom Line. There has always been a link between the commercial and military uses of nuclear energy. The potential for nuclear-weapons proliferation from civilian reactors is exemplified by France.[28] The EDF's three reactors at Marcoule were tied into the same electricity grid that produced weapons-grade material. Although these reactors are now permanently closed, two more reactors at Marcoule have explicit military functions in producing plutonium and tritium—the latter for use in the neutron bomb. (Breeder reactors produce supergrade material containing 2 to 4 percent plutonium-240, while weapons-grade is 7 percent.) The material for French Pluton missiles and nuclear weapons may also be obtained from its civilian reactors. Recent advances in laser technology have simplified the process of converting uranium wastes into weapons-grade material. The proliferation of nuclear technology thus makes the proliferation of nuclear weapons all the more likely.

In the United States, the Department of Energy is responsible both for research on nuclear energy and for the development, testing, and production of nuclear weapons. The Hanford N-reactor, now closed, once produced electricity for the Washington Public Power Supply System, but this relationship may potentially be reversed. The Hart-Simpson Amendment to the NRC Authorization Act of 1983 currently prohibits obtaining plutonium from irradiated commercial fuel, but laser isotope separation may change this. Plutonium is still available from dismantled missiles withdrawn from Europe as a result of the INF treaty. The advanced nations are nonetheless increasingly developing a system linking nuclear-weapons-production with commercial nuclear power.

This does not solve the problem of radioactive wastes. The nations possessing this capability believe stringent international controls through international organizations will prevent the recycling of nuclear wastes into nuclear weapons in nonnuclear nations. Amory Lovins, a prominent antinuclear activist, argues that it is impossible to prevent the proliferation of nuclear bombs through government policy as long as we have nuclear power.[29] Institutional arrangements for nuclear safeguards will never be adequate to prevent the diversion of nuclear materials for military purposes. Therefore, national efforts to replace oil with nuclear power are the source of the problem of nuclear proliferation.

Terrorism and Nuclear Power

Would a terrorist group be able to attack a nuclear installation and steal nuclear materials? Early in the antinuclear movement, this was one of the most emotional and symbolic issues. The initial warnings of possible danger to societies from terrorists came from Theodore Taylor and Mason Willrich.[30] In their study, they also warned of nuclear theft by criminal organizations for blackmail or sabotage and of the diversion of materials from within the nuclear industry. The increase in international terrorism was certainly a factor in the passage of the 1978 Nuclear Nonproliferation Act.

Michael Flood cogently presented an argument of why terrorists may turn to nuclear power.[31] Nuclear installations are attractive targets because the fear of radioactivity adds a new dimension to terror. Since terrorist violence is violence for effect, nuclear facilities are prime targets. Any event involving "atomic terror" would make world headlines. In the developing nations, nuclear power plants may also become symbols of imperialism to leftist groups, who may obtain the sophisticated weapons to launch an attack that might lead to a core meltdown. In an attack on the construction site of the Super-Phenix breeder reactor in France by an unknown group in 1981, Soviet-made missiles were used. Although the missiles could not penetrate the containment shelter then being built, such an attack is not beyond the resources of violent groups.

On the other hand, it could be argued that terrorist groups would never develop nuclear weapons because the theft of nuclear materials involves such a high death risk. Terrorists have many easier means to realize their goals, since a complex technological society is vulnerable in many different ways. In fact, a BDM Corporation study of the threat of nuclear installations found that most attacks have come from dissident employees or psychologically disturbed individuals.[32] Few terrorist groups have the organization and skilled personnel necessary for an attack on a nuclear site, or the technical knowledge to steal nuclear materials without exposing themselves to lethal radiation. Terrorists also tend to refrain from malevolent acts that bring mass casualties because this mobilizes public opinion against them.

However, the BDM study also documented seventy-seven terrorist attacks against nuclear facilities between 1966 and 1975. The major left-wing incident was the takeover of a nuclear power plant under construction at Atucha, Argentina, by a guerrilla band of fifteen men. From the radical right, eight people were arrested in a plot to poison a water supply in Italy with stolen uranium. Fuel rods have been stolen from nuclear power stations in France and Germany, and plutonium has been reported missing at plants in the United States. Some of the incidents in the United States since 1969 include a pipe bomb found in the reactor building of the Illinois Institute of Technology, dynamite found at the site of a Michigan reactor, a break-in at a fuel-storage facility in North Carolina, detonation of an incendiary device near the Pilgrim reactor outside Boston, and arson attempts in New York and California.

Table 3 shows the BDM study's conception of the potential sources of nuclear terrorism. It classified the sources according to private or public objectives, the source of the stimulus to the act (external or internal), and the degree of rationality or emotionality in the act. In the public

Table 3. Potential Sources of Nuclear Terrorism

Social Stimulus	Private Objectives	Public Objectives

Rational-Internal	Criminals
	  Financial gain
	  Extortion
	  Mercenary sales
	  Ransom
		Terrorists
		  Bargaining
		  Publicity
		  Social paralysis
		  Mass casualties

Rational-External	Vigilantes
	  Restoration of a social order
	  Protection of public from danger
		Paramilitary
		  Adventurism of a local commander
		  Restoration of a social order

Emotional-Internal	Psychopaths
	  Nuclear mystique
	  Ego gratification
	  Pyromania
		Sociopaths
		  Vandalism
		  Subculture of violence

Emotional-External	Avengers
	  Revenge
	  Retribution
	  Dissident employee
	  Labor dispute
		Protesters
		  Exhibitionism
		  Political statement
		  Confrontation

Source: Adapted from "Analysis of the Terrorist Threat to the Commercial Nuclear Industry," BDM Corporation (1975), pp. 33, D-5.

sphere are terrorists, protesters, sociopaths, and paramilitary groups. In the private sphere are criminals, avengers, psychopaths, and vigilantes. The range of objectives for each stereotype is also indicated.

According to the BDM study, outside assistance to terrorist activity, such as Cuban support of Latin American guerrillas and the training of Mexican guerrillas and the Japanese Red Army by North Korea, is becoming more common. The Palestine Liberation Organization is reported to have had liaisons with the Irish Republican Army, Basque separatists, and French terrorists. Thus, international cooperation among terrorists may make an attack on a nuclear installation possible.

Should a terrorist group ever acquire nuclear materials, the technical expertise to fashion a weapon might be within its grasp. Willrich and Taylor estimated that between ten and twenty-four skilled scientists with several thousand dollars' worth of equipment could fabricate a crude nuclear bomb. To obtain materials, they could engage in armed attacks, bombing, hijacking, and kidnapping.[33] A PBS television documentary entitled *The Plutonium Connection* followed the progress of an undergraduate chemistry major at MIT asked to design a bomb using only publicly available materials. The task was accomplished in five weeks.

The NRC responded to this issue in 1976 by requesting that Congress allow a special army unit to be trained for emergencies, rather than try to protect the entire nuclear fuel cycle from terrorists and saboteurs. Antinuclear activists feared that a garrison state would emerge to protect the nuclear fuel cycle. The most commonly advocated safeguard now is the underground location of nuclear facilities. The BDM study regarded the fear of nuclear energy as the most effective deterrent to theft and nuclear terror—nuclear energy frightens terrorists as much as it does the public.

But a 1985 study of terrorist incidents by the International Task Force on the Prevention of Terrorism found that the danger of nuclear terrorism is increasing. It based its finding on five factors; 1) the growing incidence, sophistication, and lethality of terrorism; 2) state support or sponsorship of terrorism; 3) the deployment of nuclear weapons in areas of intense terrorist activity; 4) the increasing number of potential targets in civilian nuclear programs; and 5) the gray market in nuclear equipment and materials.[34] The study concluded that the most plausible terrorist threat would be a credible hoax involving nuclear weapons or materials that would result in mass hysteria and social disruption.

Of fifty-two serious incidents cited by the task force, thirty-two were in Spain. Over a six-year period, the Basque separatist group ETA bombed, kidnapped, murdered, and made guerrilla attacks with machine guns, grenades, and explosives in Spain. Most of the terrorist activity was directed against the Iberduero nuclear power plant, near Lemoniz. The manager of the power plant and the chief engineer were killed in separate incidents, and four workers were killed in three of the bombings. In 1983, the last reported incident, a car bomb exploded outside a plant at Tafalla, Spain, killing the occupants.[35]

Three serious terrorist incidents occurred in France, one involving the Iranian Liberation Army. Two bombings have occurred in the United States, where there have also been several bomb threats (two involving the Indian Point reactors in New York). In Toronto, a Litton Industries plant, which makes guidance systems for cruise missiles, was bombed by terrorist demolition teams from Europe, who were suspected of getting help from the Front for the Liberation of Quebec, who themselves had trained at PLO camps in Lebanon.[36]

Bombings have also been reported in Italy, Japan, Belgium, and Holland. In South Africa, the African National Congress sabotaged a nuclear reactor at Koeberg. The most bizarre nuclear plot was hatched by the Ugandan dictator Idi Amin. Hours after his downfall in 1979, documents were discovered that described Operation Poker, a plot to build nuclear bombs small enough to fit into suitcases and be carried worldwide into Ugandan embassies by suicide diplomats.[37]

The threat of sabotage and bombings of facilities can be removed simply by closing the facilities. In the Philippines, the Communist guerrilla New People's Army blew up twenty-six transmission towers connected with the Bataan nuclear power plant grid, but the plant has since been ordered dismantled.

The list of terrorist groups that may possibly become motivated to "go nuclear" is a long one. In addition to those mentioned above, there are FALN and Macheteros in Puerto Rico; the Secret Army for the Liberation of Armenians; the U.S. United Freedom Front; Sendero Luminoso and Tupac Amaru in Peru; the Red Brigades and the Armed Proletarian Nuclei in Italy; the Red Army Faction and Revolutionary Cells in West Germany; the Irish Republican Army; the Belgian Communist Combatant Cells; revolutionary groups in El Salvador, Chile, and Colombia; a wide range of Middle Eastern terrorist groups; and right-wing organizations in the United States such as the Aryan Brotherhood, the Posse Comitatus, the Ku Klux Klan, and the Order. Right-wing groups are thought to be more indiscriminate and less predictable than left-wing terrorists.[38]

Terrorists have attacked nuclear installations and corporations connected with nuclear power and have committed sabotage and theft of nuclear materials. There have been seventeen fatalities, mostly in bombings and armed assaults by Basque separatists. State-sponsored terrorism centers on Libya, Iran, and Syria, but other nations such as Cuba, Angola, Vietnam, East Germany, North Korea, Ethiopia, Bulgaria, South Yemen, Nicaragua, and the Soviet Union could be included, depending on the definition of terrorism used.[39]

Antinuclear Demonstrators Are Not Terrorists. It is terrorists, not demonstrators, who are likely to damage a plant and cause radioactive release, to steal nuclear materials or weapons, or to attempt to make a crude nuclear device. Generally, antinuclear activists have not emphasized the terrorist threat to nuclear power plants (but plans for emergency evacuation must also take this into consideration).

There is considerable debate among experts as to how easy it would actually be to construct a crude nuclear device using stolen or diverted plutonium. It is estimated that eight kilograms of plutonium would be sufficient to make a crude nuclear weapon and that over four hundred metric tons of plutonium will exist in the world as a result of nuclear-fuels reprocessing by the year 2000.[40] One study by the International Task Force on the Prevention of Nuclear Terrorism concludes,

In the 1990s, large quantities of weapons-usable plutonium will be in routine commerce. The plutonium fuel cycle will include several points where separated plutonium or fresh, irradiated plutonium fuel will be more accessible for potential diversion to weapons: reprocessing plants, plutonium fuel fabrication facilities, reactors using plutonium fuels, and the many transit routes between facilities.[41]

Pilot or functioning reprocessing facilities exist in fifteen countries.

One response has been to develop low-enriched fuels for research reactors and to discourage reprocessing, since uranium is more plentiful than it was once thought to be. Thorium reactors would also take plutonium off the market. Eliminating extensive reprocessing facilities and scaling back plans to develop fast breeder reactors that utilize recycled plutonium solve one problem but leave unresolved the issue of what to do with radioactive wastes. Proposals have also been made to strengthen the regulatory power of the International Atomic Energy Agency.

In the United States, the NRC is under criticism for not taking the steps necessary to adequately protect nuclear power plants from terrorists. The agency has no mandate to protect reactors from more than one insider; from three external attackers; from coordinated teams of attackers; or from an enemy of the United States.[42] Tamper-proof controls within nuclear plants to protect against insiders do not exist, nor do reactors have bunkered emergency core-cooling systems or other backup systems resistant to terrorist attacks, as exist in West Germany.[43] The NRC acknowledges the vulnerability of plants to truck-bomb attacks, but it has not ordered nuclear power plants to install the expensive security defenses to protect against them.[44]

Inga Thorsson, a task force member, summarizes a personal perspective on the problem:

No serious discussion of the threat of nuclear terrorism can disregard the most decisive threat to our survival—the existence of nuclear weapons. The threat of nuclear terrorism is the result of this fundamental fact and of the production of electrical power by nuclear reactors. Consequently, and as aware as I am that knowledge of evil—in this case, the splitting of the atom—can never be taken away from mankind, the political renunciation of nuclear weapons and nuclear-produced electric power is a prerequisite to removal of the terrorist nuclear threat. In the final analysis, all states possessing nuclear weapons are nuclear terrorists, keeping the peoples of the world hostages to their political aims, to be achieved, if necessary, by the use or the threat of use of nuclear weapons.[45]

Public Opinion and Nuclear Power

Public opinion is a fourth area of impact of the antinuclear movement and a measure of the success or failure of the movement. The various public-opinion polls of attitudes toward nuclear power indicate not only how the antinuclear movement has influenced public opinion, but who is more likely to oppose nuclear power plants and which social categories are the support base of the antinuclear movement.

Public opinion surveys should probably be divided into pre- and post-Three Mile Island—the 1979 event was a "Watergate" in the nuclear controversy. Although Three Mile Island affected public sentiment toward nuclear power, a survey by ABC News two weeks after the accident showed that 47 percent of the public still favored the construction of new nuclear power plants, while 45 percent were opposed. Eighty percent of the public rejected the idea of a permanent shutdown of all power plants, while 71 percent wanted more nuclear power plants *with stricter government supervision.* However, a majority of people opposed the location of nuclear power plants in their local community. These data do not tell us if those who opposed nuclear plant construction were crossovers after Three Mile Island or were predisposed against nuclear power before the accident.[47]

Two of the most comprehensive pre-Three Mile Island surveys were conducted by Louis Harris and Associates in April 1975 and August 1976 for Ebasco Services (a company that supplies technical services to the nuclear industry).[46] The methodology followed and the questions asked do not suggest any systematic bias or deliberate distortion in the surveys. Although these two surveys are not recent, they do show the wellsprings of antinuclear sentiment. The year between the two surveys was one of the most intensive in the movement, so the later one is a good measure of shifts in public attitudes toward nuclear power that may in part be attributed to the antinuclear movement.

Table 4 indicates public opposition to nuclear power in the United States in 1976. First, subgroups of opponents are defined by such criteria as region, age, income, sex, and race. The second column shows the percentage of each subgroup who opposed nuclear power. Opposition was concentrated in the East—40 percent of all those opposed lived in that region (although only 29 percent of all easterners were opposed to nuclear power development). The South had only a small minority of nuclear opponents, and there were moderate levels of opposition in the West and Midwest. Most of the opposition came from those living in urban areas, while rural areas (where most nuclear power plants are sited) expressed little opposition. People over fifty years of age were the least likely to be opposed; most who were opposed had had some college education but were not college graduates (although college graduates were more likely to oppose nuclear power). Scarcely any opposition came from blacks, and women were much more likely to be opposed than men.

There was a pattern to these beliefs: easterners, the young, and those who opposed nuclear power were more likely to identify major problems.[48] In the year between the two surveys, the number of people opposing nuclear power grew by about 8 percent among college graduates and among those living in the West or Midwest. Support for nuclear power lost ground among urban dwellers and the young, while slight increases in support for nuclear power occurred among rural dwellers, southerners, blacks, and those with low incomes.[49] Although women were more likely than men to be opposed to nuclear power, the percentage difference between the sexes was affected by the fact that twice as many women as men were not sure about their attitudes toward nuclear power.

Table 4. Nuclear Power Opposition in the United States

	Nuclear Power Opponents by Subgroup (% of all Opponents)	Nuclear Power Opponents within Each Subgroup (% of Subgroup)
Region		
East	40	29
Midwest	25	19
South	15	14
West	20	25
Residence		
Cities	43	29
Suburbs	27	22
Rural	18	18
Small towns	22	18
Age		
18–29	35	27
30–49	37	24
50+	28	17
Education		
Some high school	24	18
Some college	48	21
College grad	27	31
Income		
Under $5,000	16	22
$5,000–9,000	24	25
$10,000–14,999	21	23
$15,000+	—	19
Sex		
Male	41*	19
Female	59*	25
Race		
White	85	19
Black	8	22

*Approximate percentage
Source: 1976 Harris Survey, p. 100.

Radioactive-waste disposal was the main concern of all groups, particularly college graduates, while those with some college education were more concerned with radioactive discharges into the atmosphere and with theft of plutonium by revolutionaries. People who expressed concern about hazardous problems frequently drew the conclusion that nuclear power plants are safe. In 1976, solid majorities believed that nuclear power plants are either very safe or somewhat safe, while only about one-fourth of the public believed that they are unsafe or dangerous.

The Harris surveys also measured public confidence in various individuals and groups concerning nuclear power. They most trusted scientists—58 percent of respondents had a great deal of confidence in scientists in both surveys. The credibility of environmentalists grew by 34 percent in 1976 (a 12 percent increase), while about 40 percent had confidence in the Nuclear Regulatory Commission. Slightly more than one-fifth of the public expressed confidence in Ralph Nader, but even fewer had confidence in elected officials, the nuclear industry, the utilities, or newspaper commentators.[50]

A 1976 Gallup survey revealed social characteristics of respondents ignored in the Harris surveys: political affiliation, religion, occupation, and whether they followed the discussion about nuclear power. As Table 5 shows, Republicans were somewhat more likely than Democrats to be receptive to a plant being located in their neighborhood, and Protestants were more receptive than Catholics. Those in the lower-middle-class occupations of clerical and sales work were much more likely to oppose a nuclear power plant than professionals and manual laborers. This is consistent with the Harris data, for those with only some college education were generally opposed to nuclear power and were also most concerned with the emotional issue of the theft of plutonium by radical groups. High levels of knowledge were not associated with opposition to nuclear power; 71 percent of those who opposed a nuclear power plant being located in their neighborhood did not follow discussions about nuclear power.[51]

The surveys demonstrate that opposition increases if a nuclear plant is to be located in the vicinity of one's own neighborhood. A government study of residents of Hartsville, Tennessee—where a power plant was actually going to be located—found that those less favorable to the proposed plant emphasized its potential hazards, while those who favored it were interested in economic benefits that would accrue to the community. Again, people in business professions and laborers were most favorable, and women were the most adamant opponents, along with a small majority of farmers. Opponents placed a high value on the way of

Table 5. Receptivity To a Nuclear Plant in Neighborhood

	Favor (%)	Oppose (%)	No Opinion (%)
Political Affiliation			
Republican	48	43	9
Democrat	38	47	15
Southern Democrat	43	38	15
Independent	45	45	10
Religion			
Protestant	45	42	13
Catholic	39	51	10
Occupation			
Professional and business	50	43	7
Clerical and sales	32	59	9
Manual workers	45	42	13
Nonlabor force	41	43	16
Followed Discussion	46	46	8
Haven't Followed	29	71	<1

Source: 1976 Gallup Poll, p. 99.

life that then characterized Hartsville and were concerned with the plant's effect on noise levels, traffic congestion, crime rates, school overcrowding, the number of taverns and bars, and drug problems. They were also concerned about water and air pollution, radiation, accidents, and sabotage of the plant. Nevertheless, over 60 percent of the Hartsville community surveyed favored the construction of the proposed plant.[52]

A 1986 sociological study of opposition to the Diablo Canyon plant among a population living near it found that high levels of information are associated with resistance to licensing the plant.[53] Some previous surveys had shown that high levels of knowledge were more associated with support of nuclear power, but not among populations living near nuclear power plants—with the exception of the Hartsville study (in the region of the country with the least opposition to nuclear power).

Concern about safety issues was the primary source of opposition to Diablo Canyon; pronuclear sentiments were based on the perceived need for energy. The latter attitudes were predominant among older, less-educated, higher-income males with children, particularly if they lived more than twenty miles from the plant.[54] Multivariate analysis found income, age, and the perception of health risks to be the prime determinants of opinion on Diablo Canyon. Because Mothers for Peace was among the most active groups opposing the plant, male-female differences were an important focus of the study. Some differences in attitudes were related to different patterns of socialization between the sexes and between generations and whether or not men had children. (Women and men without children were more opposed to licensing of the plant.)

Those who favored nuclear power for economic reasons also assumed that nuclear power is inexpensive—a point contended by antinuclear activists. Much antinuclear literature argues that nuclear power is actually the most expensive form of energy and that it is heavily dependent on government subsidies. Amory Lovins, for example, argues that nuclear power programs provide a disincentive to seek alternative-energy sources, and that nuclear energy does not result in a saving of oil. "Further confirming the loose coupling between nuclear output and oil saving, between 1978 and 1979 the United States reduced by 16 percent the amount of oil used to make electricity, while U.S. nuclear output simultaneously fell by 8 percent: the oil saving came instead from conservation and coal and gas substitution."[55] In other words, many of the basic arguments of antinuclear activists have not yet filtered into the public mind.

The cumulative effect of the antinuclear movement on public opinion cannot be precisely determined by these surveys, but trends are apparent. The three-to-one margin favoring nuclear power in the early 1970s dropped considerably by 1979. Although many beliefs of the antinuclear movement had become incorporated into public opinion—such that conservation and development of alternative-energy sources are needed—the public view that nuclear power plants may be a necessary evil still prevails by a small margin.

David Lilienthal, first chairman of the Atomic Energy Commission, sees opposition to nuclear power as part of a broader set of attitudes.

The citizen protest against atomic energy plants here and abroad was not raised against nuclear hazards alone. Nor would it be satisfied if all nuclear plants were to be closed tomorrow. To a large extent, it has been a protest against the misuse of science, the misdirection of enormous forces that human ingenuity has brought into being. It is a protest against the abuses of industrial technology that poison the land instead of nurturing it, that sour the air and foul the water, that devour marsh and woodland and make hazardous to health and peace of mind the cities and factories in which people live and work. It is a protest against governments— all governments—that spend billions in an endless, insane atomic arms race that consumes the cream of the world's resources and much of its brightest talent. It is a protest against the uses of science and technology that are antihuman and antilife.[56]

Accidents such as those at Three Mile Island and Chernobyl have a greater impact on the attitudes of people living near nuclear power plants. Opposition to nuclear power rose from 19 percent in 1975 to 78 percent in 1986 among the general public following Chernobyl, and similar shifts of attitudes occurred in Europe. We must keep in mind that no nuclear power plants had been ordered anyway in the United States and a public opinion survey on whether or not *existing* plants should be shut down would have different results.

Conclusion

The antinuclear movement has succeeded in pressuring the government to redefine and enforce safety regulations in nuclear power plants more than in getting it to completely revamp energy policy. The greatly increased number of government regulations has made nuclear power more expensive and less desirable to the utilities industry.

In 1976 the nuclear issue helped to propel Jimmy Carter into the White House. His campaign and the Democratic party capitalized on his credibility as an expert in the field of nuclear energy. Many goals of the antinuclear movement were realized in his administration: government reorganization, including the abolition of the Atomic Energy Commission; a slowdown of research on the liquid-metal fast-breeder-reactor program; a temporary moratorium on plutonium recycling and nuclear-fuels reprocessing; international efforts to control nuclear technology and nuclear-weapons proliferation; increased government regulation of the safety of nuclear power plants; steps to protect the nuclear fuel cycle from terrorists; increased funding for solar and other alternative energy systems; and incorporation of public opinion into energy-policy decisions rather than a strict reliance on scientific, military, and industrial elites.

The Reagan era may prove to be an aberration in the history of public policy toward nuclear power, for trends in the 1980s have given more credence to the steps initially taken by the Carter administration. Future policy decisions must rest on the fact that energy growth has slowed to 1.8 percent rather than followed the projected 7 percent growth rate and that uranium reserves have increased. This points to an end to nuclear reprocessing and the breeder reactor as major issues in the United States, important programs for President Reagan. U.S. support for nuclear-fuels reprocessing and the breeder reactor in Europe is not likely to be as strong for similar reasons, and because less support would minimize the terrorist threat and the proliferation of nuclear weapons from the plutonium fuel cycle.

In an effort to gain markets in the Third World, the United States may increasingly turn to research on more intermediate, smaller-scale technology under the favorable conditions of political leadership. This would benefit both the United States and the developing nations. Competitive efforts by other nations to capture the potentially immense nonnuclear-energy market in the Third World are already having some impact. Many nuclear plants will be nearing the end of their thirty-year cycle within the next several decades, so government policy must at some point become concerned with alternative-energy technologies. Clean coal and gas, co-generation, small hydro dams, solar energy, advanced energy-efficiency technology, and other such alternatives will probably be increasingly seen as viable. Two major accidents have dramatically affected the growth of nuclear power: a third (especially one involving terrorism) would probably permanently seal the fate of nuclear power with the public.

The storage of commercial nuclear wastes is still the most unresolved issue. Antinuclear activists may be expected to oppose their use in the manufacture of nuclear weapons and their reprocessing as increasing the terrorist threat. The possibilities of entombing wastes at nuclear-power-plant sites and proposed permanent repository loom as continuing controversies, here as in Europe.

The antinuclear movement has been highly successful in influencing public policy and public attitudes. In its institutionalized stage, as environmentalist and scientist groups lead it, it is becoming intrinsic to the decision-making process throughout the nuclear fuel cycle. But its source of strength is still mobilized local groups and populations. The U.S. antinuclear movement has not succeeded in accelerating the phase out of *existing* nuclear power plants as called for in many referendum efforts. Seabrook remains its most symbolic loss or victory in the 1980s, though new issues always loom on the horizon with nuclear power.

Chapter Six

The Antinuclear Movement in Perspective

Social movements are groups of people involved in the process of social change. The antinuclear movement is one of the most significant social movements to emerge in the twentieth century. It has raised concerns about the gravest problems yet faced by human society: how to control the spread of nuclear weapons, how to prevent lethal radioactive materials from afflicting large populations, and how to provide the energy that is crucial to the survival of society.

How society should be organized for the production and distribution of social wealth is central to the ideology of many social movements. The egalitarian goals of modern social movements are frequently a response to large-scale changes in the social order brought about by technological innovations. However, the antinuclear movement is not basically an anti-technology movement, no matter how much the ideology of particular groups questions the value of technological progress.

Energy—the ability to do work—is the basis of all surplus wealth in a society. Relatively abundant and therefore inexpensive sources of energy once greatly increased the wealth of industrial societies, but abundance is quickly turning to scarcity as developing nations attempt to make use of their own depleting natural resources. Governments must now emphasize conservation, not only as an energy policy but as a way of preventing the instability and gradual erosion of social institutions under the pressures of scarcity. Nuclear technology has the potential to ensure continued high levels of energy production (if we could also ensure the safety of the technology).

Anthropologist Leslie White believed that the culture or civilization of mankind could be regarded as an organization of energy. He developed the law of cultural evolution, which asserts:

Culture develops when the amount of energy harnessed by man per capita per year is increased; or as the efficiency of the technological means of putting this energy to work is increased; or, as both factors are simultaneously increased.[1]

This succinctly expresses an underlying problem in modern society. Advanced societies faced with dwindling supplies of fossil fuels must implement efficient and new means of producing energy. If social evolution is a consequence of technological evolution, as White argued, a social system may retard progress if it resists new technologies. Either the technology or the social institutions must give way. Over forty years ago, he warned of the depletion of fossil fuels and speculated about the potential of both nuclear and solar energy. He quoted a research associate in physics as having said that with atomic energy,

the face of the earth will be changed. . . . Privilege and class distinctions . . . will become relics because things that made up the good life will be so abundant and inexpensive. War will become obsolete because of the disappearance of the economic stresses that immemorially have caused it. . . . The kind of civilization we might expect . . . is so different from anything we know that even guesses about it are futile.[2]

In retrospect, these views seem wishful thinking, for nuclear technology has made war not obsolete but even more probable, while economic stresses in societies have intensified. Political structures of control become more centralized with nuclear technology, enforcing elitism and powerful bureaucracies in both scientific and political institutions. If nuclear power is to be a step forward in technological evolution, it must add to, not damage, positive changes taking place in the social and political structure of both modern and developing societies. It must create an infrastructure that allows people to adapt to the new technology.

Nuclear power demands greater structural differentiation in the institutions of societies. Specialized occupations emerge at all levels with the technology, bringing new problems of social organization. Increased safety precautions must be taken to protect workers, who, like Karen Silkwood, may be risking their lives just by working in plants and factories. Technicians and plant operators must be better trained to prevent accidents such as those at Three Mile Island and Browns Ferry.

The positivist belief in evolutionary progress demands that societies make such adaptations in order to gain the benefits from a new technology. Sociology first developed from the positivism of Auguste Comte, at a time when social phenomena were interpreted through the laws of natural science. In one branch of positivism, dubbed social energetics,[3] man and society were viewed as energy apparatuses, with their history subject to the processes of the transformation of energy. Culture was thought to progress through the transformation of crude energy into useful energy, while society was viewed as an arrangement for the better utilization of energy.

As documented by Pitirim Sorokin, the social-energetics school attempted to explain the social phenomena of change, differentiation, equalization, domination, and general historical progress through the basic laws of thermodynamics. These theorists predicted an increasing social entropy that would be manifested in egalitarian and socialistic movements. Although Sorokin believed these assertions were unscientific extrapolations that caricatured scientific law and disguised the meaning of social facts, social energetics contributed to positivism by arguing that science could reconstruct society if the state were to guarantee the efficient use of maximum energy.[4]

The positivist view suggests, then, that nuclear technology is the epitome of technological evolution. Despite all its problems, nuclear energy represents historical progress in science and an enormous potential for resolving the energy crisis. The positivist view holds that it is the role of government to assure the implementation of a technological system that can continue the survival of society, which exists primarily to create surpluses through the efficient use of energy. There is no alternative to nuclear power in this view.

Alvin M. Weinberg, a senior nuclear scientist at Oak Ridge National Laboratory, is an articulate advocate of continued reliance on nuclear energy.[5] Weinberg argues that the need for fission depends on the availability of alternative sources of energy, and that coal is the only abundant alternative. Since solar technologies have not yet proved feasible on a large scale and oil is scarce, he argues we must rely either on nuclear fission or on coal or on a combination of both. Technological innovations such as the electric car and the heat pump may further increase the demand for electricity. However, Weinberg points out, coal still has serious environmental drawbacks and is not readily available to the rest of the world. He characterizes coal as a "sword of Damocles" because burning it results in carbon-dioxide emissions into the atmosphere that could one day lead to an ice-free Arctic and change the world's climate. Weinberg says that we should resort to nuclear fission and fusion energy, including even the fast breeder reactor, and work toward reducing the probability of accidents through technical improvements.[6]

Such positivist views are also present in the arguments of antinuclear activists. Amory Lovins, also a physicist, asserts that we can resolve the energy crisis by making more efficient use of existing nonnuclear sources of energy, including coal, which can be made environmentally safe through technical improvements and does not bring the threat of atomic warfare.[7]

In opposing nuclear power plants, do antinuclear groups accept a negative view of evolutionary processes? The destructive consequences of modern technology are all too apparent, including the automobile, chemical wastes, and the burning of fossil fuels. The antinuclear movement resists technological evolution in terms of large-scale, centralized nuclear power stations, but it affirms the belief in creative innovation and evolutionary change by seeking progress in solar energy and a more decentralized social structure.

Who Will Make the Decisions?

Government policy on energy has long been characterized by a bureaucratic commitment to nuclear power. The technology of nuclear power and its complex nuclear fuels demand the centralization of both productive and political functions. Its large-scale use places a great responsibility on the state to provide both military and operational security for nuclear power plants. Centralization of state control over the nuclear fuel cycle is also necessary to ensure that citizens are safe from radioactive wastes and nuclear accidents.

Antinuclear activists see this centralization as leading to the abuse of government power and the deprivation of citizens' civil liberties. One activist's view was given in a comment on the proposed final environmental statement on the liquid-metal fast breeder reactor:

Intolerance of minorities, pervasive domestic intelligence, centralization, technological priesthoods, human engineering, specialization, inequity, epidemic paranoia, and dilemmas already stressing the institutions of a disoriented society: nuclear technology will affect these dilemmas, and if effects compound the stress to some ultimate threshold, then the apocalyptic means of resolution will bear no resemblance to the arid bureaucratic cant that appears in the draft statement. . . . Sabotage is a terrifying prospect where we may be creating a quasi-military private army system under government directives, which may be impossible to totally monitor.[8]

Antinuclear groups do not desire state control of energy production, particularly if private interests prevail in decision-making. They argue that the role of large energy corporations in formulating energy policy must be minimized, while the public role should be expanded.

Antinuclear activists see their movement as functioning in the public interest. They justify their social action in the name of the people. Although a majority of the American and Western European populace does not appear to oppose nuclear power, activists persist in identifying the nuclear industry, oil corporations, and government agencies as private interests.

But the antinuclear movement should also be evaluated in terms of the possibilities that it has introduced for the survival of society. The energy crisis created a generalized social crisis that demanded new values to guide political action, new directions in energy policy, a new ordering of priorities, and public participation and support for new alternatives. The movement must be given credit for pressuring the government to consider the viability of a nonnuclear future through greater use of coal, solar energy, geothermal energy, and synthetic fuels, and through conservation.

These alternative-energy technologies also seem to mean the diffusion of social control and the decentralization of energy production. The viability of alternative sources of energy such as solar, hydroelectric, and geothermal systems, seems to depend on changes in other areas of the social order. At present, solar energy is not suitable for the large-scale demands of industrial societies. The use of solar energy would necessitate the reorganization of social institutions along lines of communal cooperation, such as those that existed in frontier society, so that energy is not wasted. Population growth would have to be slowed. Consumer patterns would have to drastically change so that expanding economic growth is not seen as a necessity. New directions in the use of leisure time would have to be forged, and productive activities found for those now dependent on energy-intensive industries must be found. Conservation and self-reliance would become a way of life, while cooperative societies would have to assure that the basic needs of all humans are met. Public transportation systems would have to replace the extensive use of the private automobile. Most important, government would have to change to prevent new forms of inequity from emerging.

Is this a utopian and visionary ideal that can never be realized, or does it represent the direction that societies must now take as they enter an era of scarcity with increasing populations? Citizen participation has already brought an end to secrecy in matters concerning nuclear power development, and the inability of political elites to develop a policy assuring a continued supply of safe energy has helped the antinuclear movement prepare the way for creative adaptation to a precarious situation.

Government must be actively involved in coordinating efforts to implement diverse sources of energy and in funding the necessary scientific and technological research. Capital expenditures for these efforts will be so great that social resources must be distributed to meet these efforts. However, if citizens are not involved in this decision-making process, they may by default contribute to the creation of a leviathan state that has enormously increased power over its populace.

The role of scientists in making decisions about nuclear power has become quite complex. Even though nuclear technology itself is proof that science does not produce perfect systems, public confidence in scientific authority remains high. Thorstein Veblen, a maverick theorist in the development of American sociology, once observed that scientists now have the ultimate answers to questions that other types of social authority used to have.[9]

But when scientists break from the cryptic barriers of rationalization and become prophets or social activists, they open themselves up to criticism that they have gone beyond their areas of competence. Talcott Parsons once wrote that

professional authority, like other elements of the professional pattern, is characterized by "specificity of function." The technical competence which is one of the principal defining characteristics of the professional status and role is always limited to a particular "field" of knowledge and skill.[10]

Thus, charges of irresponsibility often face scientists who are social activists. Richard Wilson, a professor of physics at Harvard University, leveled such a charge at Linus Pauling when he wrote to Representative

Hosmer of the Joint Committee on Atomic Energy that Pauling had exaggerated the cancer hazard associated with nuclear power—"scared the living daylights out of people"—and that this same exaggeration "is now plaguing the peaceful application of nuclear energy."[11]

To the public, even a Nobel laureate who warns of the danger of nuclear power has a great deal of credibility. Within the sciences, an unknown technician may have greater knowledge and experience with nuclear power than the Nobel laureate. It is true that some antinuclear scientists make judgments outside of their technical sphere of competence. Nuclear engineers have competence over specific aspects of nuclear technology, but they are more likely to be pronuclear. The engineer may have a narrow perspective that goes along with his narrow speciality, and he often cannot adopt a critical role without jeopardizing his career. Nuclear engineers may have an intrinsic interest in the status quo. As Amory Lovins points out, nuclear power is "a highly bureaucratized high technology that must be permanently run by a self-perpetuating (and probably paramilitary) technical elite, likely to be remote from their clientele."[12]

Scientist activists may sometimes be regarded by their peers as misrepresenting scientific authority for other social rewards, but these activists have freed themselves from many of the social constraints placed on scientific elites. Scientists, by virtue of their education, are also likely to be highly informed on issues and thus have difficulty segregating their roles as citizen and scientist. Thus, groups such as the Union of Concerned Scientists are able to combine political activism with exceptional technical criticisms of nuclear power.

On What Basis Will Decisions Be Made?

Will the economics of nuclear power ultimately decide its future? Capital investment in nuclear power plants is already astronomical, and it requires heavy government subsidies. The government and the nuclear industry would have to amortize billions of dollars' worth of debts if the nuclear power program were to come to a complete halt. The nuclear industry is already facing a crisis because it is prepared for a diminishing market that does not now seem to exist. However, the market has not disappeared entirely in developing nations. And although some labor unions oppose nuclear power, most are supportive, including the United

Auto Workers, the United Steel Workers, and the International Brotherhood of Electric Workers. (The nuclear industry has argued that over 200,000 jobs will be lost if the current obstructions to nuclear-power-plant construction continues.) While nuclear power plants have encountered significant opposition in local communities, many welcome the jobs, the increased property-tax base, and the general contribution of the nuclear power plant to community interests. Thus, any decision involving the future of nuclear power must take into account the needs of developing nations, local communities, and labor.

Opponents of nuclear power also assert that the future of light-water reactors cannot be considered independently of fast breeder reactors and the recycling of plutonium, as the government has done. Similarly, if radioactive wastes continue to accumulate at the site of nuclear power plants, steps should be taken to begin providing for their permanent disposal underground. Finally, if the United States is going to participate with other nations in agreements to control nuclear power, decisions must be made as to whether or not this will include American support of nuclear-fuels-reprocessing plants and breeder reactors in these nations. The trend in the 1990s is toward an international fuel cycle in Europe, which may provide governments with a basis of cooperation in political spheres in matters other than nuclear power.

Even if the United States does eventually abandon nuclear power, problems are still with us. Radioactive wastes are produced in the manufacture of nuclear weapons and electricity, and no one nation has a monopoly over nuclear energy anymore. But we must resist a worldview that sees nuclear energy as inherently evil and solar and alternative sources as inherently good. Solar energy, hydroelectric power, and geothermal energy may not be the solutions to energy problems; nor may conservation. As Gerald Garvey of Princeton University writes, "Despite exhortations to conserve energy, the logic of modern American history points in the opposite direction—that is the dominating fact of energy planning today."[13]

As religious leaders and organizations have shown, nuclear energy is a moral dilemma that individuals must confront. The ultimate moral question raised by the antinuclear movement is whether succeeding generations should be saddled with the problems created by the present generation. Radioactive wastes remain lethal for centuries and may afflict people even in nations without nuclear power plants. Bequeathing a future generation with the technological means of total destruction is hardly a positive contribution from the moral perspective. The Right Reverend Mortimer, bishop of Exeter, observes that

new scientific discoveries and advances increase human power and, therefore, moral responsibility. . . . The ability to employ nuclear energy is an immense advance in human power to control and adapt man's environment and an immense increase, therefore, in human responsibility. [14]

On the other hand, excessive moralism can retard the progress of society. Moral absolutism threatens the existence of a social system because it compares the society to its own standards, which are never perfectly fulfilled. Italian political theorist Gaetano Mosca once argued that the individual of average morality was better adapted for the struggle for existence than either the morally deficient or the individual with an unusually delicate moral sense. [15] We must at least leave succeeding generations with the means to control nuclear energy, if not abandon it altogether.

In the final analysis, it is up to individuals to decide our energy future and to take social responsibility for that future, through actions as mundane as installing wood-burning heaters or solar panels or walking instead of driving whenever possible. Political action might take the form of a letter to one's congressman or to the president of the United States, or it might involve chaining oneself to the gate of a nuclear power plant. Expressing an opinion is better than allowing someone else to make decisions by default. This is the responsibility of all members of society. As eminent historian and social philosopher Barrington Moore, Jr. wrote,

If human society is noxious for anybody, why then does it exist? The obvious and banal answer is that by means of the division of labor, possible only in and through society, human beings enormously enhance their capacity to adapt to and control their environment. And even if it is obvious and banal, it is true. Without the invention of human society, *Homo sapiens* might well have become extinct long, long ago. [16]

Postscript on Green Politics

As a social movement, the antinuclear movement has been absorbed into the Green movement in West Germany and France. The Green party in West Germany has obtained up to 9 percent of the vote, but a much smaller percentage in France. The U.S. antinuclear movement has also been absorbed *somewhat* back into the environmentalist movement, and an incipient Green movement appears to be emerging.

The Greens fuse together the ecological, peace, and feminist movements with success. Ideologically, Greens are to some extent nonviolent anarchists, rejecting both liberal and left-wing politics while attempting to break through the "conservative barrier."[17] In the postmaterialist society of the United States, ecological lifestyles based on values of self-reliance, communalism, and personal liberation have been adopted by many, who also incorporate values of "eco-feminism," political ecology, and the peace movement into their activist outlooks. The Greens criticize bureaucratic, centralized states and exploitative, concentrated capitalist economies without resorting to either the methods or the ideology of Marxism.

Antinuclear goals are an intrinsic part of Green politics, but the inclusion of peace, feminist, and lifestyle objectives as goals diffuses the identity of the antinuclear movement as such. Institutionalized environmentalist and scientists' organizations are still the building blocks of the antinuclear movement, but the mass base of the movement is drifting increasingly toward the Greens.

Appendix A:
The Antinuclear Movement and Sociological Theory

Despite a burgeoning literature on the subject of energy, only a few social scientists have studied the citizen-action groups concerned about nuclear issues. In the late 1960s, both scientists and citizens opposed the construction of a nuclear power station on the shore of Cayuga Lake in New York state. In 1971, Dorothy Nelkin documented the conflict between those who recognized a need for growth in the electric-power industry and those who believed the plant would damage the ecology of Cayuga Lake.[1] Nelkin's case study demonstrates the difficulty of attaining consensus when scientists disagree about the extent of ecological harm that might ensue from a nuclear power plant. The study was prophetic, in that the role of the scientific community in the controversy is as critical now as it was in the late 1960s.

Whom are we to believe in the controversy over nuclear power? While most of the public is willing to trust the trained judgment of scientists, there is notable disagreement within the scientific community itself as to whether nuclear power is a safe technology. The political system is not structured to keep the views of scientists distorted for political ends, either by supporters or by opponents of nuclear energy.

The role of experts and the use of scientific and technical information in nuclear-power-plant-licensing hearings before the now-defunct Atomic Energy Commission was the subject of analysis by two political scientists. In 1974, during their months as participant-observers in hearings in Michigan and Vermont, Steven Ebbin and Raphael Kasper examined the roles of conflicting parties in these hearings, concluding that the licensing process

is neither fair nor expeditious nor democratic in any substantive or meaningful way. It is marked by manipulation of scientific information by all parties in order to substantiate their predetermined points of view. It is a system evidently designed for lawyers for the consideration of legal issues and as such does not resolve important issues of science and technology and human and physical ecology which are likely to accompany the construction and operation of nuclear power plants.[2]

Distortion of fact is commonplace among politicians. Consider this statement on nuclear energy by the presidential nominee of the Republican party in his 1980 acceptance speech: "It must not be thwarted by a tiny minority opposed to economic growth which often finds friendly ears in regulatory agencies for its obstructionist campaigns."[3] What are the underlying assumptions of such a statement? Are antinuclear activists opposed to economic growth or to nuclear power (or both)? Are they obstructionist, or do they present viable alternatives to energy policy? Are they a tiny minority, or are their views actually representative of a substantial part of the electorate? Political statements often raise more questions than they answer and take us away from a factual consideration of the issues.

Social scientists have the role of presenting balanced and objective analyses of political and social problems so that those who have the responsibility for making decisions will be better informed. In a democracy, it is important that the voting public be as informed as those elected to public office.

By understanding the antinuclear movement as a social movement, the entire panoply of issues raised by opponents to nuclear power should be more clear. The case studies by Nelkin and Ebbin and Kasper were written before the energy crisis of the early 1970s enabled antinuclear groups and organizations to coalesce into a movement.

Social movements are collective attempts by groups and organizations to change an aspect of society or the state. They are among the more difficult phenomena to explain by social scientists, for movements have complex organizational structures and often complex ideologies or justifications of the changes they seek. In the discipline of sociology, there are many competing theoretical explanations of why movements emerge.

Resource-Mobilization and Social-Action Theory

One recent theoretical perspective in sociology, known as the resource-mobilization school,[4] is concerned with what makes a social movement succeed or fail. Its main thesis is that organizations within a social movement must gain access to external resources in society, such as mass-media publicity, economic sponsorship, or legitimation of their symbolic worth, in order to succeed. Most social movements are not loosely structured associations of discontented individuals, as was once assumed, but consist of organizations that do many of the same things that all organizations do in order to survive. The main difference is that social movement organizations frequently choose dramatic and unconventional ways of gaining attention to their cause.

Although social-movement organizations always seek to maximize their use of resources available in society, they may also have varying levels of internal resources. Some movements may have leaders that give extraordinary strength to them, as Martin Luther King, Jr. gave to the civil rights movement. One internal resource of the antinuclear movement is the cadre of scientists who have devoted a substantial part of their personal and professional lives to the movement.

The resource-mobilization perspective enables the researcher to specify conditions that lead to the successful organization of a social movement. The strategies and tactics used by movement groups to attempt to gain power in the political arena are in large part determined by the need to coordinate and unify the various groups in the movement, and also are affected by the reaction of those in positions of formal authority to the movement.

A more general approach to the antinuclear movement is social-action theory.[5] The basic tenet of this theory is that behavior is purposive and motivated and that it is guided by symbolic processes.[6] From this perspective it examines the orientations of groups or collectivities as they interact with the external world. The resource-mobilization school correctly points to the need to discover the support that a movement obtains, but social-action theory focuses on the values and beliefs that bind members of a social movement together.

The first sociologist to apply social-action theory to the study of social movements was Rudolph Heberle.[7] His work emphasized that although movements have organizations within them, they are not conventional organizations, with roles independent of individuals and with social relationships that are merely functional. Heberle observed that social movements require a similarity of sentiments and a sense of group solidarity and identity among their members. Social movements have "constitutive values," or ideas and beliefs that form the spiritual-intellectual foundation of group cohesion and solidarity.[8] As we saw in chapter 1, the ideology of the movement includes its goals as well as conceptualizations of the alternative direction social change might take. The ideology of the antinuclear movement includes core beliefs and values that unite diverse antinuclear groups.

These values and beliefs define the general direction that collective action takes. In a large nation such as the United States, it is difficult to understand how a movement could really occur. When antinuclear activists are arrested during a demonstration in Seabrook, New Hampshire, what impact does this have on groups in California and Tennessee? Since *events* are the substance of movements, the actions of a group in one part of the nation become significant to groups in another part. The need to identify with other activists and to have a sense of solidarity with them is characteristic of people in social movements. If the core values of the movement diffuse sufficiently throughout the country, then the movement is more integrated despite geographical separation.

Antinuclear groups and organizations are extremely diverse, ranging from voluntary associations in local communities, such as the Women's Club in Linwood, New Jersey, to Friends of the Earth in California. There must be constitutive values that have symbolic importance in integrating and maintaining cohesion within the movement.

Social movements are often a means through which a society makes a transition from traditional modes of organization to a new social order. The version of social-action theory propounded by Neil Smelser suggests that people who are attracted to social movements have been dislodged from traditional social ties but are not yet integrated into a new social order.[9] These people feel psychological strain and are susceptible to the appeals of the social movement. The movement gives them an opportunity to define new social norms and values. The energy crisis contributed to basic alterations of American social structure. One way people cope with fundamental changes in their economic situation is to redefine individual goals and to change collective social values. A simple act in everyday life, such as walking, may take on new significance and people who purchase large automobiles may find themselves the object of criticism rather than envy. Instead of feeling that it is important to vacation in Hawaii, the national park a few hundred miles away looks more appealing.

Conservation of resources at both the individual and the societal level becomes more desirable.

Individual Motivations to Participate

The argument that social movements appeal to people who are experiencing psychological strain and individual discontent has always been one of the more controversial themes in social science. For example, a study of the Boston antibusing movement found that social cohesion increased protest against busing among Boston residents, but that discontented individuals were more likely to protest than others.[10] These contradictory findings in the same study are characteristic of the uncertainty in social science as to why certain individuals are motivated to participate in social protest or in a social movement.

When an individual joins a movement, his motivation may be either intentionally concealed by him or unknown to him. Rather than argue vaguely that frustrated individuals under stress are the ones who join, Heberle simply constructed four types of motivation out of the complexity of individual motives,[11] based on the typology of orientations to social action developed by classical social theorist Max Weber. The *emotional-affectual* orientation emerges when an individual has experiences that arouse his or her emotions against the people or conditions that the movement attacks, or when he or she has affection for the leaders and followers of the movement. The *value-rational* orientation holds that the goal of the movement is desirable; and its success is desirable for the sake of the cause it advocates. In the *purposive-rational* orientation, the individual has expectations of personal advantage, and in the *traditional* orientation, the status characteristics of the individual (such as social class or ethnicity) motivate participation in the movement.

Social movements involve the individual more intensively than do formal organizations. Individuals who break from established cultural traditions are often prone to alienation and anomie. If the movement is in rebellion against social conditions, its support groups lessen the negative effects of their deviance. At one extreme, the individual's identity becomes almost totally dependent on the social-movement group.

A common set of values emerges that sets participants in a social movement apart from the mainstream of social life. This is perhaps a necessary condition of movement formation. Although the individual's motives for "conversion" to the movement may be too complex to determine accurately, the basis of collective social action is the values and orientations of groups in the movement.

There is a strong tendency to impute personal motivations to social activists, often by opponents of the movement who wish to discredit the leaders by questioning their moral character. Such a Machiavellian perspective is characteristic of the historical sociology tradition, exemplified by Hans Gerth and C. Wright Mills. [12] Although they were social-action theorists (and Mills a radical activist), these sociologists looked for "inner" motivations of historical figures that differed from their publicly revealed motives. Motivations, they argued, are found in the psychic structure of individuals, as social action is ultimately subjective in nature. They did not accept the idea that common value orientations are necessary for the formation of a movement, asserting instead that individuals have various motivations that may converge or coincide with the movement's direction. [13]

That there may be as many motives to join a movement as there are individuals who join suggests that the stated ideology of activists is not necessarily the reason for their participation in the movement. Ideology integrates events and goals of movement activists into comprehensive explanatory schemes that can help to mobilize groups into collective action. [14] Possibly, people do have distinct motivations for participating at various stages in the life span of a social movement. For example, Heberle suggests that at the beginning, movements attract men and women who are devoted to the goals of the movement and who are often original and idealistic thinkers. [15] As the movement gains power, ambitious and careerist individuals join, at which point the moral and intellectual caliber of the movement may begin to deteriorate. The ideology of the movement is also affected by a generation's political experiences. The general conditions of life in an historical period of war or peace, prosperity or depression, have particular impact on movement activists.

Sequential Stages in Social Movements

The idea that social movements go through stages is a major theme of theories and models of movements. Movements may have *careers* that pass through stages such as social unrest, popular excitement, formalization, and institutionalization. [16] During the stage of social unrest, agitators emerge who develop an esprit de corps and a supportive morale. At this point an ideology forms, and the strategy and tactics of the movement take shape. The agitation phase has the function of dislodging people from traditional ways of life, liberating them for movement in new directions. Leaders have different roles during the course of the movement. The role of agitator is usually associated with the stage of social unrest, and that of the prophet with popular excitement. When the movement becomes more organized and formal, leaders must become statesmen. At the final stage, social-movement organizations may become institutionalized, and their leaders are then administrators of the organization. The history of the NAACP follows this model.

Another widely accepted model of the stages of social movements sets forth six determinants that explain the development of social movements.[17] These determinants proceed in sequence. The first is that of *structural conduciveness*. For instance, one of the reasons the antinuclear movement emerged was the failure of the political elite to formulate a comprehensive energy plan. Beginning under the Nixon administration, the energy crisis and the high cost of oil made nuclear energy appear to be the most feasible alternative. A number of environmentalist voluntary associations with access to government channels of communication were well aware of some of the risks of nuclear energy that were not known to the public. There is vagueness and generality in the concept of structural conduciveness, for innumerable conditions could be specified that were conducive to the emergence of the antinuclear movement.

The second determinant is *structural strain*. There must be some sort of disturbance in the social system that contributes to psychological strain in affected people. The energy crisis contributed to severe economic hardship for large numbers of Americans, although not necessarily the people who became antinuclear activists. However, movement members who held ecological values did perceive other forms of energy technology—such as solar energy—to be less threatening and dangerous than nuclear power. We could say, therefore, that conditions of structural strain had existed.

The third determinant is the growth and spread of a *generalized belief*. This is the most critical stage if the social movement is to develop. At the common-sense level, we could simply say that antinuclear activist groups came to believe that nuclear power was not a safe form of energy and that it produced harmful radioactive byproducts, while solar energy was a safe, plentiful, and clean form of energy. These beliefs involve the totality of individuals' wishes and desires and their perception of situations that cause them to redefine the direction of their activities. Generalized beliefs assume that there are extraordinary, threatening, and conspiratorial forces at work in the universe. In this sense, there is a psychological element involved in generalized beliefs. It is true that some antinuclear activists believe that plutonium is the ultimate evil creation of man or that nuclear power plants will explode like nuclear bombs or that people who live next to a nuclear power plant will probably die of cancer. On the other hand, many antinuclear groups, like the Union of Concerned Scientists, have high levels of knowledge and information about nuclear technology and radiation, and their opposition is based on that knowledge as well as on their social values.

Precipitating factors follow the spread of generalized belief. Events like the nuclear accident at Three Mile Island and the fire at Browns Ferry crystallize beliefs into action. The movement gets under way as precipitating events lead to the mobilization of participants for action. Groups form, leaders emerge, coalitions and mergers of organizations take place, and demonstrations or other forms of tactical action occur. At this stage the mobilization of external resources—finances, mass-media attention, defection of members of the opposition, public support—becomes critically important.

The final determinant is the operation of *social control*. As dissent magnifies, those in positions of formal political authority must act. The National Guard may be called out to arrest demonstrators, concessions will usually be made, government agencies may be reorganized, and leaders of the movement may themselves become more moderate. Dissent between moderates and radicals may splinter and weaken the movement, or drastic tactics, particularly if they are violent, may turn away public support from the movement.

The core assumption of this six-determinant theory of collective behavior is the idea that conditions of social strain create ambiguous and difficult situations for individuals. Generalized beliefs restructure and redefine these ambiguous situations through a psychological process that provides simple answers to a complex situation—a circuiting process that reduces the stress of ambiguity.

Generalized beliefs help maintain group solidarity for those in the movement. If the "enemy" is regarded as diabolically powerful and threatening to movement activists, a sense of persecution and apprehension will bring solidarity to the movement.[18] The belief that the nuclear industry is engaged in conspiracies may give its representatives the face of a superhuman enemy against which drastic measures must be taken. Some observers claim that Manichaeism, a view of the world in terms of saints and sinners or good and evil, gives members of a movement a sense of elite status.[19] This is particularly true when members feel that organization is a social constraint contrary to the spirit of change. Social-movement organizations have a management function, for their members must identify with the movement or they will leave. Unlike conventional organizations, members are not dependent on the movement for an economic livelihood and are free to leave with no adverse consequences. There are of course exceptions—many leaders are professional social-movement entrepreneurs,[20] and in some cults desertion may even bring death, as it did for the people who lived in Jonestown.

Psychologists also theorize that individuals have a frame of reference, or a generalized point of view, that determines their specific attitudes and psychological motivations.[21] A frame of reference is learned as a normal part of the socialization or learning process and defines the meaning an individual gives to his or her life. When the individual is presented with a chaotic external environment that is difficult to interpret, he or she becomes highly suggestible. Leaders of social movements exploit slogans and symbols to stimulate individuals to perceive their experiences in a new way without being critical. Thus, the psychology of suggestibility explains partly why people join a movement.

In a similar vein, some argue that social movements draw people who have personal problems and are therefore predisposed to the movement.[22] Susceptibility to the appeals of the social movement increases if such a person believes that he or she must take action to solve the problems. Personal resentments may be exploited by movement leaders.

People may also turn to the movement for solutions to their personal problems, such as paranoia, in dead-end situations, perhaps searching for a sense of community. Eric Hoffer notes that a "full-blown mass movement is a ruthless affair, and its management gives an appearance of spontaneity to consent obtained by coercion."[23] In other words, a movement may exploit an individual who is in a dependency situation by indoctrinating him or her.

When an individual undergoes "conversion" to a movement, he or she usually has a precipitating experience.[24] The conversion of a disillusioned person is the result of a discrepancy between his or her conventional beliefs and psychological realities. This theory is anathema to informed political activists, for they do not wish to believe that their activities are the result of a distorted view of social reality or of frustrated personal needs. Such psychological theories are also generally held in some disrepute by sociologists, who are more interested in external social events and conditions that produce an activist response.

The Social Organization of Movements

The motivations of individuals joining a social movement are also important for the organizational structure of the movement. All groups and organizations must have some division of labor, even one that emerges spontaneously with tacit agreement among members on what their role is in the group. Some major problems are the nature of the relationship between leaders and followers, the interrelationships among different movement organizations, and the relationship of the movement to political parties.

Inevitably, a status hierarchy develops in movement organizations, usually in the nucleus of the group and among the core members. Competition for leadership is endemic to social movements, and this often diverts the movement from unified action. Charismatic leaders may be a source of gratification and identification, but eventually more bureaucratically oriented leaders begin to dominate the organization. As rules and regulations develop and leadership roles become more formal, the organization devotes increasing time to maintaining itself rather than to acting on the goals of the movement.[25] In this transformation, one can distinguish between centripetal forces, through which groups coalesce while keeping their local autonomy, and centrifugal forces, in which a small group gathers around a charismatic leader and other groups spin off as the movement expands.

Resource-mobilization theory in particular emphasizes the organized nature of social movements. But movements vary greatly as to the degree of organization or centralization. Herbert Blumer distinguishes three different types of movements.[26] In the *general* social movement, collective efforts to change aspects of society are uncoordinated, episodic, formless in organization, and often inarticulate. This type of movement is merely an aggregation of individual activities. On the other hand, *specific* social movements have a definite organization and structure. Finally, the *expressive* social movement does not seek changes in institutions but has profound effects on the persons involved. We could think of the labor and peace movements as general social movements, from which more specific movements emerged. The antinuclear movement would be a specific social movement in this typology. Hippies, on the other hand, were part of an expressive social movement that changed the life-styles of individuals rather than seeking specific changes in social institutions. To some extent, the antinuclear movement is also an expressive movement, for many groups desire not only the abandonment of nuclear power but an entirely new way of life based on alternative social values.

Social-action theory helps analysis of social movements by providing a way to classify groups that are part of the antinuclear network. Other insights into the movement derived from social-action theory have to do with *dilemmas of orientation* that activists may experience.

Individuals in a social movement have an ambiguous status outside the movement, and they often experience this conflict subjectively as a dilemma between the self and the collectivity. Their status may have a broad or generalized significance to them—that is, they may be alienated from technological systems in general and perhaps even from the entire political system as the conflict with political authorities grows sharper. On the other hand, their status significance may be quite specific. For instance, if their main criticism of nuclear power plants is that radioactive wastes are produced, a satisfactory solution to this problem could soften their opposition to nuclear power. There is much variation in the intensity of participation over time in a social movement. Events can drastically change the public image of activists, and the government may choose to intervene by suppressing the movement.

Leadership of the antinuclear movement is diffused throughout the movement in a kind of *acephalous* (headless) leadership structure. To some extent, Ralph Nader is a charismatic leader, and Nader organizations took the "lead" role in many phases of the movement. But the antinuclear movement has generally involved so many diverse groups and organizations that it is almost impossible to ascertain which are the most important.

Strategy and tactics are the core activity of social-movement organizations. A study of the strategy and tactics of antinuclear groups, primarily in New England, found that the main strategy of antinuclear groups was to win publicity for their cause.[27] This need resulted in some groups deciding to maintain a single-issue orientation, rather than broadening the focus to an attack on capitalism or including other issues such as disarmament or gay rights as part of the strategy. For much the same reason, civil disobedience and nonviolent action had to be carefully defined by activists in their protests against the Seabrook nuclear power plant and other nuclear installations.

Tactics are extremely important to a movement in forming its public image and identity. Since movements use noninstitutionalized means of advocating a cause, tactics can very easily determine success or failure. Initially, antinuclear activities consisted of interventions in nuclear-power-plant-licensing hearings, but as the movement grew and more diverse groups became involved, tactics changed.

Tactics diffuse throughout a movement if they are successful, but they must advance the goals of the movement without causing splits.[28] Therefore they must be flexible and innovative. In some cases, however, the tactics of a movement are more important than the goal, as is often the case with boycotts and strikes in the labor movement. At other times, the tactics serve the expressive needs of group members.

Interrelationships among movement organizations are a problem especially important to the antinuclear movement. Coordination of activities among diverse groups is rare at the national level. Only a few demonstrations in Washington, D.C., pulled together the whole range of groups involved. The antinuclear movement is an amalgamation of several social movements, including the environmentalist movement and segments of the labor, peace, women's, and gay rights movements. In addition, many groups established during the 1960s decade of activism found new life in the antinuclear movement. (Many counterculture figures also became involved, and well-known music groups such as Peter, Paul, and Mary devoted their talents to the new cause.) There has not been any noticeable competition among these movements for leadership of the antinuclear movement. But there has been, in the last several years, a substantial countermovement inspired by the nuclear industry to block the efforts of antinuclear activists.[29]

Of particular interest in an analysis of the antinuclear movement is its relationship to the major political parties, particularly to the Democratic party. As Heberle observed, "In order to enter into political action, social movements must, in the modern state, either organize themselves as a political party, or enter into a close relationship with political parties."[30] The antinuclear movement has not closely affiliated itself with the Democratic party, but many of its goals were "coopted" by the Democrats for their own political advantage. The Carter administration, however, was extremely ambiguous in terms of actual support for antinuclear goals.

Social movements are so much a part of the American political system that they have become institutionalized much in the same way that interest groups have. In one sense, social movements are part of the normal functioning of the social system, revitalizing social structures and introducing—or resisting—innovative changes. Social movements are more often than not the bearers of significant social change, and this role determines their function in a modern society. When we consider the consequences of the antinuclear movement, we should be aware that movements have recognizable functions within a political system.

Research Difficulties

Both social-action theory and the resource-mobilization perspective on social movements facilitate a better understanding of what occurs when groups seek change through collective action. However, it is almost impossible to assess modes of communication and psychological interaction among members of a movement.[31] Newspapers and social-movement literature become primary sources for our knowledge of the sequence of important events, but their relative significance to the movement must be left largely to the analytical abilities of the observer.

The sequence of events pertinent to the antinuclear movement can be found in the movement literature as well as in major newspapers over a specified time period.[32] This longitudinal method is much more useful than a cross-sectional analysis of movement groups at a particular point of development. Do the groups change over time by getting larger? Do they merge into coalitions, or do they gain publicity and then drop from the public arena? Answers to these questions are incomplete due to the selective inattention of the mass media, but if certain groups appear continually in newspaper items and have the resources to continue producing their own literature, they may be identified as important organizations in the movement.

A more difficult methodological problem is finding a way to discover how social conditions are related to social movements at individual and collective levels. Much of the classical sociological literature focuses on the relationship of social or economic deprivation and frustration to individual participation in movements. But social movements become a part of the conditions of life for their participants, who experience the significant events in the history of the movement subjectively. The beliefs of participants become in part a new definition of their social conditions, and in some instances they may not be related to the original life situation at all.

The problem of the origin of the antinuclear movement is somewhat distinct from the problem of how antinuclear groups and organizations survived and developed as a movement. The resource-mobilization school gives us excellent clues on how to analyze the organizational growth and decline in the movement.[33] Resources such as power, labor, publicity, and finances are all used by both pronuclear and antinuclear groups to struggle with the issue.[34]

The problem of how social conditions contribute to individual participation in a movement is identical to the problem of analyzing the motivations that propel individuals into collective action. Perhaps the resolution of this problem lies in the orientations, values, and beliefs held by *groups* rather than essentially idiosyncratic individual motives. Social conditions should not be ignored. The general political and economic conditions during the life span of the movement—the energy crisis of 1973–74 and the ensuring years of recession and political anxiety—were obviously sources of collective action by antinuclear groups.

Theoretical Studies of the Antinuclear Movement

The nonsociologist should be aware that the many sociological theories of movements can all be applied in some way to the antinuclear movement. The variety and diversity of sociological approaches enrich our understanding of a phenomenon with complex, interrelated dimensions and ramifications.

Social scientists have explicitly drawn upon the antinuclear movement to illustrate theories of social movements. The *political process* model utilizes the concept of *structure of political opportunities* to refer to the receptivity of a political system to organized protest by challenging groups.[35] Herbert Kitschelt used this framework in a comparative study of the antinuclear movement in France, Sweden, the United States, and West Germany. In all four countries, the antinuclear movement grew out of the environmentalist movement, but the four political systems had varying degrees of openness that either constrained or facilitated the input of the antinuclear movement in formulating national policy.[36]

The degree of structural openness depends on many factors, including the nature of the system's political parties, the executive and legislative branches of government, and the relative independence of the judiciary and the government agencies regulating nuclear power. Sweden and the United States have open political systems; there, the antinuclear movement was able to adopt *assimilative* strategies by working through multiple points of access in established institutions. France and West Germany's political systems are more closed, so the antinuclear movements there had to adopt more *confrontational* strategies, such as public demonstrations and acts of civil disobedience.[37] For example, referendums are not allowed in the French and West German political systems, and participation in licensing proceedings are not allowed in France or Sweden. Kitschelt viewed antinuclear demonstrations and civil disobedience in the United States as "temporary aberrations from the American pattern of assimilative protest."[38] He argued that the rise of the Green movement in France and West Germany is related to the greater nonresponsiveness of the political systems in these countries to antinuclear demands.

The theoretical application of the "structure of political opportunities" approach to the antinuclear movement does point to obvious limiting factors in the development of the movement in each country. But there are also many exceptions in the evidence that contradict this simplified approach. For example, in the United States mass demonstrations and civil disobedience occurred at a time when the system was *most* open to demands—in the Carter administration—and assimilative strategies were used when it was *least* open—in the Reagan era.

Kitschelt did not see pronuclear movements as particularly important in determining differential movement impact because in each country the nuclear industry, electric utilities, and state agencies promoting nuclear power were firmly committed to it. But a study of the pronuclear movement utilized the resource-mobilization approach.[39] Bert Useem and Mayer Zald showed that the pronuclear movement evolved from a pressure group to a social movement by first becoming a countermovement. It arose as a result of lessening government support in the late 1970s for the nuclear industry in the face of the strong antinuclear movement.

One wing of the pronuclear movement emerged from the nuclear industry, while another wing was based in local communities. The nuclear-industry wing was represented by the Committee on Energy Awareness, Edison Electric Institute, and Nuclear Energy Women. Westinghouse Corporation also trained people as debators for college campuses. The community wing was represented by such groups as the New Hampshire Voice of Energy, whose working-class and nonprofessional middle-class membership who sponsored a rally of four thousand persons in Manchester, New Hampshire. The Massachusetts Voice of Energy consisted of nuclear engineers and graduate students in nuclear engineering. The industry wing support hurt the legitimacy of the community wing and actually helped solidify antinuclear alliances in the face of a common enemy.[40] The pronuclear movement got an endorsement from leaders of the NAACP, who thought nuclear energy would promote economic growth and opportunity, but it also attracted the John Birch Society and the Ku Klux Klan.

The authors noted that the pronuclear movement ultimately bolstered antinuclear arguments that with nuclear power, civil liberties would be violated—pronuclear groups collected information on antinuclear groups to disrupt their activities.[41] Useem and Zald found that these negative activities also included taking pictures of antinuclear demonstrators, copying their license plate numbers, and maintaining files on individuals.[42] The U.S. Labor party sent infiltrators to Clamshell Alliance meetings and gave information to the New Hampshire State Police and the FBI. The Georgia Power Company operated a surveillance program for "dirt gathering" on the "commies and queers" involved in the protests in Georgia. The U.S. Labor party also persuaded Republican Governor Meldrim Thompson of New Hampshire that the demonstrations outside Seabrook were a cover for terrorist activity.[43] It is difficult to view the pronuclear movement as anything but a countermovement in the light of nuclear-industry efforts to use smear tactics in an attempt to suppress legitimate political protest.

The antinuclear movement and the related Green movement are not Marxist "new social movements"[44] but are unique outgrowths of the earlier environmentalist and other nonviolent middle-class movements (with unconventional middle-class values). The growing connection of the antinuclear movement to the peace and feminist movements is worth exploring. Arthur Meir, for one, has described the peace movement in terms remarkably resonant of the antinuclear movement. The peace movement draws upon a similar population with similar goals—to challenge technocratic power in the nuclear age.[45]

Appendix B:
The Economics of the Nuclear Industry

Electrical power is essential to the existence of industrialized societies and an important stimulus to the economic growth of developing ones. Some antinuclear groups have contested the assumption that a growth economy based on increased energy consumption is really necessary. Nevertheless, the technological foundation of an industrial society is an abundant energy supply.[1]

The Energy Policy Project of the Ford Foundation predicted in 1974 that, as natural gas and oil production leveled off by the year 2000, nuclear power would supply 25 percent of U.S. energy needs. The researchers assumed that although use of coal and alternative forms of energy would increase, nuclear power consumption would grow even more in proportion, ultimately reaching 60 percent of electric power generation. (However, in the 1980s nuclear energy produces less than 18 percent of U.S. electricity.[2])

An increase in the use of nuclear power would not necessarily reduce dependence on foreign oil, for oil provides only 5.5 percent of electricity generation. Most oil use is in transportation—this is the reason for continuing dependence on foreign oil.[3]

Electricity generation does require vast amounts of energy, and if the need for electricity increases, more power plants will have to be constructed. The cost of producing energy is a major factor in the energy problems of the United States. According to the 1974 Energy Policy Project, the consumption of energy in the industrial and transportation sectors will continue to increase, while household and commercial use of energy will rise moderately because the United States has an advanced

159

energy infrastructure.[4] This study, however, underestimated the effects conservation policies could have.

In the United States, energy and energy-intensive industries account for at least 10 percent of all employment: 3 percent in energy industries, and 7 percent in energy-intensive manufacturing. A 1973 study by the House Committee on Science and Astronautics shows where these employees are located.[5] These employment figures, summarized in Table 6, do not reflect the large numbers of transportation employees and government and scientific personnel involved in energy research and development.

Table 6. Employees in U.S. Energy Industries

Industry Classification	Number of Employees	Total Employment (%)
Employment in energy industries	2,190,000	2.96
Coal mining	138,000	0.19
Oil and natural gas	261,000	0.35
Pipeline transportation	18,000	0.02
Petroleum and coal products	191,000	0.26
Electric and gas companies	464,000	0.63
Combination companies	190,000	0.26
Gasoline service stations	618,000	0.84
Petroleum bulk stations	212,000	0.28
Fuel and ice dealers	99,000	0.13
Employment in energy-intensive industries	4,828,000	7.31
Primary metals	1,178,000	1.60
Stone, clay, and glass	588,000	0.80
Food products	1,582,000	2.10
Paper products	635,000	0.90
Chemical products	845,000	1.10
Total	7,603,000	10.27

Source: Committee on Science and Astronautics, *Energy Facts 1973* (Washington, D.C.: Government Printing Office, 1973), p. 144. These 1971 figures have probably substantially changed in the 1980s, but the chart is intended to show the *extensiveness* of employment in energy and energy-intensive industries. No comparable study in the 1980s was available, nor figures on employment in the nuclear industry itself.

Energy is also related to inflation. In the year ending January 1974, the U.S. wholesale price index rose by 20.8 percent, and two-thirds of that increase was due to food and fuel prices. The mechanization of American agriculture is so intensive that the increase in food prices was itself energy related; oil is important in the manufacture of fertilizer as well. Fuel costs rose by 74 percent; the blast furnace and steel industries were the most affected, followed by petroleum refining, paper milling, and plastics and synthetics.[6]

The cost of producing all forms of energy has continued to escalate. Growth in energy consumption in the 1980s was slower than predicted, helping to reduce the general inflation rate; the price of oil produced by foreign nations dropped. But in the United States this has not reduced the cost of nuclear power plants, nor the cost of mining coal, nor the cost of producing domestic oil and gas. A recession in the oil-producing American states occurred as they were unable to compete with lower foreign-oil prices.

Nuclear power supplies almost 18 percent of the total electricity generated in the United States in the late 1980s. Currently, 108 nuclear power plants are authorized to operate within the United States and approximately 370 reactors are operating worldwide in noncommunist countries. Approximately thirty reactors are to come on line during the next decade in the United States. The ordering of new nuclear power plants remains at a virtual standstill, although many construction projects are near completion.

The greatest growth in nuclear power had been planned for New England. The costs of coal-generated electricity there were seen as simply too high: transportation of low-sulfur western coal to eastern markets is expensive, as are stack gas scrubbers that reduce air pollution from coal-fired plants. Moreover, meeting the stringent air-quality standards in the Northeast increases the cost of coal-fired stations by as much as 20 percent. (The same standards do not exist in the Midwest, but winds carry midwestern emissions to the Northeast, where they contribute to the region's serious acid-rain problem.)

But the costs of nuclear energy are also high. One reason for these costs is the plants' unreliability and inefficiency. The environmental director of Businessmen and Professional People in the Public Interest, David Comey, asserted in 1975 that nuclear power plants run at a lower capacity than coal-fired plants and are often out of commission for safety checks or refueling. Comey calculated that if capacity fell below 55 percent, coal-fired plants would be cheaper to operate than nuclear power plants—even though coal plants generally run at 60 percent of capacity.[7] (Capacity figures for nuclear power plants are based on statistical means. For example, in May 1975 the mean capacity at which plants operated was 57 percent. Yankee Rowe operated at 97.6 percent and the Palisades reactor at 19.7 percent of capacity.[8]) On the average, nuclear power plants spend 40 percent to 45 percent of their time undergoing repairs or routine service.[9]

Nuclear power plants are also expensive to build. It is increasing capital costs that lead to most cancelations of and construction delays in nuclear power plants. Construction costs quadrupled between 1970 and 1985. (The increase was comparable for coal plants.)

There is no clear economic advantage for nuclear power plants over coal plants. Some utilities have even divested themselves of nuclear plants; Con Edison, for example, sold its Indian Point reactor to the state of New York. Thus, the slump in the nuclear industry has been due to financial obstacles as well as to environmentalist opposition to nuclear-power-plant construction.

Yet much of American industry would now appear to have a direct or indirect interest in the nuclear industry, even though for much of its history nuclear power was a government monopoly. In 1973, the House Select Committee on Small Business found that energy companies were buying up and merging with other types of energy companies. In particular, oil companies were acquiring coal properties, uranium, and natural-gas supplies. The committee reported that the major oil corporations owned 84 percent of refining capacity, 72 percent of natural-gas production, 30 percent of coal reserves, and 25 percent of uranium-milling capacity.[10] The Exxon, Gulf, Sohio, Continental, and Phillips oil companies all now have significant interests in the nuclear industry.

Many companies are also involved in the manufacture of nuclear reactors. Westinghouse and General Electric are the most important manufacturers of nuclear equipment, but the Thomas register indicates that nuclear-reactor components are also manufactured by Atomics International, Rockwell, Kaiser Engineers, and over thirty smaller companies. And even Westinghouse and General Electric play a relatively minor role in nuclear-power-plant construction compared with the utilities. There simply is no separate, monolithic nuclear industry; much of American industry is tied into it.

Appendix C:
The Nuclear Fuel Cycle

It is an error to assume that anyone who is not an engineer or physical scientist is incompetent to research the esoteric subject of nuclear technology, as political scientist Robert Dahl has noted. Social scientists are capable of grasping at least the technical complexities of physical sciences that pertain to their own research.[1] One outstanding characteristic of many antinuclear activists is their high level of knowledge of nuclear technology.

One fundamental distinction that *must* be kept in mind when analyzing nuclear power is the distinction between a fission reaction and a fusion reaction. Uranium is a *fissionable* material, for when its nucleus absorbs a neutron, it can split, or undergo fission, into two smaller nuclei. The process releases significant amounts of energy and two or three neutrons. All nuclear reactors opposed by movement groups operate on the fission principle.

In the *fusion* process, hydrogen nuclei and deuterium atoms are fused to produce energy. Fusion reactors remain at the research stage, but they are a potentially unlimited source of energy. Fusion is the process by which the sun produces energy. Almost by default, the antinuclear movement has precluded nuclear fusion as an alternative-energy source (as it has also had a negative effect on the development of alternative reactors such as thermal converters, which utilize thorium rather than uranium, and high-temperature gas-cooled reactors). This may well have been an unanticipated consequence of the antinuclear movement.

The issues and controversies raised by the antinuclear movement involve what is known as the *nuclear fuel cycle*. This generic term refers to all phases of production involved in using nuclear energy as a com-

163

mercial power source. An understanding of the nuclear fuel cycle provides insight into the aspects of nuclear power that concern antinuclear groups.

Uranium is the basis of fuel for nuclear power (but it can be used in its natural state only in a specific type of plant manufactured in Canada). Thus, *uranium mining and milling* are the first stage of the nuclear fuel cycle. To become fuel for most reactors, uranium oxide must then undergo an expensive and complex industrial process to *convert and enrich* it. The third major stage is *nuclear-power-plant operation,* followed by *fuel reprocessing* and *storage of the radioactive wastes.* There are many types of nuclear reactors, several alternative methods of uranium enrichment, and many different kinds of radioactive wastes.

Uranium Mining and Milling

In the first stage of the nuclear fuel cycle, natural uranium is mined in open pits and through strip mining (presenting still another environmental problem). Uranium mines in the United States are concentrated in the Wyoming Basin, the Colorado Plateau, and the Gulf Plains. The cheapest recoverable reserves are in New Mexico, Wyoming, Texas, Utah, and Colorado. In addition, the United States imports about one-third of the uranium produced worldwide. (An embargo that prohibited uranium-ore imports has been phased out.) Canada, South Africa, Sweden, Spain, France, Gabon, Niger, and Australia all have large reserves.[2] More large reserves were found in Canada and Australia in the 1980s. (This, however, does not mean that some nations will no longer be dependent on others for their uranium supply; nor does it solve environmental and safety questions.)

After uranium is mined, it is milled, or crushed, to a concentrate containing about 85 percent uranium oxide, or "yellowcake."[3] Since uranium ore contains only about 1 percent uranium, large amounts of wastes, called "tailings," accumulate. These radioactive wastes discharge radon-222 gas into the air, and the presence of thorium-230 makes the tailings radioactive for thousands of years. (The EPA estimates that individuals in the surrounding population receive radioactive exposure in their lungs from the radon releases.[4] Union of Concerned Scientists studies also indicate that the tailings piles are hazardous to the health of miners.[5])

Projections of future uranium reserves are based on many factors, such as the location and depth of the ore, the percentage of uranium oxide in the ore, the cost of extraction technology, and the transportation facilities available.

Stockpiles of uranium exist for nuclear-weapons programs, but the adequacy of future reserves depends on the future of the liquid-metal fast breeder reactor, whose technological advantage is that it produces more fuel than it consumes. Proponents of nuclear power believe that the perfection of the fast breeder reactor for commercial use will solve the problem of the fuel supply. But if the breeder is successfully blocked by the antinuclear movement, the uranium supply could become a problem. (One scientist-critic, M. C. Day, bases his antinuclear position on the fact that the technology on which the uranium supply relies is unproven. Until uranium reserves are proved adequate, Day argues, a slowdown or moratorium in the construction of light-water reactors is justified.[6])

With international use of nuclear power, uranium is becoming even more valuable as a resource. Som   ....archers have explored the possibility of a uranium-exporters' cartel, which would make the United States vulnerable to a uranium embargo in the future.[7] Since oil corporations have been expanding horizontally into uranium mining, the potential for monopolistic price-fixing by a domestic cartel is more likely. These fears were substantiated in hearings before Congress that documented the existence of a conspiracy between Gulf and Tenneco to raise the price of uranium.

Uranium Conversion and Enrichment

After the uranium oxide is milled, it is converted into uranium hexafluoride (UF_6), which is maintained in a gaseous state. UF_6 contains isotopes of uranium, including U-235 and U-238. Then the uranium is enriched.

Enrichment is the process of increasing the concentration of fissionable U-235 atoms above what occurs in natural uranium. It is the most complex step, in which isotopes are separated. The gaseous UF_6 is diffused through porous barriers so that the lighter U-235 molecules are diluted from the heavier U-238 molecules. The UF_6 gas must be continuously diffused through thousands of barriers, pumped into them by compressors driven by electric motors that consume vast amounts of electricty. Enrichment plants easily cover ninety acres of land, use about 400 million gallons of recirculating cooling water every day, and consume 1,300 megawatts of electric power.[8] The United States government owns all three U.S. gaseous-diffusion plants, which are located at Oak Ridge,

Tennessee; Paducah, Kentucky; and Portsmouth, Ohio. Conversion plants are located at Hematite, Missouri; Apollo, Pennsylvania; and Erwin, Tennessee.

Gas-centrifugal processes are also usable for the isotopic separation but are not as technologically developed as gaseous-diffusion processes. Soviet and American scientists working independently have discovered still a third process. It involves focusing a laser beam that is precisely tuned to the vibrational frequency of an isotope on to it to free it from its chemical compound. If it were used to extract U-235 from uranium ore, the process would supersede the centrifuge and diffusion methods and make enriched uranium easily available.

Uranium enrichment has become a several-billion-dollar-a-year market. At the same time, the U.S. monopoly is being eroded. Because of this, in 1969 the Atomic Industrial Forum (a trade association of the nuclear industry) proposed that uranium-enrichment facilities be put into the hands of private industry. The federal government restricts the sale of enriched uranium, but private control would make the industry more competitive with French and German firms on the world market. (The proposal was supported by President Nixon and the AEC, but it failed to gain support in Congress, which was wary that it would create an "enrichment directorate." Legislation to transfer future enrichment facilities to private enterprise was also requested by President Ford but was not pursued by the Carter administration.)

Large corporations such as Bechtel, Goodyear, Exxon, and General Electric have formed consortia to enter the uranium-enrichment field, hoping to be stronger in international competition. The industry also believes that the United States' balance of payments would benefit from increased sales of enriched uranium and reactor exports, offsetting losses suffered from OPEC policies. The fear often expressed in the antinuclear literature is that these corporations' integration produces conflicts of interests that adversely affect the pricing and competitiveness of solar-energy technologies.

The nuclear industry has been concerned with the profitability and availability of uranium for export rather than with the effective safeguarding of nuclear materials in the expanding world market. In the 1980s, there is a world oversupply of enriched uranium. France and Britain reprocess nuclear fuels, and West Germany and Japan are expected to enter the market in the 1990s. The USSR also exports uranium, and the technology has also spread to Brazil and Pakistan on a smaller scale.

Nuclear-Power-Plant Operation

The enriched uranium is converted chemically to metal or oxide. It is fabricated into fuel elements that are then clad in alloy tubing. Fabrication facilities are located in Oklahoma (Kerr-McGee)[9], California (Gulf General Atomic), Connecticut, and Virginia. The fabricated fuel elements are transported to a nuclear reactor, loaded, and irradiated for approximately three years.

Electric-power generation in nuclear power plants operates on the same principle as in fossil-fuel plants, except that steam is generated by nuclear fission rather than by the combustion of fossil fuels. Nuclear reactors are classified according to the type of fuel used, the moderator controls the fission process, and the type of coolant used. For fuel, plants use either natural or enriched uranium. The moderator may be ordinary or "light" water; carbon; or "heavy" water, which contains deuterium. Heavy water is the best moderator, but it is very expensive. Carbon is cheap, but it cannot serve as both a moderator and a coolant, as water can. Since water can, light-water reactors are the most common. But light water cannot moderate well enough to sustain a chain reaction in natural uranium, so it must be used with enriched uranium. Heavy water and carbon may be used with either natural or enriched uranium, and in more advanced reactors molten salt and gas are used as coolants.[10]

Individual reactor units have a capacity of up to 1,200 megawatts. The plants have lower thermal efficiency than modern fossil-fuel plants and, therefore, a higher conversion loss of energy. Plants with open cooling systems discharge heat into lakes, rivers, canals, and evaporation ponds. To protect the environment, many nuclear power plants now have closed cooling systems that transfer heat directly into the atmosphere through cooling towers or recycle the cooling water back to the condenser.[11] Nevertheless, thermal pollution remains a major concern of antinuclear groups.

At this stage in the nuclear fuel cycle, a nuclear accident may occur if the plant's cooling system malfunctions and contributes to a core meltdown. This would release large amounts of radioactive materials into the environment. The nuclear industry has taken an important precaution to prevent radioactive materials from being released in an accident: containment enclosures have been constructed around reactor cores.

Fossil-fuel plants produce sulfur oxides, carbon monoxide, nitrogen oxides, hydrocarbons, and dust. Nuclear power plants produce radioactive materials largely contained within the reactor fuel elements; radiation emitted from normal plant operation is minimal.

Bernard Cohen, a nuclear physicist, has argued that the air pollution produced by a coal-fired plant kills more people every few days than a nuclear power plant would kill in thirty years (without an accident). [12] On the other hand, environmentalist David Comey claims that if all nuclear power plants are built as scheduled, 5.7 million deaths will occur over the next 80,000 years. Since most would occur outside the United States, this would be "a paradigm example of imperialism."[13]

Fuel Reprocessing

Spent fuel from nuclear reactors is removed, and the highly radioactive material is shipped in heavy lead casks to nuclear-fuel reprocessing plants. Nuclear-fuel reprocessing involves recovering the transuranium wastes that uranium and plutonium have produced during the fission of U-235 in normal power-plant operation.

In a reprocessing plant, spent fuel assemblies are unloaded under water and cooled. They are mechanically chopped into small pieces and dissolved by a Purex process. The dissolved fuel is run through extraction cycles to separate the uranium and plutonium from the waste fission products, and the solid wastes are buried near the plant. Krypton-85 is released to the environment during reprocessing, and 25 percent of the tritium is also emitted. Only a minute percentage of uranium and plutonium remains in radioactive wastes after reprocessing.

Until the 1960s, all nuclear-fuel reprocessing took place in government installations in Washington, Idaho, and Georgia. The first private corporation received a construction permit in 1963 for a plant in West Valley, New York. Between 1966 and 1971, radioactive emissions from this plant were so high that major modifications in its design were required. It has since been closed permanently.

The recovery of the transuranic plutonium is desired by the nuclear industry because plutonium is a primary weapons-grade material. It can also be recycled for use in the fast breeder reactor.

Plutonium is one of the most toxic substances known to man and the most toxic transuranic element. It is hazardous even if only 10^{-6} grams are deposited in lungs or bone tissue, where it tends to concentrate. The radiological hazard of plutonium is 10,000 times that of natural uranium and its daughters. The yield of Pu-239 and Pu-240 from one metric ton of nuclear fuel is seventy grams after five hundred years. With the projected five hundred or more nuclear reactors worldwide by the year 2000, there would be 25,000 tons of accumulated wastes and 24 tons of Pu-239.

After eight hundred years, fission-product decay generally drops by a factor of several million, and the wastes have a toxicity only fifty times greater than a similar volume of natural uranium does. But decay of Pu-239 takes 250,000 years.

Storage of Radioactive Wastes

Wastes are produced in each stage of the nuclear fuel cycle. Solid wastes are commonly metallic and are stored in concrete silos on site for radioactive decay. Sea disposal has been used by some countries. Highly radioactive wastes contain the bulk of radioactive fission products.

The highly radioactive liquid wastes that result from nuclear fuels reprocessing include strontium 90, which concentrates in human bones; cesium, which lodges in muscles; ruthenium and cobalt in the intestinal lining; and tritium in the entire body. Most of these isotopes have a long physical half-life.

The liquid wastes are reconcentrated and stored as slurries in underground steel tanks at Hanford Works in Washington state and Savannah River, South Carolina. Some 600,000 tons have accumulated as of the 1970s, or 90 million gallons since World War II. Leakage from these tanks has been reported, and an AEC document even speculated that a chain reaction could possibly occur from the spilled wastes.

A permanent waste-disposal plan has not been approved. Proposals have included storing the wastes in underground caverns excavated by nuclear weapons, placing them in solar orbit, and burying them under Antarctic ice. Disposal of wastes in solar orbit brings the danger of reentry burnups, such as occurred in April 1964 when a thermoelectric satellite containing nine thousand grams of plutonium disintegrated in reentry. Depositing them under Antarctic ice poses the danger that the materials will melt their way into underground channels leading into the sea. Depositing them in caverns excavated by nuclear explosions risks the creation of geologic strains.[14]

Savannah, Georgia, has been chosen as the site for interim aboveground storage, and Carlsbad, New Mexico, has been designated as a site for permanent disposal. Other sites have been suggested in poor rural states such as Maine and Mississippi. Ultimately the wastes may be deposited in salt beds or geologic caverns in New Mexico (military wastes) and Nevada. One hope is that the chemistry of fuel reprocessing may improve in the future to allow separation of the long-lived transuranium wastes from actinide wastes in order that they may be burned in fast neutron reactors.[15]

The transportation lines between enrichment plants and power plants and then to reprocessing plants and back to power plants again are critical. Because accidents may occur in the shipment of wastes and materials, antinuclear activists believe that these transportation lines may be hazardous to the public.

The Fast Breeder Reactor

One future source of energy that has been promoted by government policy and the nuclear industry is the fast breeder reactor. This reactor can "breed" nuclear fuel from natural uranium by converting it into plutonium. The plutonium can be used again in the breeder reactor or recycled as fuel in conventional light-water reactors.

The United States breeder program is considerably behind its European counterparts. France and Britain already have breeders in operation, as does the Soviet Union. The only breeder ever to go into operation in the United States is the Fermi reactor, near Detroit. But in 1966 there was a partial core meltdown of this reactor, and it was shut down. The Fermi reactor is still too radioactive to be disassembled, although a portion of it is used for joint experimental research by the United States and the Soviet Union.[16]

The two main types of breeders are the liquid-metal fast breeder reactor (LMFBR) and the high temperature gas-cooled reactor (HTCGR). The gas-cooled reactor is being developed by the Gulf Atomic Corporation at Fort St. Vrain in Colorado. Many scientists think it is the safest of all nuclear reactors, but it has not received significant federal funding. The liquid-metal fast breeder reactor is receiving government funding.

The liquid-metal fast breeder reactor is capable of undergoing a minor nuclear explosion, or hypothetical core disassembly accident (HCDA). Since the breeder also produces plutonium, the development of this reactor is greatly feared by antinuclear groups. It may cost over $10 billion in research alone and would not make electricity much cheaper, if at all. It has the advantage of providing electricity with an unlimited source of fuel. The high-temperature gas-cooled reactor partially breeds U-233 from thorium-232 and does not produce plutonium, but it does produce the same waste-fission products as light-water reactors. This reactor would expand the quantity of nuclear fuel since the United States is self-sufficient in thorium reserves.

A test installation for the liquid-metal breeder reactor, the Fast Flux Test Facility in Richland, Washington, is near completion, and the first plant utilizing the breeder concept is under construction on the Clinch River in Tennessee. The United States government has already invested $2 billion in the project, equaling its total investment in the Manhattan Project to develop the atomic bomb.

If sodium coolant is blocked off to the core of a breeder, it may reach "autocatalytic criticality" in a few minutes: the fuel is compressed and collects on the walls of the reactor core, allowing a spontaneous and uncontrolled nuclear reaction to occur. The dispersion of plutonium in such a nuclear accident would have severe consequences, for plutonium is a self-distributing aerosol that travels on small air currents. If 4.4 pounds of plutonium were released into the air, inhabitants 1,000 feet downwind would be certain to contract cancer, and forty miles downwind 1 percent of the inhabitants would get cancer. If inhaled, 1/28,000 ounce of Pu-239 oxide causes death within weeks by destroying lung tissue. Amounts five hundred times smaller can cause cancer of the lung, lymph, liver, bone, and other organs.[17]

These fearsome possibilities have made government insurance-liability limits controversial. Private insurance refused to underwrite the fledgling nuclear industry in the 1950s, so government insurance was provided—an important first step in commercializing nuclear energy. The Price-Anderson Act of 1957 provided for liability of a flat $560 million for any one accident, regardless of the number of people or amount of property damaged. Private insurance companies now make $160 million worth of insurance available to the nuclear industry, and the balance is provided by the federal government and retroactive assessments to each plant of $5 million in the event of an accident.

But estimates of property damage from a nuclear-power-plant accident range from $17 to $280 billion dollars. The government insurance program is actually being decreased and phased out under the 1974 amendments to the Price-Anderson Act. New insurance plans are under consideration, but these plans do not cover all phases of the nuclear fuel cycle, only normal power-plant operation.

Appendix D:
Sample of Antinuclear Groups

The initial sample of antinuclear groups for this study was taken from a list entered into the *Congressional Record* 121, no. 75(12 May 1975): 109, by Senator Mike Gravel (D-Alaska). I collected literature from each group between March 1975 and November 1976 by mailing postcards requesting information about its activities and organization. I identified myself as a doctoral candidate in sociology at Rutgers University doing research on the antinuclear movement. Many of the addresses were obtained from a newsletter entitled *People and Energy,* published by the Center for Science in the Public Interest in Washington, D.C.

Only two groups did not respond to requests for information. Several organizations, such as the Clamshell Alliance and the Environmentalists for Full Employment, never appeared on the initial list. I selected forty groups on the basis of the attention given to them by the mass media and my own evaluation of their significance to the movement for more intensive study. The literature sent to me was only one of many sources of my knowledge of their activities.

Three asterisks indicate that the group was selected for intensive study and two asterisks show that it was only of secondary importance. One asterisk indicates that the group was contacted for information (not all groups were contacted). The categories for the groups are my own creation.

National or Regional Antinuclear Groups
***Businessmen and Professional People in the Public Interest
    (Chicago)
 *Common Cause

***Consolidated National Intervenors
***New England Coalition on Nuclear Pollution, Inc.
***People for Proof
***Supporters of Silkwood
***Task Force against Nuclear Pollution
***Western Bloc

Environmental/Ecology Groups
***Congresswatch
  *Environmental Action Foundation
  *Environmental Policy Center
  **Florida Audubon Society
***Friends of the Earth
    Hudson River Sloop Restoration, Inc.
***National Resources Defense Council
    Piedmont Organic Movement
***Sierra Club
  *Wilderness Society
    Zero Population Growth

Farmer Organizations against Nuclear Power
    4-H Earthkeepers (Croton, New York)
    Jefferson County [Wisconsin] Farm Bureau
    Kansas Farmers Union
    National Farmers Organization (Wood Falls, Wisconsin)
  *Nebraska Low-Energy Agriculture Project
    Vermont Natural Food and Farming Association

Labor Unions against Nuclear Power
    Amalgamated Meat Cutters and Butcher Workmen, Executive
        Board, Local 525 (Asheville, North Carolina)
    American Association of Retired Persons, Chapter 727 (Tuckerton,
        New Jersey)
  *Central Labor Union (Catawba, South Carolina)
    Communication Workers of America, Executive Board, Local 5503
        (Milwaukee)
    UAW Community Action Program Council (Lima, Ohio)

Local Environmental/Antinuclear Groups
 Alternative Energy Coalition (Turners Falls, Massachusetts)
 Americans for Safe Energy (Lafayette, Indiana)
 Anti-plutonium League (Urbana, Illinois)
 Biocides Recycling Group (Denver)
 [North] Carolinians for Safe Energy
 Citizens Action for Safe Energy (Oklahoma)
 Citizens against Nuclear Dangers (Berwick, Pennsylvania)
 Citizens Association for Safe Energy (Croton, New York)
 Citizens Association for Sound Energy (Dallas)
 Citizens Committee for Protection of the Environment (Ossining,
     New York)
 Citizens Energy Council (Allendale, New Jersey)
 Citizens Energy Council of West New York
 Citizens for a Safe Environment (Harrisburg, Pennsylvania)
 Citizens for Environmental Action (Iowa City)
 Citizens for Safe Power (San Antonio, Texas)
 Citizens for Tomorrow (Wisconsin)
 Citizens League for Education about Nuclear Energy (New
     Rochelle, New York)
 Citizens to Preserve the Hudson Valley (Catskill, New York)
 *Citizens United for Responsible Energy (Iowa)
 Coalition for a Safe Environment (Seattle)
 Coalition for the Environment (Fort Wayne, Indiana)
 Columbia County Survival Committee (Germantown, New York)
 Committee for Nuclear Power Plant Postponement (Wilmington,
     Delaware)
 Concerned Californians (San Pedro)
 Concerned Citizens for Nuclear Safety (New York)
 Concerned Citizens of Highland, New York
 Concerned Citizens of Tennessee
 Connecticut Citizen Action Group
 Delaware Valley Committee for Protection of the Environment
 Delaware Valley Conservation Association (Stillwater,
     New Jersey)
 Detroit Area Coalition for the Environment (Michigan)
 Dubuque Environmental Coordination Committee (Iowa)
 Dutchess County Environmental Association (New York)
 Eau Claire Area Ecology Action (Eau Claire, Wisconsin)

Ecology Alert (Bloomsburg, Pennsylvania)
Ecology Information Center (Sacramento, California)
Energy Conservation Organization (Hilyard, Oregon)
*Environmental Action of Colorado
**Environmental Coalition on Nuclear Power (Jenkinstown,
    Pennsylvania)
*Eugene Future Power Committee (Oregon)
Hudson Valley Citizens Watch on Nuclear Safety (New York)
Illinois Citizens for a Nuclear Moratorium (Chicago)
Kansas League against Nuclear Dangers
Keys for Education for Environmental Protection (Summit, New
    Jersey)
Knob and Valley Audubon Society (Louisville, Kentucky)
*League against Nuclear Dangers (Wisconsin)
Mid-America Coalition for Energy Alternatives (Kansas City,
    Missouri)
Minnesota Environmental Control Citizens Movement
North Anna Environmental Coalition (Charlottesville, Virginia)
*New York State Safe Energy Coalition
Ohio Valley Citizens Concerned about Nuclear Pollution (Ohio)
People against the Atom (New York City)
People for Energy and Environmental Responsibility (Lacomb,
    Oregon)
People's Action for Clean Energy (Connecticut)
People's Energy Project (Lawrence, Kansas)
Prince Georges County [Maryland] Environmental Coalition
Protect the Peninsula's Future (Sequim, Washington)
Rhode Islanders for Safe Power
*Safe Power for Maine (Stockton Springs)
Sassafras Audubon Society (Bloomington, Indiana)
Save Solanco Environment (Quarryville, Pennsylvania)
Southeastern Confederation for Safe Energy (Asheville, North
    Carolina)
Southerners for Safe Power (Nashville)
**Stop Nuclear Power (Margate, New Jersey)
Stop Nuclear Power Plants (New Orleans)
Vermonters against Splitting Atoms
York [Pennsylvania] Committee for a Safe Environment
Wappinger Conservation Association (Wappinger Falls, New York)

Political/Quasi-governmental Organizations
    California Democratic Council
    Iowa Democratic party
    Natural Resources Council of Maine
    New York City Environmental Protection Agency
    New York county legislatures: Ulster, Greene, Columbia, Niagara, Dutchess
  *New York State Conservation Council
    Oregon state Democratic party
    Washington Environmental Council (Seattle)

Scientists' Antinuclear Groups/Health Groups
    *Committee for Nuclear Responsibility
***Federation of American Scientists
    *National Health Federation
    Northern Michigan Medical Society
***Union of Concerned Scientists

Student Organizations
    Central Pennsylvania Committee on Nuclear Power (State College)
    *ENACT (Ball State University, Indiana)
  **Public Interest Research Groups: Iowa, Massachusetts, New Jersey
    Purdue Environmental Action
    *University of Texas (Austin) student government
    *Vanderbilt Energy Study Group (Tennessee)

Women's Groups against Nuclear Power
    American Association of University Women (Peekskill, New York)
    *Women's Club (Linwood, New Jersey)
    Church Women United of Tennessee
    Housewives Involved in Pollution Solutions (Illinois)
    League of Women Voters (Riverhead/Southold, New York)
***National Organization for Women
    Stewardess Alumnae Association (Florida chapter)
    Women's Christian Temperance Union (Quarryville, Pennsylvania)
    Women for Peace (Chicago)

Religious Groups against Nuclear Power
   Council of Churches (Springfield, Massachusetts)
   Dubuque Council of Churches (Iowa)
***National Council of the Churches of Christ
   New Jersey Friends (Quaker) Council (Princeton, New Jersey)
   Religious Society of Friends (Quakers) (Harrisburg, Pennsylvania)

Notes and References

Chapter One

1. The first Maine referendum, in 1980, was on a proposed Nuclear Fission Control Act that would have prohibited electric-power generation by nuclear-fission power plants in Maine, including by existing facilities. This would have shut down Maine Yankee, the state's only nuclear power plant. The 23 September results were 59.1 percent no and 40.9 percent yes (*Maine Sunday Telegram*, 28 September 1980, 24A). One year later, a referendum to elect public-utilities commissioners and formally to define state energy policy in terms of nonnuclear alternatives was also defeated. Undaunted, the Maine Nuclear Referendum Committee tried to put on the ballot in 1985 a referendum to close down Maine Yankee in five years by public mandate. A 1987 referendum to close any facility producing nuclear wastes was defeated by a margin similar to that of the first referendum.

2. For a history of the Atomic Energy Commission between 1947 and 1952, see Richard G. Hewlett and Francis Duncan, *Atomic Shield* (University Park: Pennsylvania State University Press, 1974).

3. A good analysis of these early struggles against the military may be found in Stuart S. Blume, *Toward A Political Sociology of Science* (New York: Free Press, 1974).

4. Franz Schurmann, *The Logic of World Power* (New York: Pantheon Books, 1974).

5. For an insightful view of this decision, see Barton J. Bernstein, "Roosevelt, Truman, and the Atomic Bomb, 1941–1945: A Reinterpretation," *Political Science Quarterly* 90 (Spring 1975):23–69.

6. See Walter and Miriam Schneir, *Invitation to an Inquiry: Reopening the "Atom Spy" Case* (Baltimore: Penguin Press, 1973).

7. See Aaron Wildavsky, *Dixon-Yates: A Study in Power Politics* (New Haven, Conn.: Yale University Press, 1962).

8. Corbin Allardice and Edward Trapnell, *The Atomic Energy Commission* (New York: Praeger, 1974).

9. Reported in Richard S. Lewis, *The Nuclear Power Rebellion* (New York: Viking, 1972).

10. See Francis Parkin, *Middle Class Radicalism: The Social Bases of the British Campaign for Nuclear Disarmament* (Manchester, England: University of Manchester Press, 1968).

11. Lewis, *Nuclear Power Rebellion.*

12. Ibid.

13. Two studies of cancer rates near Maine Yankee did find higher than normal rates of cancer, but not the types known to be caused by radiation. Reported in "Deaths near N-plants studied," *Evening Express* (Portland, Maine), 5 February 1988.

14. *Report of the President's Commission on the Accident at Three Mile Island* (Washington, D.C.: U.S. Government Printing Office, 1979).

15. Arthur C. Upton, "The Biological Effects of Low-Level Ionizing Radiation," *Scientific American* 246 (1982):41–50.

16. Dorothy Nelkin, *Nuclear Power and Its Critics: The Cayuga Lake Controversy* (Ithaca, N.Y.: Cornell University Press, 1971), 70, 117–19.

17. Ibid.

18. Steven Ebbin and Raphael Kasper, *Citizen Groups and the Nuclear Power Controversy* (Cambridge, Mass.: MIT Press, 1974).

19. Ibid., 4.

20. John G. Fuller, *We Almost Lost Detroit* (New York: Readers Digest, 1975).

21. See Mark Hertsgaard, *Nuclear Inc.* (New York: Pantheon, 1983), for a detailed analysis of nuclear energy policy in the first years of the Reagan administration.

22. The struggle over government reorganization to meet the energy crisis is best documented in *National Journal Reports* during 1974 and 1975. For 1974, see 12 January: 59–61; 16 February: 229–34; 23 March: 439–41; 20 April: 588–91; for 1975, see 1 March: 305–13; 22 March: 419–29; 4 May: 647–58; 29 June: 962–68; 5 July: 983; 2 November: 1635–44; 14 December: 1868–70.

23. This synopsis of events was constructed from a variety of sources, mainly the *New York Times* and *People and Energy—News of Citizen Action on Energy,* a newsletter published by the Center for Science in the Public Interest in Washington, D.C., during 1975 and 1976. The items are too numerous to warrant separate footnotes, and the events during this time period were carefully followed by the author.

24. Srouji reappeared with a published book, much of which focused on Silkwood. See Jacque Srouji, *Critical Mass* (Nashville, Tenn.: Aurora Publishers, 1977).

25. This summary of events during 1977 is taken from items appearing in the *New York Times.*

26. See the *Philadelphia Inquirer,* 1 April 1979, for a detailed account of the Three Mile Island crisis.

27. This was the second death of an antinuclear demonstrator. The first had occurred during a demonstration in Fessenheim, France, in 1977.

28. A first report on the Whyl demonstration appeared in the *New York Times* on 28 August 1975 in the article "West German Farmer's Resistance Forces Review of Nuclear Power Plants." A follow-up analysis by William Sweet, "The Opposition to Nuclear Power in Europe," appeared in the *Bulletin of the Atomic Scientists* 33 (1977): 40–47. See also John J. Berger, *Nuclear Power: The Unviable Option* (New York: Ramparts Press, 1977), 330–34. Whyl was the first demonstration of its kind in Western Europe.

29. Dorothy Nelkin and Michael Pollack, "Political Parties and the Nuclear Energy Debate in France and Germany," *Comparative Politics,* January 1980, 127–41.

30. Ibid., 129.

31. Etienne Bauer et al., "Nuclear Energy—a Fateful Choice for France," *Bulletin of the Atomic Scientists* 32 (January 1976): 37–41.

32. "Giscard's Nuclear Salesmanship," *New Statesman* 99 (25 January 1980):112.

33. Swedish nuclear opposition is documented in Lennard Daleus, "A Moratorium in Name Only," *Bulletin of the Atomic Scientists* 31 (1975):27–33.

34. Peter James, "The Nuclear Issue in Swedish Politics," *World Today,* December 1979, 499–507.

35. Nancy E. Abrahams, "Nuclear Politics in Sweden," *Environment* 21 (12 July 1980):75.

36. Brian Trench, "Massive Protest May Stall Reactors," *New Statesman* 98 (9 November 1979): 716.

37. "Spain Sets Up Shop," *Economist* 273 (12 July 1979):75.

38. Sweet, "Opposition to Nuclear Power," 40–47.

39. *New York Times,* 21 February 1980, 10.

40. "Going Nuclear, Slowly," *Economist* 273 (22 December 1979):50–51.

41. Gabriel Tonay, "First Victory for East Europe's Anti-Nuclear Lobby," *New Statesman* 98 (9 November 1979): 716–17.

42. Robert C. Paehlke, "Canada—Three Nuclear Inquiries Conclude," *Environment* 21 (May 1979):41.

43. Hertsgaard, *Nuclear Inc.,* 216.

44. These inferences are drawn from a survey of articles concerning nuclear power that appeared in the *New York Times* between 1980 and 1984.

45. Financing the construction of nuclear power plants bankrupted Public Service of New Hampshire in 1988, but other utilities faced with these difficulties continue to operate. Washington Public Power Supply System still exists as a public utility, despite its large default.

46. These policy changes were the subject of an intensive analysis in Hertsgaard, *Nuclear Inc.,* 210–39.

47. This descriptive account is based on Bennett Ramberg, "Learning from Chernobyl," *Foreign Affairs* 65 (1986):304–28; "Chernobyl: The Emerging Story," *Bulletin of the Atomic Scientists* (August/September 1986): 18–60 (twelve

articles); Mike Edwards and Steve Raymer, "Chernobyl—One Year After," *National Geographic* 171 (1987):632–53; and articles appearing in the *New York Times* on 30 April and 7 May 1986.

48. Edwards and Raymer, "Chernobyl—One Year After," 640. The figure of 24,000 exposed to radiation is obviously controversial.

49. Estimates of future deaths are even more controversial. I have not attempted to give more credence to one prediction over another.

50. Serge Schmemann, "Chernobyl and the Europeans: Radiation and Doubts Linger," *New York Times,* 12 June 1988.

51. Ellen Graham, "Jump in 1986 Death Rate Sparks Dispute—Did Chernobyl Cause Surge in U.S. Mortality?" *Wall Street Journal* 8 February 1988.

52. Matthew L. Wald, "Need for Bombs, Jobs, Safety Affect Fate of Plutonium Plant," *New York Times,* 14 February 1988.

53. Task Force against Nuclear Pollution bimonthly *Progress Reports,* from September 1974 to September 1975, Washington, D.C.

54. See Gary L. Downey, "Ideology and the Clamshell Identity: Organizational Dilemmas in the Anti-Nuclear Power Movement," *Social Problems* 33 (1986):357–73, and Anna Gyorgy and Friends, *No Nukes: Everyone's Guide to Nuclear Power* (Boston: South End Press, 1979).

55. Upper Great Lakes Green Network newsletter *Green Net,* December 1987.

56. Northern Sun Alliance newsletter *Northern Sun,* March 1988.

57. Social-action theory has important roots in the work of Talcott Parsons, a social theorist affiliated with Harvard University until his death in 1979. Parsons contributed to sociological theory in two main areas. First, he developed the perspective known as structural functionalism, which has dominated American sociology for at least a quarter of a century. Basically, structural functionalism is a way of analyzing societies by looking at how institutions, cultural values, and social norms function to integrate people into a working society. Critics have frequently argued that this focus on society as an integrated entity excludes analysis of the conflicts that exist between social classes and other social groupings. This criticism has often obscured Parsons's contributions to the general theory of social action. A good summary can be found in "An Outline of the Social System," in *Theories of Society,* ed. Talcott Parsons et al. (New York: Free Press, 1961), 30–79.

58. Talcott Parsons, *The Structure of Social Action* (New York: Free Press, 1937).

59. This typology is developed by Talcott Parsons and Edward A. Shils in *Toward A General Theory of Action* (Cambridge, Mass.: Harvard University Press, 1951), part 2.

60. A complete list is available from the Union of Concerned Scientists, 26 Church Street, Cambridge, MA 02238.

61. The concept of instrumental activism derives from the social theory of Talcott Parsons and has been used in a variety of contexts. For example, see Jackson Toby, "Inadequacy, Instrumental Activism, and Adolescent Subculture,"

in *Explorations in General Theory in the Social Sciences,* ed. Jan Loubser et al. (New York: Free Press, 1976), 407–14.

62. Bennet M. Judkins, "The Black Lung Movement: Social Movements and Social Structure," in *Research in Social Movements: Conflict and Change,* ed. Louis Kriesberg (Greenwich, Conn.: JAI Press, 1979), 105–29.

63. Parkin, *Middle Class Radicalism.*

64. Tahi L. Mottl, "The Analysis of Countermovements," *Social Problems* 27 (June 1980):620–34. See also Stanley Albrecht, "Environmental Social Movements and Counter-Movements," in *Social Movements: A Reader and Source Book,* ed. Robert R. Evans (Chicago: Rand-McNally, 1973), 244–62.

65. Atomic Industrial Forum news release "The Nuclear Industry in 1974: The $80 Billion Giant as Underdog," December 1974, New York.

66. W. Donham Crawford, "Energy Demand and the Electric Utility Industry," in *Energy and Public Policy* (New York: Conference Board, 1972), 49–51.

67. A typical pronuclear argument is that there were fewer casualties at Chernobyl than at Bhopal in India. For example, Alvin M. Weinberg, "A Nuclear Power Advocate Reflects on Chernobyl," *Bulletin of the Atomic Scientists* (August/September 1986):57–60.

68. *Bangor Daily News* (Maine), 17 September 1980, 1–2.

69. See chapter 4 for an analysis of the California referendum.

70. Save Maine Yankee, "Maine Yankee Shutdown Referendum Fact Sheet," Augusta, Maine, 1980.

Chapter Two

1. For diverse approaches to the environmentalist movement, see Richard P. Gale, "Social Movements and the State: The Environmental Movement, Countermovement, and Government Agencies," *Sociological Perspectives* 29 (1986):202–40; Rice Odell, *Environmental Awakening: The New Revolution to Protect the Earth* (Cambridge, Mass.: Ballinger Publishing Co., 1980); Allan Schnaiberg, *The Environment: From Surplus to Scarcity* (New York: Oxford University Press, 1980); and Hans Kruse, "Development and Environment: A political Science Approach," in *The Politics of Environmental Policy,* ed. Lester W. Milbrath and Frederick R. Inscho (Beverly Hills, Calif.: Sage Publications, 1975).

2. Michael McCloskey, *The Sierra Club and Nuclear Power* (San Francisco: Sierra Club, 1975).

3. This account is drawn from materials and legal briefs supplied by the Florida Audubon Society, particularly "Comments upon the Draft Environmental Impact Statement, Westinghouse-Tenneco Offshore Power Systems Development, Blount Island, Duval County, Florida," in *Florida Audubon Society, Maitland, Florida, v. Howard Callaway, Secretary of the Army,* civil no. CA-1692–73, 4 September 1973, before the United States District Court for the District of Columbia. The issue dates back to the early 1970s, and it did not end until 1980.

4. Edward T. LaRoe, "Report to the Florida Audubon Society on the Blount Island Westinghouse-Tenneco Project" (Naples, Fla.: Collier County Conservancy Inc.).

5. Sean Devereaux, "Slanting the News to Destroy a Marsh," *Audubon* 78 (May 1976): 135–37.

6. This controversy over nuclear power in New Jersey was documented by Laura J. Lewis and David Morell in "Nuclear Power and Its Opponents: A New Jersey Case Study" (Princeton, N.J.: Center for Environmental Studies, Princeton University, 1977). Further accounts appear in the newsletter of the Center for Science in the Public Interest, *People and Energy* vols, 1–2 (May 1975–November 1976).

7. The account of this hearing in Atlantic City is based on my own observations at the city hall on 29 March 1976 and on follow-up stories over the next few days in the Newark *Star-Ledger.*

8. See 1976 publicity materials of the Friends of the Earth, San Francisco.

9. Ibid.

10. See various Environmental Alert Group, Public Interest Reports ("Nuclear Terrorism," "Commercial Doomsday Machines," "Breeder Reactors and the Plutonium Economy," "Nuclear Power Plants").

11. Quoted in the newsletter *Critical Mass—the Citizen Movement to Stop Nuclear Power* 1 (April 1975).

12. Mottl, "The Analysis of Countermovements."

13. See *Critical Mass—the Citizen Movement to Stop Nuclear Power.*

14. Ralph Nader, "The Nuclear Advocates," letter to the editor, *New York Times,* 21 April 1974, 38.

15. Augusta, Maine, PIRG, *News and Views* 1 (1975).

16. New Jersey PIRG, "One Year in Review," (Trenton) (1976).

17. New Jersey PIRG, "Everything You Wanted to Know about Nuclear Power But Were Afraid to Find Out," (Trenton). Unfortunately, Rutgers University students voted to discontinue supporting PIRG from student fees in 1977.

18. William Clark, "What's in a Name?" *Portland Press Herald* (Maine), 18 August 1975.

19. Rob Burgess, "A Pricetag on the Constitution?" Augusta, Maine, PIRG *News and Views* 1 (December 1975): 2.

20. See annual reports (1971, 1973, 1975) of Business and Professional People in the Public Interest.

21. Thomas B. Cochran, *The Liquid Metal Fast Breeder Reactor* (Baltimore: Johns Hopkins University Press, 1974).

22. Natural Resources Defense Council, "Can We Afford a Plutonium Economy?" NRDC newsletter 3, no. 2. See also, "Citizens Guide: The National Debate on the Handling of Radioactive Wastes" (1975).

23. This reactor has also been criticized by antinuclear groups as having inadequate containment in the event of an accident.

24. Department of Energy report released by Senator John Glenn (D-

Ohio), chairman of the Senate Governmental Affairs Committee, as reported in *Portland Press Herald* (Maine), 14 February 1988.

25. The Bustamente Amendment appeared to have been shelved pending the outcome of the November 1988 general election.

26. Personal observations at DOE meetings at Portland City Hall in Maine during 1987.

27. The Massachusetts referendum went through a constitutional challenge by the owners of Pilgrim and Rowe nuclear power plants, but the state Supreme Court ruled that it could be put before the voters.

28. Dianna Solis, "Texas Nuclear Plant Enters Critical Stage," *Wall Street Journal*, 8 March 1988, 6. The plant reportedly began low-power operation in September 1988.

29. Brochures made available by Comanche Peak Citizens Audit, Fort Worth, Texas.

30. Consumer notice of People's Medical Society, Emmaus, Pennsylvania.

31. Environmentalists for Full Employment, *Jobs and Energy*, no. 1 (1976).

32. See Rebecca Logan and Dorothy Nelkin, "Labor and Nuclear Power," *Environment* 22 (March 1980): 6—12.

33. Ibid.

34. Steven E. Barkan, "Strategic, Tactical, and Organizational Dilemmas of the Protest Movement against Nuclear Power," *Social Problems* 27(October 1979):19–37.

35. See W. B. Devall, "Conservation: An Upper-Middle-Class Social Movement," *Journal of Leisure Research* 2(Spring 1970):123–26.

36. U.S. Labor party, "Stop Ralph Nader—the Nuclear Saboteur" (New York: Campaigner Publishers, 1977).

37. H. A. Cavanaugh, "Where Do the Antis Get Their Money?" *Electrical World*, 15 April and 1 May 1980.

38. Ibid.

39. This information is drawn from James F. Raymond, "A Vermont Yankee in King Burger's Court: Constraints on Judicial Review Under NEPA," *Boston College Environmental Affairs Law Review* 7 (1979):629–64.

40. Ibid, 664.

41. This conclusion is also reached by Alan Schnaiberg in *The Environment: From Surplus to Scarcity* (New York: Oxford University Press, 1980), 418.

Chapter Three

1. The term *ultraelite* is used by Harriet Zuckerman in her study of Nobel laureates, *Scientific Elite* (New York: Free Press, 1977), 11. Elite scientists are

those who have been elected to membership in the National Academy of Scientists. I have used the term somewhat more loosely in this study.

2. This term is also used by Harriet Zuckerman in "Stratification in American Science," *Sociological Inquiry* 40 (Spring/1970): 235–57.

3. See Robert Gilpin and Christopher Wright, *Scientists and National Policy Making* (New York: Columbia University Press, 1964).

4. Robert Gilpin, *American Scientists and Nuclear Weapons Policy* (New York: Basic Books, 1962), 342.

5. Don K. Price, *The Scientific Estate* (Cambridge, Mass.: Harvard University Press, 1965), 83.

6. Ibid., 271.

7. See Edward Shils, *The Torment of Secrecy* (New York: Free Press, 1956) and Michael Rogin, *The Intellectuals and McCarthy* (Cambridge, Mass.: MIT Press, 1967), for documentation of this dark age for American scientists.

8. Daniel Bell, *The Coming of Post-Industrial Society* (New York: Basic Books, 1973), 229.

9. Fred Cottrell, *Energy and Society* (New York: McGraw-Hill, 1955), 207.

10. Federation of American Scientists, *Public Interest Report*, Special Issue with Nuclear Policy Ballot, Washington, D.C., 1975.

11. This history is drawn from Stuart S. Blume, *Toward a Political Sociology of Science* (New York: Free Press, 1974), 160–65.

12. This account is drawn from Arell S. Schurgin and Thomas C. Hollocher, "Lung Cancer among Uranium Mine Workers," in *The Nuclear Fuel Cycle*, ed. The Union of Concerned Scientists (San Francisco: Friends of the Earth, 1974), 116–48.

13. Ibid., 141.

14. Ibid., 129.

15. This account is drawn from Daniel F. Ford and Henry W. Kendall, "Catastrophic Nuclear Accidents," in *The Nuclear Fuel Cycle*, 75–91.

16. U.S. Atomic Energy Commission, "Theoretical Possibilities and Consequences of Major Accidents in Large Nuclear Power Plants (WASH-740)" (Washington, D.C.: U.S. Government Printing Office, 1957).

17. The nuclear industry has not compiled statistics on the number of deaths of construction workers or nuclear-power-plant workers, but newspaper accounts of accidents are common.

18. Bernard J. Cohen, *Nuclear Science and Society* (New York: Doubleday, 1974).

19. David R. Inglis, "Sweet Voice of Reason," *Bulletin of the Atomic Scientists* (September 1974): 50–52.

20. Paul Jacobs, "What You Don't Know May Hurt You," *Mother Jones* 1 (February—March 1976): 35–39.

21. Zuckerman, "Stratification in American Science," 239.

22. Union of Concerned Scientists, "Voter Information Kit" (Cambridge, Mass., 1988).

23. Ben A. Franklin, "Nuclear Agency Assailed by Staff," *New York Times,* 6 March, 1988.

24. Matthew L. Wald, "The Peach Bottom Syndrome," *New York Times,* 27 March 1988.

25. Matthew L. Wald, "Nuclear Agency Said to Lag in Seeking Out Crime," *New York Times,* 31 January 1988.

26. Daniel Utroska, "Holes in the U.S. Nuclear Safety net," *Bulletin of the Atomic Scientists* (July/August 1987):36.

27. Michael Adato and the Union of Concerned Scientists, *Safety Second, the NRC and America's Power Plants* (Bloomington: Indiana University Press, 1987).

28. Ibid., 18.

29. Ibid., 111–15.

30. Ibid., 159.

31. Union of Concerned Scientists, "Voter Information Kit" (1988).

32. See the newsletter of the Committee for Nuclear Responsibility, *Common Sense* (1975). The information on the work of the Nobel laureates is from Zuckerman, *Scientific Elite,* 282–90.

33. Committee for Nuclear Responsibility, "Letter from Jack Lemmon," 1975.

34. Egan O'Connor, "Remarks to a Gathering of Washington D.C. Religious Leaders," in *Congressional Record,* 94th Cong., 1st sess., 1975, 121, no. 124.

35. Ibid.

36. Ibid.

37. Common Cause, "Legislative Report," 1976.

38. National Council of the Churches of Christ, "The Plutonium Economy," 1975.

Chapter Four

1. See the bimonthly "Progress Reports" of the Task Force against Nuclear Pollution, September 1974 to September 1975.

2. Ibid.

3. Mike Gravel, "The Anti-Nuclear Movement." Testimony before the House Energy and Environment Subcommittee, 28 April 1975, *Congressional Record* 121, no. 75: 107–9.

4. Hamilton Fish, "Nuclear Powerplant Construction Ban," *Congressional Record* 121, no. 75: 42.

5. Gravel, "The Anti-Nuclear Movement," 107.

6. Information on these newsletters is available from most state energy

agencies. This sampling came from *Solar Two,* a publication of the Maine Office of Energy Resources, Augusta.

7. Energy Action Committee, "Oil Industry Profits Skyrocket since 1972," news release, 6 March 1976.

8. Letter appealing for funds, sent with Energy Action Committee news release (see note 7).

9. This account is quoted from Larry Gay, "History of Nuke Plant Birth in Rural Vermont," *Recorder* (Greenfield, Mass.), 18 January 1973.

10. Diana Sidebotham, "History and Comments by President of the NECNP," in newsletter of the New England Coalition on Nuclear Pollution, Brattleboro, Vt.

11. Nathaniel Smith, "NECNP gives Support to Nuclear Moratorium," *Recorder* (Greenfield, Mass.), 7 December 1974.

12. New England Coalition on Nuclear Pollution, "Testimony at Seabrook Construction License Hearings," Brattleboro, Vt.

13. An excellent case study of the multitude of federal hearings on the Seabrook controversy is now available. See Donald W. Stever, Jr., *Seabrook and the Nuclear Regulatory Commission* (Hanover, N.H.: University Press of New England, 1980). The book deals primarily with the licensing procedures of the NRC. See also Steven E. Barkan, "Strategic, Tactical, and Organizational Dilemmas of the Protest Movement against Nuclear Power," *Social Problems* 27 (October 1979): 19–37.

14. Quoted in Harvey Wasserman, "Showdown at Seabrook," *Nation* 223 (September 1976): 203–5.

15. Mark Traugott, "Reconceiving Social Movements," *Social Problems* 26 (October 1978): 38–49.

16. Jeannie Christie, "Maine Clamshell Alliance Groups Would Rather Stay Home and Develop Options," *Ellsworth American* (Ellsworth, Me.), 15 March 1979.

17. Jeannie Christie, "Violence Mars Clamshell Demonstration," *Ellsworth American* (Ellsworth, Me.), 15 March 1979.

18. I have followed this controversy for several years. Dozens of articles and news items have appeared in the *Boston Globe* and local Portland, Maine, newspapers concerning Seabrook. Also noteworthy is Matthew L. Wald, "House Debates Troubled Nuclear Plants," *New York Times,* 6 August 1987.

19. "The Vote for Nuclear Power," *New York Times,* 23 May 1976, 1.

20. Edwin Koupal, "The Nuclear Web," in newsletter of the Western Bloc, 1976, Los Angeles.

21. Tahi L. Mottl, "The Analysis of Countermovements."

22. Koupal, "Nuclear Web."

23. Ibid.

24. Edwin A. Koupal, "California Government Agencies v. People's Lobby: A Study in the Abuse of Power," in newsletter of the Western Bloc, November 1975, Los Angeles.

25. Koupal, "Nuclear Web."

26. "Three Engineers Quit G.E. Reactor Division and Volunteer in Anti-Nuclear Movement," quoted in *New York Times,* 3 February 1976, 12.

27. This notion contradicts the idea that persons who have no social ties are most susceptible to the appeals of a social movement.

28. See David A. Snow, Louis A. Zurcher, and Sheldon Ekland-Olson, "Social Networks and Social Movements," *American Sociological Review* 45 (October 1980): 787–801.

29. "Three Engineers Quit," *New York Times,* 12.

30. U.S. Congress, Joint Committee on Atomic energy, "Investigation of Charges Related to Nuclear Safety, 94th Cong., 2d sess., 1976, 2.

31. Ibid.

32. Ibid., 97.

33. Srouji's book, *Critical Mass,* also dwells on the alleged use of drugs by Karen Silkwood.

34. See newsletter *Critical Mass—the Citizens Movement to Stop Nuclear Power,* vol. 1 (November 1975).

35. Ibid.

36. Supporters of Silkwood newsletter, no. 1 (1976).

37. The most detailed accounts of this sequence of events that I have found are Howard Kohn, "Malignant Giant—the Nuclear Industry's Terrible Power and How It Silenced Karen Silkwood," *Rolling Stone,* 27 March 1975; and *Organizer* (November 1975), an issue prepared by Sara Nelson, national coordinator for the Labor Task Force of the National Organization for Women.

38. "The Cost of Karen Silkwood," *Economist,* 26 May 1979, 57. The settlement was later reduced to a smaller sum in federal appeals court.

39. Susan Holleran, "Who Is Karen Silkwood?" in newsletter of Supporters of Silkwood (1976).

40. James Scaminaci III and Riley E. Dunlap, "No Nukes! A Comparison of Participants in Two National Antinuclear Demonstrations," *Sociological Inquiry* 56 (1986):272–82.

41. Anthony E. Ladd, Thomas C. Hood, and Kent D. Van Liere, "Ideological themes in the Antinuclear Movement: Consensus and Diversity," *Sociological Inquiry* 53 (1983):252–72.

42. Ibid., 257.

43. Gary L. Downey, "Ideology and the Clamshell Identity: Organizational Dilemmas in the Anti-Nuclear Power Movement," *Social Problems* 33 (1986): 357–73.

44. Ibid., 367.

45. Alain Touraine, Zsuzska Hegedus, Francois Dubet, and Michael Wieviorka, *Anti-nuclear Protest: The Opposition to Nuclear Energy in France* (Cambridge: Cambridge University Press, 1982). My book review of this volume is in *American Journal of Sociology* 91 (1985):184–86.

46. Paul Schaefer, letter to author, 30 March 1988.

47. Kathy Moody, letter to author, 26 March 1988 (quoted with permission).

Chapter Five

1. Mayer Zald and John D. McCarthy, eds., *The Dynamics of Social Movements* (Cambridge, Mass.: Winthrop Publishers, 1979), 1.

2. David Lilienthal, *Atomic Energy, A New Start* (New York: Harper & Row, 1980), 31.

3. Rudolph Heberle, *Social Movements* (New York: Appleton-Century-Crofts, 1951). Heberle argues that movements are not restricted to a national society or state as political parties are, and that they are bound together more by ideology. The relationship between political parties and social movements is a major focus for Heberle, unlike the resource-mobilization school, and this relationship is important for the impact of movements.

4. The Ford Foundation, *A Time to Choose* (Cambridge, Mass.: Ballinger, 1974).

5. Jimmy Carter, "Three Steps toward Nuclear Responsibility," *Bulletin of the Atomic Scientists* (October 1976):8–14.

6. I have analyzed this television address in "Dilemmas of Energy Policy in the Carter Administration," Rutgers Graduate School Colloquia, New Brunswick, New Jersey, 1977.

7. Bernard J. Cohen, *Nuclear Science and Society* (New York: Doubleday, 1974), 139, 143.

8. Mel Horwitch, "Coal: Constrained Abundance," in *Energy Future,* ed. Robert Stobaugh and Daniel Yergin (New York: Ballantine, 1979), 103.

9. See Michael Wallace, "Dying for Coal: The Struggle for Health and Safety Conditions in American Coal Mining, 1930–82," *Social Forces* 66 (1987):336–64.

10. Federal Energy Administration, *Project Independence* (Washington, D.C.: U.S. Government Printing Office, 1974).

11. Marsha Dubrow, "The Candidates on Energy," *Boston Globe,* 12 October 1980, 9.

12. Hertsgaard, *Nuclear Inc.*

13. John R. Redich, *Military Potential of Latin American Nuclear Energy Programs* (Beverly Hills, Calif.: Sage Publications, 1972). For an analysis of possible nuclear proliferation in the Middle East, see Robert J. Pranger and Dale R. Tahtinen, *Nuclear Threat in the Middle East* (Washington, D.C.: American Enterprise Institute, 1975). A primer on this subject is Henry A. Kissinger, *Nuclear Weapons and Foreign Policy* (New York: W.W. Norton Co., 1969).

14. Congressional Quarterly, *U.S. Defense Policy,* 2d ed. (Washington, D.C.: Congressional Quarterly, 1980), 37–44.

190   *The Antinuclear Movement*

15. See Barbara Rodgers and Zdenek Cervenka, *The Nuclear Axis: Secret Collaboration between West Germany and South Africa* (New York: Times Books, 1978).
16. Serge Schememann, "Nuclear Industry under Fire in Bonn," *New York Times,* 7 February 1988.
17. See Robert Tucker, "Israel and the United States: From Dependence to Nuclear Weapons?" *Commentary* 60 (November 1975): 29–43.
18. Israel still does not acknowledge its nuclear capability.
19. Leonard S. Spector, "Clandestine Nuclear Trade and the Threat of Nuclear Terrorism," in Paul Leventhal and Yonah Alexander, eds., *Preventing Nuclear Terrorism* (Lexington, Mass.: D.C. Heath, 1987), 78–87.
20. Hertsgaard, *Nuclear Inc.*
21. The Green movement in France and its power relative to that of the Greens in West Germany have been the subject of considerable study. For example, see Herbert P. Kitschelt, "Political Opportunity Structures and Political Protest: Anti-Nuclear Movements in Four Democracies," *British Journal of Political Science* 16 (1986): 57–85, and Dorothy Nelkin and Michael Pollack, *The Atom Besieged* (Cambridge, Mass.: MIT Press, 1981).
22. Stephen Salaaf, "The Plutonium Connection: Energy and Arms," *Bulletin of the Atomic Scientists* 36 (1980):18–23.
23. David Albright, "Civilian Inventories of Plutonium and Highly Enriched Uranium," in Leventhal and Alexander, eds., *Preventing Nuclear Terrorism,* 265–91.
24. This market, however, is bottoming out. See "Nuclear Businessmen Fight to Survive in the 1980s," *Economist* 274 (23 February 1980):18–23.
25. The European response is summarized by Steven Greenhouse, "Safety Issues Test Europe's Faith in Nuclear Power," *New York Times,* 31 January 1988, 28.
26. Dennis Goulet, "The Paradox of Technology Transfer," *Bulletin of the Atomic Scientists* 31 (June 1975): 39–46.
27. A summary of Third World nuclear-power development can be found in Alvin Weinberg, Marcelo Alonso, and Jack Barkenbus, *The Nuclear Connection* (New York: Paragon House, 1985).
28. See Ronald Koven, "Nuclear Power is Alive and Well in France," *Boston Globe,* 6 June 1988, 17; and Mary D. Davis, *The Military-Civilian Nuclear Link: A Guide to the French Nuclear Industry* (Boulder, Colo.: Praeger, 1988).
29. Amory B. Lovins, L. Hunter Lovins, and Leonard Ross, "Nuclear Power and Nuclear Bombs," *Foreign Affairs* 38 (Summer 1980): 1137–77.
30. Mason Willrich and Theodore Taylor, *Nuclear Theft: Risks and Safeguards* (Cambridge, Mass.: Ballinger, 1974).
31. Michael Flood, "Nuclear Sabotage," *Bulletin of the Atomic Scientists* (October 1976):29–35.
32. Braddock, Dunn & McDonald, Inc. (BDM), "Analysis of the Terrorist

Threat to the Commercial Nuclear Industry," report submitted to the Nuclear Regulatory Commission (Washington, D.C., 1975).

33. Willrich and Taylor, *Nuclear Theft*, 51.

34. International Task Force on Prevention of Nuclear Terrorism, "The Task Force Report," in Leventhal and Alexander, eds., *Preventing Nuclear Terrorism*, 8.

35. Konrad Kellen, "The Potential for Nuclear Terrorism: A Discussion," in Leventhal and Alexander, eds., *Preventing Nuclear Terrorism*, 104–33.

36. Ibid., 132.

37. Ibid., 125–26.

38. Ibid., 119–20.

39. Jeremiah Denton, "International Terrorism—the Nuclear Dimension," *Terrorism* 9 (1987):113–24.

40. Albright, "Civilian Inventories," 266.

41. Ibid.

42. Daniel Hirsch, Stephanie Murphy, and Bennett Ramberg, "Protecting Reactors from Terrorists," *Bulletin of the Atomic Scientists* (March 1986):21.

43. International Task Force on Prevention of Nuclear Terrorism, "Task Force Report," 25.

44. Daniel Hirsch, "The Truck Bomb and Insider Threats to Nuclear Facilities," in Leventhal and Alexander, eds., *Preventing Nuclear Terrorism*, 207–22.

45. International Task Force on Prevention of Nuclear Terrorism, "Task Force Report," 11.

46. Ebasco Services, Inc., "A Survey of Public and Leadership Attitudes toward Nuclear Power Development in the United States" (New York: Ebasco Services, 1975), and "A Second Survey of Public and Leadership Attitudes toward Nuclear Power Development in the United States" (New York: Ebasco Services, 1976).

47. W. P. Hoar, "Independence for America—Energy," *American Opinion* 22 (May 1979): 5–10.

48. Ebasco Services 1975, 58.

49. Ebasco Services 1976, 69, 95.

50. Ibid., 131.

51. George Gallup, *Opinion Index*, report no. 134, September 1976, 12–16, 99.

52. Oak Ridge National Laboratory, "Executive Summary of ORNL-5124" (Oak Ridge, Tenn. 1976).

53. David L. George and Priscilla L. Southwell, "Opinion on the Diablo Canyon Nuclear Power Plant: The Effects of Situation and Socialization," *Social Science Quarterly* 67 (December 1986):721–35.

54. Ibid., 725.

55. Lovins et al., "Nuclear Power," 1150.

56. Lilienthal, *Atomic Energy*, 109–10.

Chapter Six

1. Leslie White, "Energy and the Evolution of Culture," *American Anthropologist* 45 (1943): 338.

2. Ibid., 251.

3. Pitirim A. Sorokin, *Contemporary Sociological Theories* (New York: Harper & Row, 1928).

4. Ibid., 23–25.

5. Alvin M. Weinberg, "Is Nuclear Energy Necessary?" *Bulletin of the Atomic Scientists* 36 (March 1980): 31–35.

6. Ibid., 33.

7. Amory B. Lovins, L. Hunter Lovins, and Leonard Ross, "Nuclear Power and Nuclear Bombs," *Foreign Affairs* 58 (Summer 1980):1137–77.

8. Energy Research and Development Administration (Department of Energy), *Proposed Final Environmental Impact Statement on the Liquid Metal Fast Breeder Reactor,* vol. 5 (Washington, D.C.: U.S. Government Printing Office, 1974), 3–4.

9. Thorstein Veblen, *The Place of Science* (New York: Russell & Russell, 1961).

10. Talcott Parsons, *Essays in Sociological Theory* (New York: Free Press, 1949), 38.

11. Richard Wilson, letter in *Proposed Final Environmental Impact Statement on the Liquid Metal Fast Breeder Reactor.*

12. Amory B. Lovins and John H. Price, *Non-Nuclear Futures* (New York: Harper Colophon, 1975), 6.

13. Gerald Garvey, "The Potential of Energy Remodeling," in *The Northeastern States Confront the Energy Crisis,* ed. Jay Rolison (Washington, D.C.: National Science Foundation, 1975), 195. Also see Gerald Garvey, *Nuclear Power and Social Planning: The City of the Second Sun* (Lexington, Mass.: Lexington Books, 1977).

14. The Right Reverend Mortimer, bishop of Exeter, "The Moral Aspects," in *Economic and Social Consequences of Nuclear Energy,* ed. Lord Sherfield (London: Oxford University Press, 1972), 69.

15. Gaetano Mosca, *The Ruling Class* (New York: McGraw-Hill, 1939), 121–22.

16. Barrington Moore, Jr., *Injustice: The Social Bases of Obedience and Revolt* (White Plains, N.Y.: M. E. Sharpe, 1978), 8.

17. See Johann Galtung, "The Green Movement: A Socio-Historical Development," *International Sociology* 1 (March 1986):75–90.

Appendix A

1. Dorothy Nelkin, *Nuclear Power and Its Critics* (Ithaca, N.Y.: Cornell University Press, 1971).

2. Steven Ebbin and Raphael Kasper, *Citizens Groups and the Nuclear Power Controversy* (Cambridge, Mass.: MIT Press, 1974). A more recent case study of the regulatory and hearing process was made by Stever in *Seabrook and the Nuclear Regulatory Commission.*

3. Ronald Reagan, "The Time Is Now . . . to Recapture Our Destiny," *Washington Post,* 18 July 1980, 10.

4. An excellent introduction to this school of thought is Zald and McCarthy, eds. *The Dynamics of Social Movements.*

5. Social-action theory originates from the now classical work of Max Weber, *The Theory of Social and Economic Organization,* ed. Talcott Parsons (New York: Oxford University Press, 1947).

6. See Talcott Parsons, Edward A. Shils, and James Olds, "Categories of the Orientation and Organization of Action," in *Toward a General Theory of Action,* ed. Parsons and Shils, 30–79.

7. Rudolph Heberle, *Social Movements* (New York: Appelton, 1951).

8. Ibid., 12–13.

9. Neil Smelser, *Theory of Collective Behavior* (New York: Free Press, 1962).

10. Bert Useem, "Solidarity Model, Breakdown Model, and the Boston Anti-Busing Movement," *American Sociological Review* 45 (June 1980): 357–69.

11. Heberle, *Social Movements,* 131.

12. Hans Gerth and C. Wright Mills, *Character and Social Structure* (New York: Harcourt, Brace & World, 1964).

13. Ibid., 440.

14. John Wilson, *Introduction to the Study of Social Movements* (New York: Basic Books, 1974), 118.

15. Heberle, *Social Movements,* 432.

16. Herbert Blumer, "Social Movements," in *New Outline of the Principles of Sociology,* ed. A. M. Lee (New York: Barnes & Noble, 1951), 199–220.

17. Smelser, *Collective Behavior,* chapter 1.

18. Wilson, *Study of Social Movements,* 288–89.

19. Ibid., 286.

20. See Joseph Helfgot, "Professional Reform Organizations and the Symbolic Representation of the Poor," *American Sociological Review* 39 (August 1974): 475–91.

21. Hadley Cantril, *The Psychology of Social Movements* (New York: Wiley, 1941).

22. Hans Toch, *The Social Psychology of Social Movements* (New York: Bobbs–Merrill, 1966).

23. Quoted in Toch, *Social Psychology,* 87.

24. Ibid., 117–18.

25. Wilson, *Study of Social Movements,* 338.

26. Blumer, "Social Movements," pp. 199–220.

27. Steven E. Barkan, "Strategic, Tactical and Organizational Dilemmas of

the Protest Movement against Nuclear Power," *Social Problems* 27 (October 1979): 19–37.

28. Wilson, *Study of Social Movements,* 236.

29. A conceptualization of control movements and countermovements is present in Ralph H. Turner and Lewis M. Killian, *Collective Behavior* (Englewood Cliffs, N.J.: Prentice-Hall, 1957).

30. Heberle, *Social Movements,* 150–51.

31. Smelser, *Collective Behavior.*

32. Using this methodology, Charles Tilly reconstructed collective action and prerevolutionary events in nineteenth-century Britain and France documented in historical archives. See *From Mobilization to Revolution* (Reading, Mass.: Addison-Wesley, 1978).

33. Mayer Zald and Roberta Ash, "The Transformation of Social Movement Organization," *Social Forces* 44 (1966): 327–41.

34. See part 4 of *Explorations in General Theory in Social Science,* Jan Loubser, Ranier Baum, Andrew Effrat, and Victor Lidz, eds. (New York: Free Press, 1976), for an analysis of the concept of generalized media.

35. Herbert P. Kitschelt, "Political Opportunity Structures and Political Protest: Anti-Nuclear Movements in Four Democracies," *British Journal of Political Science* 16 (1986):57–85.

36. Ibid., 62.

37. Ibid., 66.

38. Ibid., 72.

39. Bert Useem and Mayer N. Zald, "From Pressure Group to Social Movement: Efforts to Promote Use of Nuclear Power," in Mayer N. Zald and John D. McCarthy eds., *Social Movements in Organizational Society* (New Brunswick, N.J.: Transaction Books, 1987), 273–88.

40. Ibid., 277–80.

41. Ibid., 286–87.

42. Mayer N. Zald and Bert Useem, "Movement and Countermovement Interaction: Mobilization, Tactics, and State Involvement," in Zald and McCarthy, eds., *Social Movements in Organizational Society,* 261.

43. Ibid., 263.

44. See Doug McAdam, John D. McCarthy, and Mayer N. Zald, "Social Movements," in Neil J. Smelser, ed., *Handbook of Sociology* (London: Sage Publications, 1988), 701, for a discussion of the Marxist view of "new social movements."

45. Arthur Meir, "The Peace Movement: Some Questions concerning Its Social Nature and Structure," *International Sociology* 3 (March 1988):77–87.

Appendix B

1. The necessary relationship between energy consumption and economic development is no longer taken for granted, as much of the energy consumption

in advanced societies is wasted—a problem that conservation policies hope to correct.

2. The Union of Concerned Scientists, "Voter Information Kit" contains reasonably current statistics.

3. Ibid. See also Mason Willrich, *Energy and World Politics* (Riverside, N.J.: Free Press, 1975); Joseph A. Yager and Eleanor B. Steinberg, *Energy and U.S. Foreign Policy* (Cambridge, Mass.: Ballinger, 1974); Peter R. Odell, *Oil and World Power* (Harmondsworth, England: Penguin Books, 1974); and Edward Friedland, Paul Seabury, and Aaron Wildavsky, "Oil and the Decline of Western Power," *Political Science Quarterly* 90 (1975): 437–50.

4. Ford Foundation, *A Time to Choose.*

5. U.S. Congress, House, Committee on Science and Astronautics, *Energy Facts 1973* (Washington, D.C.: U.S. Government Printing Office, 1973).

6. *National Journal Reports* (Washington D.C.: Government Research Corporation, 1974), 328–30.

7. David Comey, "Chasing Down the Facts," *Bulletin of the Atomic Scientists* 31 (February 1975): 42.

8. Federal Energy Administration, *Executive Summary, National Energy Outlook* (Washington, D.C.: U.S. Government Printing Office, 1976), 46.

9. The Union of Concerned Scientists, "Voter Information Kit."

10. "Congressional Awareness of Energy Crisis: 1969–1972," *Congressional Quarterly,* 15 February 1973, 38.

Appendix C

1. Robert Dahl and Ralph S. Brown, *Domestic Control of Nuclear Energy* (Social Science Research Council, 1951). The sources used in writing this appendix were numerous and varied. For a detailed account of the nuclear fuel cycle, the reader can consult the following: Albert V. Crewe and Joseph J. Katz, *Nuclear Research U.S.A.* (New York: Dover Publications, 1964); Bernard J. Cohen, *Nuclear Science and Society* (New York: Doubleday, 1974); U.S. Environmental Protection Agency, *Environmental Analysis of the Uranium Fuel Cycle* (Washington, D.C.: U.S. Government Printing Office, 1973); Mason Willrich, *Global Politics of Nuclear Energy* (New York: Praeger, 1971); the Union of Concerned Scientists, *The Nuclear Fuel Cycle* (Cambridge, Mass.: The Union of Concerned Scientists, 1974); American Nuclear Society, *Nuclear Power and the Environment* (Hinsdale, Ill.: The American Nuclear Society, 1975); Hans Bethe, "The Necessity of Fission Power," *Scientific American* 234 (1976): 21–30; and the International Atomic Energy Agency, *Nuclear Power and the Environment* (Vienna: International Atomic Energy Agency, 1973). I would like to thank Dr. William McLean, Department of Physics, Rutgers University, for his comments on an earlier draft of this appendix.

2. U.S. Environmental Protection Agency, *Environmental Analysis of the Uranium Fuel Cycle.* (The U.S. figure of one-third is an update).

3. Willrich, *Global Politics,* 16.

4. Environmental Protection Agency, *Environmental Analysis of the Uranium Fuel Cycle,* vol. 4, 73.

5. Union of Concerned Scientists, *Nuclear Fuel Cycle,* 92–115.

6. M. C. Day, "Nuclear Energy: A Second Round of Questions," *Bulletin of the Atomic Scientists* (December 1975): 52–59.

7. Mason Willrich and Philip Marston, "Prospects for a Uranium Cartel," *Orbis* 19 (1975): 166–84.

8. Willrich, *Global Politics,* 18.

9. This facility, the plant where Karen Silkwood worked, has been closed.

10. Willrich, *Global Politics,* 14–16.

11. Environmental Protection Agency, *Environmental Analysis of the Uranium Fuel Cycle,* vol. 2, 3–5.

12. Cohen, *Nuclear Science,* 145.

13. David Comey, "The Perfect Trojan Horse," *Bulletin of the Atomic Scientist* (June 1976): 33–34.

14. International Atomic Energy Agency, *Nuclear Power and the Environment.*

15. American Nuclear Society, *Nuclear Power and the Environment* (Hinsdale, Ill.: American Nuclear Society, 1974).

16. See John G. Fuller, *We Almost Lost Detroit* (New York: Readers Digest, 1975), for an account of this accident. A critical analysis of the fast breeder reactor is Thomas B. Cochran, *The Liquid Metal Fast Breeder Reactor* (Baltimore: Johns Hopkins University Press, 1974). See also Department of Energy, *Final Environmental Statement for the Liquid Metal Fast Breeder Reactor Program* (Washington, D.C.: U.S. Government Printing Office, ERDA–1535, 1975).

17. Daniel F. Ford and Henry W. Kendall, "The Nuclear Power Issue: An Overview" (Cambridge, Mass.: Union of Concerned Scientists, 1974).

Selected Bibliography

I have included here some of the more important books that pertain to the controversy over nuclear power, including a few earlier works that are worth reading. Most of these books are cited at some point in the text. A 1988 update is included at the end.

The Energy Crisis

Cohen, Bernard J. *Nuclear Science and Society.* New York: Doubleday, 1974. By far the most readable analysis of the technical characteristics of the nuclear fuel cycle.

Energy Policy Project of the Ford Foundation. *A Time to Choose: America's Energy Future.* Cambridge, Mass.: Ballinger Publishing, 1974. Many current policy choices are still involved with growth scenarios outlined by the Energy Policy Project. It is useful for understanding one approach to resolving the energy crisis that had a definite impact on government energy policy.

Fischer, John C. *Energy Crises in Perspective.* New York: John Wiley, 1974. A comparison of sources of electricity, utilizing the concept of economies of scale.

Ford Foundation/Mitre Corporation. *Nuclear Power: Issues and Choices.* Cambridge, Mass.: Ballinger Publishing, 1977. An overview of some of the basic issues related to nuclear energy.

Friedland, Edward, Paul Seabury, and Aaron Wildavsky. "Oil and the Decline of Western Power." *Political Science Quarterly* 90 (1975): 437–50. An excellent summary of what OPEC means for Western nations.

Odell, Peter. *Oil and World Power.* Harmondsworth, England: Penguin Books, 1974. Although dozens of books on the oil crisis exist, this one has the distinction of explaining the structure of the oil industry in a low-key and nonalarmist manner.

Schuur, Sam H., ed. *Energy in America's Future: The Choices before Us.* Baltimore: Johns Hopkins University Press, 1979. This volume was prepared for Resources in the Future, Inc., and is highly recommended, although decidedly pronuclear. The chapters on the health, environmental, and catastrophic effects of energy technologies warn us that dependence on coal could be even more disastrous than dependence on nuclear energy.

Stobaugh, Robert, and Daniel Yergin, eds. *Energy Future.* New York: Ballantine Books, 1979. This is the result of a project on energy at the Harvard Business School and leans toward conservation and solar energy as the mix most likely to resolve the energy crisis.

Willrich, Mason. *Energy and World Politics.* New York: Free Press, 1975. Willrich is a professor of law at the University of Virginia and perhaps the foremost expert on the energy crisis and its implications. This book is not frequently cited but is still one of the better ones on the subject.

Nuclear Technology and Social Change

Cochran, Thomas B. *The Liquid Metal Fast Breeder Reactor.* Baltimore: Johns Hopkins University Press, 1974. Although cutbacks of the Clinch River breeder project have softened this issue, it still divides the United States and its Western European allies who are developing breeders. Cochran's book is a good, comprehensive analysis of the fast breeder.

Fuller, John G. *We Almost Lost Detroit.* New York: Reader's Digest, 1975. In the wake of Three Mile Island, this book seems better now than when it first appeared. It documents the crisis of a partial core meltdown at an experimental breeder reactor near Detroit in 1966.

Nau, Henry P. *National Politics and International Technology: Nuclear Reactor Development in Western Europe.* Baltimore: Johns Hopkins University Press, 1974. This is a very scholarly account of the development of nuclear power in Western Europe and the growth of organizations such as EURATOM.

Skolnikoff, Eugene. *The International Imperatives of Technology.* Berkeley: University of California Press, 1972. This monograph is highly recommended for those wishing to understand the role of technology in social change.

Foreign Policy and Energy

Rodgers, Barbara, and Zdenek Cervenka. *The Nuclear Axis: Secret Collaboration between West Germany and South Africa.* New York: Times Books, 1978. An account of one of the many intrigues that surround nuclear power as the technology diffuses from one nation to another.

Szyklowicz, Joseph S., and Bard O'Neill. *The Energy Crisis and U.S. Foreign Policy.* New York: Praeger, 1975. Although published in the mid-1970s, this book is still helpful in understanding the immense foreign policy ramifications of the energy crisis.

Yager, Joseph A., and Eleanor B. Steinberg. *Energy and U.S. Foreign Policy.* Cambridge: Ballinger Publishing, 1974. This book gives a panoramic view of the impact of energy on major nations and the less-developed countries, as well as the basics on international safeguards.

Nuclear Energy and National Security

Gilpin, Robert, and Christopher Wright, eds. *Scientists and National Policy Making.* Princeton, N.J.: Princeton University Press, 1962. A classic sketch of some of the issues that arise when scientists and politicians both lay claim to decision-making power.

Rogin, Michael. *The Intellectuals and McCarthy.* Cambridge, Mass.: MIT Press, 1967. This book does not deal directly with atomic energy, but it is useful reading for those who wish to understand the political environment of the late 1950s, which affected U.S. nuclear policy for many years afterward.

Schneir, Walter, and Miriam Schneir. *Invitation to an Inquest: Reopening the Rosenberg Atom Spy Case.* Baltimore: Penguin Books, 1973. This is good reading for those who are concerned about the rise of a garrison state to protect nuclear materials.

Schurmann, Franz. *The Logic of World Power.* New York: Pantheon Books, 1974. An historical study of the rise of the national security state.

Shils, Edward. *The Torment of Secrecy.* New York: Free Press, 1956. One of the most erudite sociologists reflects on the meaning of the McCarthy era.

Willrich, Mason, and Theodore B. Taylor. *Nuclear Theft: Risks and Safeguards.* Cambridge, Mass.: Ballinger Publishing, 1974. Required reading for those interested in possible dangers posed to society through the theft of nuclear materials.

Energy and the Environment

Caldwell, Lynton K., Lynton R. Hayes, and Isabel M. MacWhirter. *Citizens and the Environment.* Bloomington: Indiana University Press, 1976. This primer on citizen action contains case studies involving a wide range of environmental issues, including energy. One case involves an early struggle over nuclear energy in Oregon by the Eugene Future Power Committee.

Liroff, Richard. *A National Policy for the Environment: NEPA and its Aftermath.* Bloomington: Indiana University Press, 1976. The Burger court changed the basic meaning of the National Environmental Protection Act in cases involving nuclear power. This book indicates how the act was originally intended to operate.

Norwood, Christopher. *At Highest Risk: Environmental Hazards to Young and Unborn Children.* New York: McGraw-Hill, 1980. A book that students don't put down until the entire narrative has been read. The chapters on radiation and other environmental toxins can be extrapolated to hazards presented by energy technologies.

Odell, Rice. *Environmental Awakening: The New Revolution to Protect the Earth.* Cambridge, Mass.: Ballinger Publishing, 1980. Chapters on energy resources, problems, and analysis are provocative. The book is also concerned with chemicals and public health.

Ramsay, William. *Unpaid Costs of Electrical Energy: Environmental Impacts from Coal and Nuclear Power.* Baltimore: Johns Hopkins University Press, 1978. This book was a main source for the project on energy directed by Sam Schurr for Resources in the Future, Inc.

Schnaiberg, Alan. *The Environment: From Surplus to Scarcity.* New York: Oxford University Press, 1980. The theoretical treatise on environmental issues from a neo-Marxist perspective should be read by all environmental professionals.

Significant Case Studies

Ebbin, Steven, and Raphael Kasper. *Citizen Groups and the Nuclear Power Controversy.* Cambridge, Mass.: MIT Press, 1974. A case study of citizen intervention in Atomic Energy Commission hearings for the licensing of Vermont Yankee and Michigan's Midland plant before the antinuclear movement captured national attention.

Nelkin, Dorothy. *Nuclear Power and Its Critics: The Cayuga Lake Controversy.* Ithaca, N.Y.: Cornell University Press, 1971. Perhaps the first documentation of conflict over nuclear power, written by someone very proficient in the analysis of modern issues concerning advanced technology.

Parkin, Francis. *Middle Class Radicalism: The Social Bases of the British Campaign for Nuclear Disarmament.* Manchester, England: University of Manchester Press, 1968. The CND has reemerged in the 1980s, and Parkin's book explores reasons for the rejection of nuclear weapons by the British.

Stever, Donald W., Jr. *Seabrook and the Nuclear Regulatory Commission.* Hanover, N.H.: University Press of New England, 1980. This is the most detailed study of the regulatory process available, written by an official in the U.S. Department of Justice. The book is objective, often critical of the Nuclear Regulatory Commission, and gives interesting insights into the Seabrook controversy.

Antinuclear Literature

Adato, Michael. *Safety Second: The NRC and America's Nuclear Power Plants.* Bloomington: Indiana University Press, 1987. Shows how the NRC has failed to enforce safety measures.

Babin, Ronald. *The Nuclear Power Game.* Montreal: Black Rose Books, 1985. The most thorough history of the Canadian antinuclear movement.

Berger, John J. *Nuclear Power: The Unviable Option.* New York: Ramparts Press, 1977. Begins with an interesting fictional account of a nuclear disaster in "Santa Bonita, California" and has well-researched analyses of problems with nuclear power.

Commoner, Barry. *The Politics of Energy.* New York: Alfred A. Knopf, 1979. This book outlines the political program of the Citizens Party, of which Commoner was the presidential nominee in 1980. It advocates the abandonment of nuclear power and a transition to a solar-powered economy.

Faulkner, Peter, ed. *The Silent Bomb: A Guide to the Nuclear Energy Controversy.* New York: Random House, 1977. An edited anthology of antinuclear articles written by prominent activists.

Finch, Ron. *Exporting Danger: A History of the Canadian Nuclear Energy Export Programme.* Contends that efforts to prevent nuclear proliferation to the Third World are hampered by Canadian exports of CANDU reactors and nuclear equipment.

Ford, Daniel. *Meltdown: The Secret Papers of the Atomic Energy Commission,* revised and updated edition. New York: Touchstone, 1986. Detailed criticism of the AEC and its successor, the NRC.

Gofman, John, and Arthur Tamplin. *Poisoned Power.* Emmaus, Pa.: Rodale Press, 1971. Written by scientists whose work was suppressed by the Atomic Energy Commission.

Gyorgy, Anna. *No Nukes: Everyone's Guide to Nuclear Power,* second edition. Boston: South End Press, 1980. The first edition of this book was a handbook for antinuclear activists in the late 1970s.

Hertsgaard, Mark. *Nuclear Inc.* New York: Pantheon, 1983. The most incisive analysis of nuclear policy in the Reagan era.

Lewis, Richard S. *The Nuclear Power Rebellion.* New York: Viking Press, 1972. One of the more interesting accounts of the early phase of antinuclear activities.

Lipschutz, Ronnie D. *Radioactive Waste: Politics, Technology, and Risk.* Cambridge, Mass.: Ballinger Publishing, 1980. A Union of Concerned Scientists report on the problem of radioactive waste disposal.

Lovins, Amory. *Soft Energy Paths.* Cambridge, Mass.: Ballinger Publishing, 1979. With several other books and important articles in *Foreign Affairs,* the British environmentalist has emerged as one of the most important critics of nuclear power.

Metzger, Peter. *The Atomic Establishment.* New York: Simon & Schuster, 1972. Criticism levied at the now-defunct Atomic Energy Commission.

Nader, Ralph, and John Abbotts. *The Menace of Atomic Energy.* New York: Grossman, 1977. Nader was one of the antinuclear movement's prime movers.

Pollock, Cynthia. *Decommissioning: Nuclear Power's Missing Link.* Washington, D.C.: Worldwatch Institute, 1986. This issue becomes increasingly important as existing nuclear reactors age.

Rashke, Richard L. *The Killing of Karen Silkwood: The Story behind the Kerr-McGee Plutonium Case.* Boston: Houghton Mifflin, 1981. Gives much of the background detail on the Silkwood case.

Sugai, Wayne. *Nuclear Power and Ratepayer Protest: The Washington Public Power Supply System Crisis.* Boulder, Colo.: Westview Press, 1987. Describes the activities of the Crabshell Alliance along a model of "mass insurgency" and the ratepayer revolt focused on Initiative 394 in Washington state.

Tirman, John. *Empty Promise: The Growing Case against Star Wars.* Boston: Beacon Press, 1986. Antimissile space satellites may be nuclear-powered, a concern to the antinuclear movement.

Pronuclear Literature

Bethe, Hans. "The Necessity of Fission Power." *Scientific American* 234 (1976): 21–30. The Nobel laureate physicist cogently argues why we must remain committed to nuclear power.

Cohen, Bernard. *Before It's Too Late: A Scientist's Case for Nuclear Power.* New York: Plenum Press, 1983. An accomplished nuclear physicist makes his argument for nuclear power.

Garvey, Gerald. *Nuclear Power and Social Planning: The City of the Second Sun.* Lexington, Mass.: Lexington Books, 1977. An argument that conservation alone will not solve energy problems.

Hoyle, Fred. *Energy or Extinction? The Case for Nuclear Energy.* Salem, N.H.: Heinemann Educational Books, 1977. Considered by the Atomic Industrial Forum to be one of the best and most concise explanations of energy and nuclear power.

Lilienthal, David E. *Atomic Energy: A New Start.* New York: Harper & Row, 1980. Although extremely critical of the nuclear energy program, Lilienthal opts for research into new reactor concepts.

Ott, Karl O., and Bernard I. Spinrad. *Nuclear Energy: A Sensible Alternative.* New York: Plenum Press, 1985. The most cogent rebuttal of antinuclear arguments can be found in this volume.

Smart, Ian. *World Nuclear Energy: Towards a Bargain of Confidence.* Baltimore: Johns Hopkins University Press, 1982. An excellent source of factual information of nuclear power plant proliferation throughout the world.

Teller, Edward. *Energy from Heaven and Earth.* San Francisco: W. W. Freeman, 1979. The chapter "Reactor Safety and the Anti-Nuclear Movement" is incisive in parts but biased in others; for example, the passage "even in California the nuts are a minority" (p. 197) refers to groups seeking passage of the 1976 California Nuclear Safeguards Initiative.

Weinberg, Alvin, Marcelo Alonso, and Jack N. Barkenbus. *The Nuclear Connection: A Reassessment of Nuclear Power and Nuclear Proliferation.* New York: Paragon House, 1985. A critical examination of weak areas of the nuclear industry; highly informative for both anti- and pronuclear advocates.

Weinberg, Alvin, and Russ Manning. *The Second Nuclear Era: A New Start for Nuclear Power.* New York: Praeger, 1985. An optimistic analysis placing future hope in nuclear technology.

Regulatory Studies

Del Sesto, Steven L. *Science, Politics, and Controversy: Civilian Nuclear Power in the United States, 1946–1974,* Boulder, Colo.: Westview Press, 1979. Shows evolution of safety regulations governing nuclear power plants.

Meehan, Richard L. *The Atom and the Fault: Experts, Earthquakes, and Nuclear Power.* Cambridge, Mass.: MIT Press, 1984. Analyzes the controversy of nuclear power plant siting in California earthquake zones.

Okrent, David. *Nuclear Reactor Safety: On the History of the Regulatory Process.* Madison: University of Wisconsin Press, 1981. Historical study of the AEC's regulatory power.

Rolph, Elizabeth S. *Nuclear Power and the Public Safety: A Study in Regulation.* Lexington, Mass.: Lexington Books, 1979. A Rand Corporation research study on safety regulations at U.S. nuclear power plants.

Special Topics

Bass, Gail V., and Brian Jenkins. *A Review of Recent Trends in International Terrorism and Nuclear Incidents Abroad.* Santa Monica, Calif.: Rand Corporation, 1983. A history and chronology of nuclear terrorism and necessary safety measures to protect nuclear power plants.

Davis, Mary D. *The Military-Civilian Nuclear Link: A Guide to the French Nuclear Industry.* Boulder, Colo.: Westview Press, 1987. An interesting study of how the French generate electricity in the production of nuclear weapons.

Freudenberg, William R., and Eugene A. Rosa. *Public Reaction to Nuclear Power: Are There Critical Masses?* Boulder, Colo.: Westview Press, 1984. Analyzes citizen participation in nuclear power plant hearings.

Marples, David R. *The Social Impact of the Chernobyl Disaster.* New York: St. Martin's Press, 1986. An overview of the consequences of the accident at Chernobyl.

Papadikis, Elim. *The Green Movement in West Germany.* London: Croom Helm, 1984. Shows the origins of the antinuclear pacifist movement in West Germany.

Rochon, Thomas R. *Mobilizing for Peace: The Antinuclear Movements in Western Europe.* Princeton, N.J.: Princeton University Press, 1988. Studies European peace and nuclear disarmanent movements.

Sorenson, John, Jon Soderstrom, Sam Carnes, Robert Bolin, and Emily Copenhaver. *Impacts of Hazardous Technology: The Psycho-Social Effects of Restarting TMI-1.* Albany: State University of New York Press, 1987. Documents an interesting psychological aftermath of the accident at Three Mile Island.

Sweet, William. *The Nuclear Age: Atomic Energy, Proliferation, and the Arms Race,* second edition. Washington, D.C.: Congressional Quarterly, 1988. Studies both accidents at nuclear power plants and the consequences of the arms race.

Thomas, Steve D. *The Realities of Nuclear Power: International Economic and Regulatory Experience.* New York: Cambridge University Press, 1988. Examines the development of nuclear power in major countries.

General Studies

Campbell, John L. *Collapse of an Industry: Nuclear Power and the Contradictions of U.S Policy.* Ithaca, N.Y.: Cornell University Press, 1988. Analyzes the decline of the nuclear power industry from a political economy perspective.

Hellman, Richard. *The Competitive Economics of Nuclear and Coal Power.* Lexington, Mass.: Lexington Books, 1983. Uses case studies to compare the costs of nuclear and coal-fired plants operated by electric utilities.

Ramberg, Bennett. *Global Nuclear Energy Risks: The Search for Preventive Medicine.* Boulder, Colo.: Westview Press, 1986. Documents international cooperation to prevent nuclear proliferation through security measures for nuclear power plants.

Index